THE NEW OLD MAID

OLD MAID

Satisfied Single Women

D1596168

THE NEW OLD MAID

Satisfied Single Women

Maureen Paraventi

Chatter House Press
Indianapolis, Indiana

The New Old Maid
Satisfied Single Women

For information:

Chatter House Press
7915 S Emerson Ave, Ste B303
Indianapolis, IN 46237

chatterhousepress.com

ISBN: 978-1-937793-46-3
Library of Congress Control Number: 2017961010

Dedication

To my parents, Mary and Jack Paraventi,
who taught me about unconditional love.

Acknowledgements

I will be eternally grateful to my sister, Tina Paraventi, for her skillful proofreading and editing assistance. I am also grateful to Tina and to my brother, Sean Paraventi, for their support and encouragement. Many thanks to all of my friends and relatives who believed in me – there are too many to name, but you know who you are. And finally, my deepest gratitude to the women who shared their stories with me. I learned so much from each one of you.

Old Maid in the Garret

I have often heard it said, from me father and me mother
That goin' to a weddin' was the makings of another
If this be so, then I'll go without a bidding
or if kind providence won't you send me to a wedding?
And it's oh, dear me. How would it be?
If I died an old maid in the garret.

I can cook and I can sew, I can keep a house right tidy
Rise up in the morning and get the breakfast ready
There's nothing in this wide world would make me half so cheery
As a wee fat man who would call me his own dearie
And it's oh, dear me. How would it be?
If I died an old maid in the garret.

Oh now there's my sister Jean, she's not handsome or good lookin'
Scarcely 16 and a fella she was courtin'
Now she's 24, with a son and a daughter
Here am I, 45, and I've never had an offer
And it's oh, dear me. How would it be?
If I died an old maid in the garret.

Oh, I'm away home, for there's nobody heedin'
Nobody heedin' to poor old Annie's pleadin'
I'm away home to me own wee bit garret
If I can't get a man, I'll surely keep me parrot.
And it's oh, dear me. How would it be?
If I died an old maid in the garret.

Oh come landsman or come kinsman, Come tinker or come tailer
Come fiddler or come dancer, Come ploughman or come sailor
Come rich man, come poor man, Come fool or come witty
Come any man at all who would marry me for pity.
And it's oh, dear me. How would it be?
If I died an old maid in the garret

Contents

Introduction

"Are you some kind of a freak?"

I knew what was coming. My co-worker Rose was midway through her second chocolate martini and apparently feeling loose enough at our after-work get together to switch from talking about *her* marriage to talking about my non-marriage.

"I don't get it. Why haven't you ever been married?" she asked, in the same tone she might use to say, "Why do you have three heads that glow in the dark?"

I sighed. "You know, this is the third time you've asked me that. Remember? We had that whole conversation about it at the office Christmas party last year."

Looking deeply perplexed, she sipped at her drink, not ready to drop the subject. Apparently the vodka was interfering with her ability to take a hint. "I just mean…you're so attractive and you have such a great personality. How is it that you've never been married?"

That's what she said. What she meant was: *What's wrong with you? Are you some kind of a freak? Couldn't you get a man? Or are you man hater?*

It's possible that I was imagining more subtext than Rose intended and to be fair, she was not the first person who'd put me on the spot about my being single. She was just the one doing it at that moment.

On a fairly regular basis, people that I meet express astonishment at my never having tied the knot, taken the plunge, walked down the aisle to what is widely assumed to be a happily ever after existence. I am expected to explain myself -- to defend my choices to people I barely know -- because I am a dissonant cognition, a jigsaw piece that doesn't fit into their puzzle, an outlier and possibly, an object of suspicion.

There *must* be a reason for such a bizarre aberration as an old maid! Why would anyone want to go through life uncoupled? After all, being single – past a certain age – means being lonely and miserable, right?

Exposing the truth

The New Old Maid examines what it's like to be a single woman in a society that relentlessly promotes marriage as the normal and *only* desirable way for adults to live. The book will reveal a little known truth: that many single women truly enjoy their lives. I'm not suggesting that they – ok, *we* – go through each day in a state of euphoria, only that the disappointments and frustrations we experience are not, for the most part, due to the lack of a husband. The single life can be very satisfying – a radical notion which I'll explore with input from old maids from all over the U.S. With their help, I'll peel back the cover of stale stereotypes and expose the truth: how we old maids feel about relationships, romance, ambition, loneliness, sex, careers, children, fears about aging, financial security, the power of friendships and more, through frank, funny and sometimes painful revelations.

There's a price to pay

I've never been married. Nonetheless, I'm an accomplished, well-rounded, generally happy person who is living what I think is an interesting life.

I spent years as a morning radio personality, bringing comedy and commentary to listeners in Michigan, Ohio, Illinois and California. I got to broadcast from the back of an elephant in a circus, a hot air balloon high in the sky and a pace car making the rounds at a racetrack. I introduced bands at concert venues. Radio also had me making guest appearances on local television shows.

In between radio gigs I lived in Los Angeles for a number of years, where I worked at a Hollywood talent agency and then as a personal assistant to actor Pierce Brosnan. (Tough job. Not really).

These days, I'm heavily involved in theatre. I act in local productions and write plays that have been produced in New York City, Michigan and Florida – so far. I've written a novel, *Palm Tree Pipe Dreams*. I also sing in and write songs for McLaughlin's Alley, a pop/rock band that performs at clubs and festivals.

I've got wonderful friends. I'm close to my siblings. My annual Halloween costume party (which includes a cheesy but scary Haunted Garage) is legendary. I'm learning to speak Italian. I sew clothes for myself that sometimes turn out so well I can actually wear them out in public. Like everyone else, I've had humiliating failures and surprising successes.

The point is: there's more to me than my marital status. That's true – of course – for married women as well. It's just that they don't find themselves shadowed by the big "but," as in, "She climbed Mt. Everest and swam across the English Channel, but she never found the right guy. How sad." An old maid could find a cure for cancer, figure out a way to reverse climate change in a week and invent high heels that felt like cushy slippers when you wore them but at her funeral, people would still whisper, "She never married," as if that canceled everything else out.

I've never wanted a conventional life and I didn't end up with one, but ultimately, I've come to realize that there is a price to pay for being a square peg in a world full of round holes.

You have to explain yourself a lot.

This book is my explanation, my letter to the world that never wrote to me. Actually, the world hasn't ignored me; I just couldn't resist quoting old maid poet Emily Dickinson.

I go where I want to go on vacations, sleep in late when I feel like it and commit to time-consuming projects that appeal to me. In other words, I spend my days doing what I love to do, without having to accommodate someone else's wants, needs or schedule. Am I selfish? Yep. Did I do any prospective Mr. Rights a favor by not marrying them? Yes I did. Because I didn't especially want to be a wife, I wouldn't have made a very good one. Is it likely that I've missed out on the many wonderful things that go along with being married? Sure I have, but as Debbie – one of the women featured in this book – put it; "You can't miss what you've never had."

Bad taste, or a self-protective mechanism?

I could have avoided the discomfort, the questions from strangers, if only I'd prioritized marriage, tried harder to make relationships work with Steve (a womanizer), Jerry (a womanizer who turned out to be married), Frank (turned out to be gay), Eric (a control freak) or Paul (just plain boring). But I didn't. Maybe I subconsciously was attracted to men who weren't good husband material, because I didn't really want a husband. What seems like consistently bad taste in men may, instead, be a self-protective mechanism designed to keep me from forming the kind of attachment that would have resulted in a "Mrs." in front of my name.

I saw marriage as a choice that would limit all other choices, a partnership that would have many benefits but would also tie me down and restrict me to a daily grind in which my own needs and desires would be secondary to those of my family. What I discovered during the course of writing this book is that my attitude is shared by many women.

So although I *assumed* – somewhere in the back of my mind – that someday I'd get married, it took the hindsight reached after decades as a singleton to realize that I'd been deeply ambivalent about marriage all along.

The funny thing is, when I began looking around for women to talk to for this book, I was initially a bit worried that there might not be enough old maids around, or that they wouldn't want to discuss being old maids. Maybe they had allowed society to make them feel ashamed of it, as if they were losers or misfits.

Unwilling to "settle"

What I found, instead, was a treasure trove of strong personalities and lively opinions. The women who shared their stories and feelings with me live in small towns and big cities, range in age from 42 to 70 and include a corporate VP, housecleaner, fashion designer, high school principal, non-profit manager, stockbroker, ski bum, psychic medium, public relations professional, entrepreneur, beauty pageant winner, nurse, single mom and retired firefighter. On the surface, they have very little in common. Beneath the differences in age, location, occupations, dating histories, religious inclinations and family backgrounds, though, was one commonality: these women preferred to live as singletons rather than to "settle" for a marriage that they knew would be unsatisfactory for them. For some, that took a lot of courage. For others, it amounted to nothing more than common sense.

Most of the women I spoke with are still open to the possibility of marriage, although they have become less inclined over the years to allow incursions into the liberty they've come to enjoy. "I'd be willing to get married as long as..." was a sentiment I heard a lot.

Another thing they have in common: they're tired of being asked why they've never married. Being treated as an oddity makes even less sense when you realize the extent to which the demographic story of old maidism has changed. There are more of us these days than ever before. Fear not: we are not so numerous that the institution of marriage is in danger of crumbling away to nothing, but the numbers are sufficient to make lifelong – or at least, long-term – singledom a hot topic. That doesn't mean that old maids are no longer objects of curiosity and pity, though. It is more socially acceptable these days to be a transgender individual than to be a woman – or man – who has never married. While this book focuses on women – because that's the perspective I'm most familiar with – much of it will ring true for men, too. I've had several bachelor friends express an interest in reading it. "You know, some people are just meant to be alone," mused my friend Craig.

My choice of the 40-year-old cutoff was somewhat arbitrary, but I thought it a useful benchmark because by 40, many people have made their most important life choices: what they'll do to earn a living, where and with whom they'll live, whether or not they'll have children. That is also the age at which a rather infamous Newsweek article published in the mid 1980s declared a college educated woman's chances of finding a mate to be somewhat less than her chances of dying in a terrorist attack. The debate begun by that article continues to this day, with ever-emerging data adding fuel to the fire, but does the underlying premise still exist? That women who are still single as they age out of their 30s must be feeling desperate? I'm sure some do, but if you pay attention to online indicators (and I'll get to those), there are plenty of single women out there who *celebrate* their singledom.

This book focuses largely on heterosexual women because until recently, lesbians were not legally allowed to marry. Because of the U.S. Supreme Court's ruling on same-sex marriage, single lesbians may – not too far down the road – find themselves in the position of having to justify their non-married status to relatives and strangers just as the women in this book have had to.

Some of my best friends are married people

It's important to note that this is *not* an anti-marriage book. Some of my best friends are married, and I'm happy for them because they're happy. I'm merely pointing out that not everybody wants to or is meant to get married – and that's ok. It does *not* mean that singletons are destined to feel lonely and isolated. Being single *is* different from being married, but often those differences are pretty great.

Many of the women I interviewed thanked me afterwards. They are pleased that their point of view is finally being represented and validated.

For those women who do not, for whatever reason, get married, I hope this book will start a conversation that may save them from at least a few iterations of that unwelcome query: "How is it that you've never been married?

I have found, on first dates, that it would be better for me to announce that I've been divorced multiple times than to reveal that I've never been married. That's just one example of the bizarre conundrum that always single women face when dealing with people who can't unwrap their minds from around the marriage-is-the-only-option idea. (Note: Throughout this book, I'll be using the positive term, "always single," as opposed to the negative one, "never married.") Despite our growing numbers, old maids are still regarded as peculiar and likely flawed. While I freely admit to my flaws (I actually revel in some of them), my not having a husband does not make me a menace to society or a threat to civilization.

Why do so many people think it's strange for a woman to fly solo? Is it because men tend to be judged on their individual achievements, while women are still predominantly judged on the value we have for others – particularly men? When we're young and sexy-looking, women are sought-after objects of lust, or servers at Hooters. As wives and mothers, women are appreciated for how they take care of their husbands, children, homes and communities – contributions I am not downplaying in any way. I'm simply suggesting that women who do not choose those specific roles have value as well.

And by the way, we old maids have powerful connections to others just as married women do and are often able to make different kinds of contributions. The single woman may be the one in the office who will stay late because someone else has to leave early to pick up a sick child, the girlfriend who can drop everything and come to your aid at a moment's notice, the daughter who cares for aging parents, the favorite aunt who treats nieces and nephews to experiences their harried parents may not have time for.

So get off our backs.

Keeping it Straight

Here's a handy reference guide to the women who contributed to the conversation:

Andrea: Corporate titan turned university administrator in Indiana. Has come a long way from the cornfields.

Atheria: Psychic medium living in New Mexico. Seeker of truth.

Eleanore Wells: Marketing professional. Adventurer. Currently living in Australia.

Debbie Roszkowski: A free spirit who hit the road young and didn't stop moving for decades.

Dr. Karen Lewis: Family therapist whose practice includes many single women.

Elizabeth: Lives in Washington State, is in a long-term relationship that's a lot like marriage…but isn't.

Ellen: Taught the value of hard work by her parents, this Arizona resident left a successful business career to care for them when they were ailing.

Tiffany: Business owner, architect of her own life.

Joan White: North Carolina entrepreneur; designer of plus-sized fashions.

Jo-Sue: High school assistant principal and youth pastor, athlete and coach.

Kay: Los Angeles entertainer turned vegan educator and animal rights activist.

Lavender Moon: Single mom, foodie, dreamer of big dreams.

Leanne: High school teacher, actor. Once freed of a stifling relationship, she didn't look back.

Lucy: A pretty and petite Denver stockbroker who did not want the life her mother had.

Marcy: A Colorado ski instructor and golf enthusiast who spends every moment possible out of doors.

Michelle E. Alford: A poet/writer/director/real estate agent who balances her love of the arts with a strong practical side.

Pat Jones (P.J. Edghill): A writer/director/producer who doesn't let physical challenges slow her down.

Sally: Works in telecommunications. Collects too much stuff. A feisty redhead with a long-term boyfriend whom she has no plans to marry.

Sheryl: A Californian who works in the fashion industry. Loves salsa dancing. Does not count being single as one of her regrets.

Stephanie Schneiderman: A Michigan-based travel expert who loves introducing others to the places and people *she* loves.

Suzanne: Retired firefighter. Eternal optimist. Sees the best in the men she dates – even when her friends don't.

Tish: A Pennsylvanian who enjoyed her career as a nurse anesthetist and is enjoying her retirement even more.

More detailed information – including websites and Facebook pages – can be found in the "About the Women in this Book" chapter.

The Benefits of Being a Single Woman

It hardly needs to be said that women who remain single lead very different lives than their married counterparts. So why am I saying it?

Society has long focused on what single women don't have – husbands – while ignoring what we *do* have: independence and autonomy. The freedom to do whatever one wants, whenever one wants to do it was a recurring theme raised by the women that I talked to for this book.

Traditionalists may find this threatening. If women stop assuming their natural, biologically-driven role of mating and procreating, the human race could, in time, vanish! Or at the very least, mothers won't get the chance to go wedding dress shopping with their daughters and bully them into buying a ball gown when what they really want is a fit and flare.

People who remain unmarried are *not* undermining the institution of marriage. In fact, the opposite is true. How many divorces occur because women *and* men who aren't meant to get married take that fateful walk down the aisle simply because they feel that it's expected of them?

(Admit it: you've sat in a church or synagogue pew – probably more than a few times – watching the proceedings and thinking to yourself, "This is a mistake. It'll never last." Of course, that didn't stop you from insincerely congratulating the happy couple afterward, eating a piece of their wedding cake and dancing to the music of the d.j. they'd hired for the reception.)

But let's get back to the benefits of being single (there *is* a downside to singledom which I'll explore later).

A hot second

Early in my career as a radio personality, when I'd worked my way up from teeny tiny markets to the small market of Champaign, Illinois, I got a job offer from a radio station in San Francisco. San Francisco! In one move, I could more than double my salary, which at that time kept me just above the poverty level. Of greater importance to me was the opportunity to work with major market personalities and reach many more listeners than I ever could in Champaign. Additionally, I could go from the Midwest to an exciting city in California.

I thought about it for a hot second, and then said "Yes!"

I didn't have to ask a husband if he wanted to move. If he would be able to transfer or find a new job in the Bay Area. If he would be willing to leave behind friends and family, forego the recreational softball team for which he'd played third base for so many summers, abandon the garden he'd lovingly hewed out of the wilds of the backyard. If we'd had children, the decision would have been even more complicated. What about their schools? Little Susie and Bill would pout for months after we moved because they missed their friends. Grandma and Grandpa would lay the guilt trip on us for taking their grandchildren so far away from them.

I was able to make a major decision based solely on what *I* wanted to do, and I must be honest; it was exhilarating. With the exception of the job interview I'd flown in for, I'd never even been to San Francisco, but I was thrilled as I packed up and hit the road for a new position in an unfamiliar city.

Ironically, that job turned sour pretty quickly, for reasons that had nothing to do with its location. I stuck it out for a year, because that would look better on my resume than a quick departure. Then I left for greener pastures (ok, Chicago) just as easily as I'd headed for San Francisco. And that wasn't my last move, by the way.

Imagine if I'd uprooted a husband, convinced him to go to the Bay Area to start a whole new life there, and then turned around in a year's time and told him that I'd changed my mind. If he had objected to moving yet again – which would have been completely reasonable on his part – I might have been stuck indefinitely in a job I hated. And I would likely have brought that bitterness home from work every day, where it would have affected my marriage.

A stepping stone v. a dead end

To a large degree, my decisions to move from place to place were motivated by ambition, which is still considered by some to be an unattractive trait in a woman. I wanted to advance in my career; earn bigger salaries and add more prestigious markets to my resume. Did my goals prevent me from finding the right guy at the right time, and in the right place? It's possible. For instance, I was dating a nice man early in my radio career, after I'd toiled away as an unpaid, overworked intern in a major market and was working full-time as a news director and anchor in a very small town. The job was a stepping stone, but it would have been a dead end if I'd chosen the man over the career, since he made it clear that he intended to remain in that small town. Forever. If I'd stayed with him, I would have spent years – maybe even decades – reporting on town council meetings ("the library wants $50 to buy some new books – who wants to make a motion?") and what passed for local crime ("vandals knocked down two more mailboxes last night").

I also would have continued to earn a miniscule salary, become quickly bored with small-town living (I'm a "city gal," as the people there correctly called me) and ultimately, felt trapped in a stagnant situation. Two people with opposite preferences may be attracted to each other, but will they stay together, happily, for very long? I'm too much of a pragmatist to believe that love conquers all. Sometimes love is the thing that gets conquered.

So, yes, career choices can play a significant role in the decision to not get married.

Attracted to the male version of herself

Andrea, for instance, grew up in rural Indiana and went on to spend decades as a high-level corporate executive before embarking upon her second and current career, which is in higher education administration. She worked for large firms in mergers and acquisitions, regulatory compliance and internal auditing. Her climb up the corporate ladder required her to move to various locations in the U.S. and to travel all over the world.

Andrea radiates a positive energy and a leadership vibe. She smiles a lot, listens as much as she talks and favors impeccably cut business suits -- a look she softens by wearing her hair long and pulled back in a pony tail. Her colleagues and friends describe her as a natural "connector" – someone with a talent for bringing people and opportunities together in ways that enrich both. She loves to entertain and is especially known for her holiday galas.

Andrea has had a lot of boyfriends over the years, but ironically, she found that the kind of man who would be compatible with her career would not, in fact, be compatible with *her*.

"I would not have been able to pick up and move every couple of years, nor would I have been able to probably get as many promotions as I've had or do as much travel as I needed to if I had been married to the kind of person that I've been attracted to over the years," she says. "Because the type of powerful, dynamic man that I'm drawn to – the male version of myself – can't pick up and move across the country every couple of years. A househusband who would follow me around and be supported by somebody like me, I'm not attracted to. And I would have felt very taken advantage of by someone like that."

She has no regrets about remaining single, because she's gotten to have the life she dreamed about since she was a young girl.

"I wanted to be one of those women who wore suits and carried a briefcase and worked in a board room," Andrea says. "I had absolutely no concept of that, obviously, growing up in the cornfields of central Indiana. I don't know if I saw somebody like that on TV, or in a movie. I just got that picture in my head, and that's what I wanted to be, and that's what I ended up being, for 26 years. And I loved it!"

"I had no idea where I wanted to go"

Stephanie Schneiderman doesn't move from place to place, but she does travel – more or less constantly. As the owner of Tia Stephanie Tours, Stephanie has found a way to combine business with pleasure. She takes clients on off-the-beaten-path visits to Mexico and Colombia, venturing to provinces far outside of the usual touristy destinations where they can see ancient landmarks, dance in local festivals and buy traditional textiles and folk art.

At first glance, Stephanie appears to be a resident of one of the locations she visits. Even when she's back home in the States, she often wears traditional Mexican attire: woven or elaborately embroidered dresses and skirts and colorful dangling earrings and other folk jewelry. Dark-eyed and dark-haired, Stephanie is enthusiastic when she talks about her passion for traveling – something she says she's always had. That's not surprising, given her multicultural upbringing. Stephanie's father was an international banker. She was born in Havana, Cuba and lived in St. Thomas in the Virgin Islands, Panama and Mexico before her family moved to Coral Gables, Florida when she was 13.

She spent a summer working on lobster boats in Maine in her early 20s, sailed on a 144' square rigger from Miami to Panama and traveled to Europe many times on her own.

"Once I flew to Italy and landed in Milan and I literally had no idea where I was going to go," Stephanie says. She saw a sign that said *Buses to the Lake District.* "I said, 'Well, I guess I'm going to the Lake District.' And I got on a bus! Having these wonderful travel adventures as a young woman was very inspiring for me. I loved it."

When she was in her early 20s, Stephanie was in a serious relationship with a banker – a "great catch," according to her friends. He proposed to her, but she turned him down. "I was too young. I just said 'No, because I'm not ready to get married. I want my life.' I knew that if I got married at that age, I would just be the banker's wife, and that's not what I wanted to be. I knew that my life was still unfolding and developing and I was happy with that."

After another breakup with another boyfriend, Stephanie was sad for awhile, but then realized: "Wow, this is kind of a blessing because I can go to graduate school and then I can go anywhere I want. I always sensed that it gave me a freedom to realize things on my own and have my own life and I feel very lucky for that. I like it."

Stephanie got her MBA and then created a business – and a lifestyle – that is perfectly suited to her. Could she have this life if she were married?

"If it was a traditional marriage, then no," she says. "There's no way I could do what I'm doing. But if it was an open-minded marriage, where people kind of respected that each person has their own life, I think it could be done, sure. With the right person."

But even with that right person, marriage would almost certainly limit Stephanie's roaming – which would not be good for someone who runs a travel business.

"There are instances when I can be gone for quite a few months at a time," she admits. "Or, it could involve, depending on that partner, that they would come and see me."

Does she ever feel as if she should have taken a more conventional path?

"I wouldn't change my life for the world! I'm living life on my terms. It's my life! Whose else is it? Life is different for different people. And for me, I've enjoyed doing the things I want to do. I never grew up like many little girls, fantasizing about going down the aisle, the dress. Those weren't my fantasies, as a kid: what's my wedding going to look like? Never."

"I had a very, very fulfilling single life"

Tiffany, a business owner, also loves to travel. Blue-eyed and fresh-faced, her lipstick glossy and her blonde hair cut in a bob, Tiffany – I suspect – probably looks polished even while trekking through the Australian outback or lying on a beach in Tahiti. (I look like a wreck if I'm away from home more than a few nights, because by then I've managed to misplace my blow dryer and drop my open mascara in the toilet of whatever hotel I'm staying in.) Her manner is friendly but firm, with an enthusiasm that's rooted in pragmatism. Tiffany is the kind of person that makes things happen.

She is a committed singleton, but she is not an old maid. Tiffany was married briefly and has been divorced for years. "I didn't get married very young, so I had a very, very fulfilling single life before I got married. My marriage wasn't very fulfilling to me, so for me it was more about putting my life back to the way I had it once the marriage ended."

Tiffany is currently in a relationship but she doesn't allow that to curtail her activities – as a former boyfriend tried to do years ago, when she came across a terrific travel deal for Australia, with an optional stopover in Hawaii.

"I told him about it," she recalls. "He didn't want me to go and he didn't want to go. So we had a conflict about that. I said, 'You know, I really think I shouldn't pass this up. I'd love to have you go but if you can't go, I really want to go myself.' It didn't sit well with him but I went anyway, and there never was another deal anywhere close to that. So I tell people: 'Do not put your life on hold for anybody or anything.' I practice no regret living and I don't put off living."

"I love my life"

Another single woman who has crafted a life that is ideal for her is Marcy, a ski bum in her late 50s. Actually, I'm being ironic. The word "bum" is hardly applicable; the hard-working Colorado resident is a five foot tall bundle of energy who talks as fast as she moves. Marcy teaches skiing every winter and works at a golf course every summer, doing a physically demanding job usually performed by teenagers. If that weren't enough, she is also a server for a catering company, which she calls, "lots of fun." (I did catering jobs when I was young, and "fun" wasn't the word I would have used to describe them.) In the spring and fall, Marcy travels, to Hawaii; Reno, Nevada; Mexico and to special events like Austin City Limits in Austin, Texas.

In spite of all the time she spends in the sun, Marcy is fair-skinned, with blue eyes, dark brown hair and what friends describe as a "force of nature" personality. "If you go skiing with her," says one, "you have to be prepared for her to call out all of the way up the lift to all of the people she knows who are skiing below her!"

"I love to work," Marcy says. "I couldn't ski every day of my life. I like teaching and having free ski days, but I don't think I could just ever not work. I love my life and I live in a beautiful place."

At her golf course job, "I'm the cart person that pulls up and loads your clubs up and picks up the balls. I'm outside 24/7, meeting and greeting people." On her days off, the fitness enthusiast is more likely to be found hiking in the mountains than lounging at home.

Marcy grew up in Southern California but gravitated to the Rocky Mountain ski resort town she's lived in for three decades due to her love of skiing.

When she was young, she thought she'd be the first one in her family to get married.

"So I started traveling and doing other things because I thought when I settled down and had kids and had a family, I wasn't going to have time to do that. I think it was a little bit selfish on my part but I wanted to travel. Then I ended up never finding the right person. And I'm happy with me, just being me. I don't need another part. I don't want or need to get married, because I'm so independent that I think I'm selfish, in a way. I like to be able – at the drop of a hat – to travel, to do things I want to do. I love my life."

"We have these interesting lives"

That sentiment is echoed by Eleanore Wells, a stylish African-American woman who looks at least ten years younger than her age. Eleanore is fashion forward and wears her short hair natural, with coppery highlights. Not unlike the main characters in *Sex in the City*, she is blunt and hilarious, with *lots* of opinions about dating, relationships and being single. At the age of 60 – when many people are feeling settled – Eleanore moved from New York City to Australia for a new job.

"One of the things that's so awesome about being single, with no kids, is I thought about it for five minutes and said, 'Yes!'" says the marketing professional. "I didn't have to think. I didn't have to consult with anybody. I didn't have to figure out what I was going to do with the kids. Are they going to like it? I had complete freedom. One of my favorite lines is that, as a single woman, I am free to spend my money and my time however I want, always. And this is a perfect example of that. This is something that sounds exciting. I'm going to do it. And you know what? There's not a soul else who I have to consider as a part of this. I love that."

Eleanore's experiences, which include climbing the High Atlas Mountains in Morocco, scuba diving at the Great Barrier Reef (in spite of being afraid of deep water) and exploring a rainforest with an Aboriginal guide, beg the question: are unmarried women more likely to be risk-takers? More open to trying new things? Or is it simply that we can indulge in our inner free spirit to a greater extent than our married counterparts because we don't have the same kinds of responsibilities?

"I think that many women who are lifelong singles and love it are much more adventurous than other people," she says. "That's sort of why we have these interesting lives, because we're adventurous about trying something new and different and not being scared. I love to travel. I want to go everywhere and I pretty much can because, as a single woman with no kids, my time and my money are my own and I get to spend both however I want. So traveling is what I do."

One thing Eleanore *won't* do again, though, is mountain climbing. "Here's the thing: I hated every f------ second that I was on that mountain! I continued to fantasize that entire week; 'Why don't I have any rich friends who could send me a helicopter and pluck me off of here and get me the f--- out of there?' But here I am, a year later and I reflect on that all the time. There were so many things that I learned and was exposed to that even though I would never do it again, it really was an important part of my recent life. I think I described it as horrific and wonderful at the same time, and that's kind of what it was."

As with a lot of the women that I spoke to, marriage was not something that Eleanore specifically ruled out; it was something that just didn't happen – despite the fact that most of her boyfriends have wanted to marry her.

"I don't know that I consciously ever made the choice that I will never get married. More likely, when asked, I would say: not right now. And not right now became never. For as long as I can remember, I know that I've never felt that burning desire for marriage and kids that I guess most little girls do. I don't think I ever consciously said, 'I don't ever, ever, ever want to get married.' I just always felt like, this is not the time. You know, maybe some other time, but not right now. And, you know, here we are."

Eleanore not only embraces her singledom, she's turned it into a brand, Spinsterlicious, with a blog, Facebook page and book (*The Spinsterlicious Life: 20 Life Lessons for Living Happily Single & Childfree*). "Being single makes a big difference in the kind of life that you live, the chances that you take and the decisions that you make," she says.

Eleanore looks forward to meeting new men in Australia. "I love dating, and I date a lot."

"If a man comes along, that's icing on the cake"

For Kay, a sixty-something Los Angeleno, getting married took a back seat to her career as an entertainer. After avoiding what she regarded as the too-conventional life her parents wanted for her, the slender, blue-eyed brunette sang with traveling show bands for more than a decade.

"We would spend two weeks on average per city, at a Sheraton or a Hilton, and do floor shows and dance sets and dinner sets and work six nights. On the seventh – every other Sunday – you'd pack and travel to the next town. Afternoons were rehearsals. Life kind of revolved around traveling from place to place."

It was a career choice to which her parents were adamantly opposed.

"My parents were very against me – 1,000 percent – going into show biz," she remembers. "They did not encourage that at all. From age 11, I wanted to take acting classes and they wouldn't drive me to them. When I started being successful – then they became the proudest braggarts around! But they didn't support my choices, emotionally. I always was jealous of other kids who had parents who were like, 'Yes, you can do anything you dream of doing!' Those were not my parents. They said things like, 'Stay in your hometown. Get a safe job working for a local insurance company or the state government, a stable job with benefits. Don't pick the scary, iffy unknowing kind of job. But that's what I was drawn to, so I didn't listen."

Kay's two sisters fulfilled their parents' wishes by staying put, marrying in their 20s and having children, but for Kay, getting married "was so back burner because career, career, career was primary. So that became the norm for me. My life was just the way I had set it up. And that was fine, because those were my priorities.

"To me, it was like, make yourself happy. Follow your dreams. Do what you're here to do. And if a man comes along, that's icing on the cake, but that was not in the plan. So I put it in the 'improbable' box because it wasn't on my list of goals."

Kay, who loves yoga and salsa dancing and often dates younger men, has had several long-term relationships, none of which tempted her to tie the knot.

The vegan and animal rights activist eventually transitioned from entertaining people to educating them about the relationship between food, health and the future of the planet through a nonprofit organization she runs. "That seemed so much more important than acting. I could really change the world by changing people's diets. Anybody could do the next acting role.

"That really became my life, and I actually met a guy the first year I was involved with that. We got very serious. When he broke up with me everyone said, 'He broke up with you? Was he crazy?' And I said,

'I don't know. I guess he is.'" Nevertheless, she remains friends with him to this day.

"I don't want to be told I can't do it"

Do some women remain unmarried because they feel adventurous and don't want to get tied down? Or is the circumstance of being single something that allows people to trek farther and wider than they would have if they were married? In my case, it was a happy coincidence that my career choice required me to move around. I was terrified of being stuck in one place. The steady job and sense of connection to one location that gave my parents such a sense of security would have made me feel trapped.

Fifty-something Debbie didn't discover that she was a gypsy until she broke up with a very controlling boyfriend at the age of 24. Finding herself free of that longtime romantic entanglement and stuck in a dead-end job, Debbie hit the road, and she didn't stop moving for decades.

First, she impulsively decided to move from Michigan to San Diego, California, where she would be able to share an apartment with a friend who'd relocated there earlier. Aside from that, however, Debbie had no firm plans; no job lined up, no car of her own, no contacts beside her friend. She did, however, have plenty of youthful confidence.

"Just like that I decided that I was going to do it. Within a couple of months I was gone."

Thus began a long, vibrant odyssey filled with new places and interesting experiences. Unlike Andrea, Debbie is not career-driven. She has worked at fast food restaurants and retail stores, and at jobs as disparate as hotel chambermaid, nanny, ice cream truck driver and housecleaner – whatever pays the bills and lets her enjoy her free time in the ways that she likes.

Debbie left San Diego for Los Angeles when some friends from back home asked her to manage their band – a gig which also took her to Boulder, Colorado, for a year. After that, it was back to L.A. and then on to Seattle, Washington.

"I used to think about all the things I did after I broke up with that boyfriend," says Debbie, a lean, curly-haired brunette who hates to sit still and *looks* like she once managed a rock band. "I thought: I did more in those couple of years that was so exciting, that was all my own, you know? I didn't have to compromise. My boyfriend sometimes didn't want to do things. I also had to deal with his jealousy. He was always accusing me of things. There was always a compromise. I felt; 'Damn, this is my life. I don't want to be told I can't do it.'

"I just did so much, and it was all without anyone telling me 'No.' All those decisions I made – they were all my own, and I just did what I wanted to do. I would have never been able to do this if I'd have stayed with him, or anybody else. I just thought: if I've already gone this far, gone all the way across the country, what else could I be doing? If I get married, I'm not going to be able to say what I want to do. I'm going to have to compromise."

Debbie loved living in Seattle. She worked as a hotel chambermaid and was soon offered a full-time supervisory position. She found an apartment and lived by herself, with no roommates, for the very first time in her life.

"I just flew into high gear right away," she remembers. "I have this new city, I'm downtown, I have my own apartment after all these years." When she wasn't working, Debbie went hiking, clubbing and for outings on friends' boats. She traveled to Hawaii, Boston, California and Louisiana and hosted friends who came to visit her.

Of her many moves, Debbie says; "I just get bored with stuff after awhile. I need something new. I don't really have a plan. I just feel the urge to go. If I want to get up and go somewhere, I'm just going to get up and get going. With a boyfriend, you have to actually ask, 'Hey, do you think this is a good idea?'"

"I am pretty ambitious"

Being single can free up a woman's time to get *a lot* done. Calm down: I'm not suggesting that married women don't accomplish many wonderful things, just that in order to do so, they have to manage their time and juggle the needs of others to an extent that singletons can't even imagine. We have the luxury of being able to focus – perhaps selfishly – on our own goals.

Michelle E. Alford, for instance, is a published writer and poet, playwright and director, real estate agent, and certified life coach. She has hosted a radio show, modeled, founded the Spoken Word Artist Association and Network (SWAAN) and Spoken Word Billboard awards, and competed in the *Miss Plus America Pageant*. In other words, she's crazy busy, mostly with creative pursuits.

"I put a lot of energy into doing things because I am not married," says Michelle, a fun-loving free spirit with dark brown skin, natural fine hair and a Mona Lisa smile. "I'm single and I only have one child, who's grown. And, although it may seem like a lot of things, it really isn't a lot to me because I enjoy doing them. But yes, I am pretty ambitious, because I feel like I want to have a positive impact on people I come into contact with in my own life, in service to humanity."

Michelle concedes that if she was *Mrs*. Alford, her resume would be nowhere near as full as it is.

"Even in the natural realm of just being in a boyfriend-girlfriend type of situation, sometimes men are intimidated by women who want to accomplish things," says Michelle. "So if you think in terms of marrying someone, you are kind of obligated to make decisions with that person. A lot of times, if you have things you want to accomplish, and you're married, your partner may not share that same support for you in doing so. So it would limit you, because you're married and you should respect your partner. That can cause friction in a marriage because you have a person that wants to accomplish something as an individual but they're married, so they have to confide in or seek – I don't want to say *permission* – but they have to consult with their partner and sometimes their partner may not be in favor of you doing something that you want to do in life.

"You never want to feel like, had I not been in this marriage, then I could have done this that and the other. You don't want to spend your marriage regretting not doing some of the things you wanted to do because you got married. So that plays a part in why I am not married now."

One area of interest for Michelle: the pageant world, where she went from being a contestant to a director. She was doing some modeling when several friends suggested she look into the Miss Plus America competition. At first she demurred *("I'm not a glamor girl")*, but when she explored the possibility, something clicked.

"We know what the traditional pageants are about, but I found a pageant that was spiritually based. It's more of a ministry type – helping others, because that's something that's near and dear to my heart. It wasn't just about beauty. It was about community service, service to humanity and all of those things that I like to be involved with."

Competing in 2014 as Miss Missouri, Michelle placed fourth runner up out of 53 women from across the nation.

"I got my trophy and everything. I couldn't believe it. I was stunned that I had gotten to that point. Somebody had told me that the number four was going to be significant in my life and that I was going to touch many lives across the nation and in the four corners of the world – that I was going to touch a lot of people globally with my life, and so that sort of resonated with me. I was supposed to place fourth runner up and I did."

That led to an opportunity for her to become pageant director for the Missouri area.

"I feel like everything that I'm doing, it's because I want to do it and I enjoy doing it," she says. "And for me, most of the things that I'm involved in are because it's a ministry for me, and not in the way that other people will view ministry. Ministry is just touching a life and being of service to people across the board – not with any type of religious influence, but again, going back to the spiritual influence. That's who I am as an individual, loving to be positively impactful to be other people's lives. I enjoy being creative, being spiritual, being involved."

Her feeling of satisfaction has grown over time. "Single women in our age bracket have a lot to say. We know what we want. We have careers, we have expectations."

Michelle has had a number of serious boyfriends (more on that in the chapter on dating and relationships) but when she is not part of a couple, she has no hesitation in going solo to events and social activities that are geared mainly toward couples.

"That's the interesting thing about me. If I want to go, I just go by myself. I don't want to sound mean about it, but I don't really care about what people think about me when I want to enjoy myself, doing something. If you go out, you may just meet that person that you're meant to be with. But the things that I do go to, like theatre, those are mostly in group settings."

"I thrive on those relationships"

High school assistant principal Jo-Sue is also someone who is involved in many activities that positively affect the lives of others – in her case, teenagers. Ironically, the 40-something educator knows that if she had a family of her own, the demands on her time and energy would prevent her from working with young people as much as she does now.

"I have a tremendous relationship with a lot of the students at my school, the girls that I coach, the girls in my Bible study and the youth that I youth pastor at the different churches," she says. "I absolutely love teenagers. I thrive on those relationships, on encouraging them and seeing their lives turned around by the encouragement. I know that I would not be able to do those kinds of things if I was married and had my own kids."

Jo-Sue is 6' tall – which, she says, adds to the challenge of finding a prospective mate. Thoughtful and rather quiet, she tempers her naturally reserved personality with an open, easy smile. An athlete in college, she now coaches girls' basketball, track and cross-country and officiates volleyball. As a youth pastor, she conducts a girls' Bible study group at her home every other Saturday.

Doesn't her single status pose a challenge when dealing with teenage girls, who are very interested in – obsessed about, really – relationships and romance?

"I haven't had any of them say, 'What do you know about it because you're single?' But they know I have a lot of the same feelings as teenage girls. The feelings of being rejected – or of being afraid of being rejected, whether or not you're a confident person.

"We've talked about the fact that I'm single a lot," she says. "It comes up quite a bit. And I say, 'You know, sometimes I do have down moments when I wish I was married and I wish I had kids, but if I was, I would not be able to do everything that I do.'"

She admits that because she's single, she doesn't have the answers to all of their questions. She tells them: "'I'm more than willing to pray with you and give you counsel, but you ultimately have to make the decision about what your relationship is going to be like.' But for the most part, they're very open and honest with me about what they're feeling. They know I've had a desire to get married and that just hasn't happened. Some of them are in relationships. Some of them have chosen to wait until they feel like they're more mature. They know where I come from, because I'm very open with them about it."

"I've been on my own, my own boss, my own person my whole life"

There are times when remaining single can protect you from the consequences of someone else's problems. That's the case with Sally, a sassy, 50-something redhead who has been with her boyfriend Frank off and on – mostly on – for more than 20 years. Astoundingly, they've never even discussed the possibility of getting married. That's fine with Sally, because she has no intention of tying the knot with Frank. She loves him, but…

"He makes bad choices, and I'm not going to be impacted by those bad choices. If we had been married, I'd have divorced his ass over those bad choices," says Sally, who is both forthright and funny. She'd make a good stand-up comic. She is also utterly confident, giving one the distinct impression that she's a woman who knows exactly who she is and what she wants from life.

Money is at the core of many of their differences. Sally has owned her own home in a quiet, well-maintained neighborhood for many years; it's nearly paid off. Frank decided to buy a house at a time when housing was overvalued and "the house cost way more than it was worth," says Sally, who is very good with money. Frank lost his job *and* his house. They'd lived together previously for a time – an experience which motivated Sally to make the very practical suggestion that Frank go and live with his mother instead of moving in with *her*.

"You'll be taking care of her and bringing her spirits up while she's thinking she's taking care of you," she told him. "And, she's going to cook for you and clean for you and *I'm not doing any of those things*.'

"'Not to mention, this is *my* house. If you move in, it'll be like it was before, where I have to make room for you, in my house. If we move somewhere together, then it's our house. Even if I bought it, it's still our house, or space. We set it up. But I've lived in my house for 20 years. It's my house. It's my way.'

"He can't just come in and tell me how he wants the furniture."

The two have been though a lot together (more on that in the chapter on relationships) and seem deeply committed to each other. Why not make it official?

"Because things that I can tolerate when we're not married I wouldn't be able to if we *were* married," says Sally. "People say if they won the lottery, they'd quit their job. I always say, 'I wouldn't.' If you don't *have to* work, and at any minute you can say, 'This pisses me off, bye,' it's not that bad of a job. It's when you have no options that it is misery."

One of Frank's mistakes occurred when he was arrested for drunk driving. If they'd been married, Sally says, that incident would have had a big impact on her.

"It impacted me anyway, but not the same way. If he makes bad choices I'm not happy, but they're his to make. If we're married, they're not his to make. *I'm* making them, which, obviously, he's not liking that concept, either!"

Sally works for a telecommunications company and has done quite well for herself. She enjoys being able to manage her finances without input from Frank, although she admits to some financial bad habits.

"I spend money on *crap* more so than I should. I have a three-bedroom house with a finished basement, two-and-a-half car garage, two-bedroom cottage with a garage and a three-and-a-half car two-story pole barn, and I don't have enough room for my things!"

Getting married would mean including Frank in spending decisions. "At this point, I don't want to, because I've been on my own, my own boss, my own person my whole life. If we got married and he thought that I was going to talk over with him whether I was getting a new couch or not – I ain't! If we're not married, I don't have to. He still doesn't like that too much."

"Call it single"

Like Debbie, Leanne's revelations about the joys of singlehood came after the breakup of a serious relationship. In her case, that serious relationship was a marriage. Leanne is included in this book because like Tiffany, she identifies as a single woman.

"On forms, when it says, 'Are you married, single, divorced, widowed?' I check 'single,' because I consider myself single," Leanne says. "Two years after my divorce, I might have considered myself divorced, but it's been so long since I've been married that I don't identify as divorced. That marriage was a whole other life. A whole other Leanne ago.

"So for me, if you're one of those people who gets married, gets married, gets married, divorced might be a state for you. But for people who tried it and found out that that wasn't going to work and have remained unmarried since then, I say: 'Call it single.' You are! You don't have to drag that anchor with you the rest of your life.

"I am seriously independent when it comes to that. I am me. I am *not* half of something that's broken."

Articulate and poised, Leanne is a brown-eyed 40-something brunette with a heart-shaped face, expressive features, and a chameleon-like appearance. She is as comfortable teaching in a classroom (her day job) as she is acting onstage (her real passion, theatre).

Looking back on the dissolution of her marriage, Leanne says she remembers a defining moment when she realized that getting divorced – however painful – was going to yield exciting new possibilities for her.

Devouring things "like a buffet"

"I was in a marriage where I had a very dominant partner, and for people who know me, that's saying a lot, because I hold my own quite well. But this particular person had developed quite a few personality issues that had become boorish and overbearing and overpowering. For someone like me, who is independent and confident and a self-starter, to suddenly be subsumed by that personality was something that I didn't really notice was happening at first, but my family did.

And they commented; 'Leanne, what do *you* want to do? Why are you doing everything that *he* wants to do? Where are *your* hobbies?' And I would say, 'Well, it's important that I try and support what he's doing.' What happened was that I got sort of lost in the process, in order to make sure that his needs were met and he was happy."

Meeting her husband's needs was apparently not enough to make the marriage last. When the reality of the impending divorce sunk in, Leanne went online to look for a new place to live.

"I would find these descriptions, and I remember thinking, 'Oh, God, he would hate that. He would not want that at all.' And then my next instinct was to start giggling like a girl, and think, 'But *I* would, and I get to, because this will be *my* house.'"

The freedom of not having to consider her husband's preferences was exhilarating. The genie was out of the bottle. After that revelation, Leanne resumed activities she'd previously loved, and went on to try many new ones.

"I made a list, about six years out from my divorce, of things that I had done that I thought were pretty exceptional and cool, and every now and then I'll look at that list and go, 'Dang, girl!' I took a hot air balloon ride. I went to England. I learned how to ballroom dance and I competed in ballroom dance competitions. It was all of this celebration of stuff that I was not allowed to do when I was married that I then just devoured like a buffet once I got free of that."

"It forces you to confront who you really are"

One issue that seems to divide single women is whether or not to travel alone. I have done it, and I still wonder whether it's worth doing. For many years, the trips I did take were to visit friends in cities I already knew, so I was choosing the safe and familiar instead of venturing out into the wider world, just because I didn't want to go alone. I've also traveled with friends, which can be great fun. When I have taken that vacation by myself, I've enjoyed my ability to make spontaneous decisions about where I would go and what I would do on any given day, but it would have been nice to have had someone along with whom I could have shared the experience. At times, I found myself feeling awkward and self-conscious – the odd woman out – in venues that catered to families.

Leanne travels by herself – although she concedes that initially, she was very apprehensive about it.

"The first time I did it I was scared to death. I thought; 'I'm going to be a total loser, sitting in my hotel room with room service.' But not at all. I have some of the best times traveling all by myself, because it forces you to confront who you really are, but also, every single thing is a blank slate. Nobody knows you. Nobody has a preconceived notion. You can be whoever you want to be. If you're feeling confident that day, you can exude confidence. If you're feeling shy and withdrawn, that's cool, too. I *love* traveling alone."

Leanne goes to the Stratford Festival in Ontario, Canada, each year to indulge in her love of theatre. She books herself into her favorite bed and breakfast and makes reservations at the nicer restaurants in town. "If I'm going to go, to hell with it. I'm going!"

On one occasion, she was sitting all by herself at a five-star restaurant when she began listening to a conversation going on at a nearby table, among two couples in their 40s.

"When I dine out alone, I have the best time eavesdropping on what's going on around me," she confesses. "The fascinating conversations that you hear. And I started laughing at something they were saying at their table and they noticed, which was *mortifying*.

"One of the women said, 'I'm sorry, are we bothering you?' They were nice about it. I said, 'No, *I'm* sorry. I overheard what you were saying and it was very amusing.' And one of the women said, 'Oh, are you here all by yourself?' I said, 'Yes, I am.' She said, 'At the restaurant? Or are you traveling alone?' I said, 'No, I'm here alone. I bought tickets to the show and I'm staying at a bed and breakfast. I'm here all by myself.'

"And both women in perfect unison went, 'Oh, that's so cool! You get to order what you want for dinner and pick out your shows.' And the two men are like, 'Uh, hello?'

"They were just so amazed that, here I am, sitting there, ordering half a bottle of champagne and filet mignon and I'm having a high old time all by myself. I was ready for the whole, 'Oh you poor thing, can't you find anybody?' And what I got was total sisterhood. It was nothing but envy from that table.

"I think it is changing. The tide is turning. And even women who are in apparently happy marriages are like, 'Oh, that's so great.'"

The Downside to Being an Old Maid

Dr. Karen Gail Lewis is angry that society promotes the notion that if a woman is not married, it's somehow her fault.

"Too many women buy into that self-blame," says the family therapist, whose practice includes many women who are trying to come to terms with their single status.

"I'm mad that so many smart, professionally successful, delightful women beat up on themselves because they aren't married or haven't stayed married or haven't remarried. They feel as if they have somehow failed. They haven't met the standard. The big one is 'What's wrong with me that I'm not married? What's wrong with me that I can't meet a man?'"

Dr. Lewis says this self-blame leads to a desire for what she calls, "the fix-it solution." A patient may feel that if she has a problem and Dr. Lewis can help her fix that problem, she won't have to be single anymore. "The assumption is, as soon as I help them not be shy or not scare men off or not be afraid of intimacy, they are going to meet a man that they're going to partner with."

Blaming themselves for being single

Women have many ways in which they blame themselves for being single. Dr. Lewis has heard them all. She's compiled a list that includes: they're too fat; too skinny; too intelligent; not intelligent enough; they scare men away; they're afraid of intimacy. Women get reinforcement in their tendency toward recrimination from loved ones, self-help books and even, sometimes, mental health professionals. Among the messages they hear and absorb: "You don't give a man a chance," "You're too choosy," "You're too set in your ways," "You aren't feminine enough."

Dr. Lewis does *not* help women "fix" themselves so that they can skip happily down the road toward certain matrimony. Her goal, instead, is to help "wise, competent, successfully single" women:
- feel good about themselves
- make good choices about their lives
- take control of the things in their lives where they do have control and let go of the areas where they don't
- deal with the "worst part" of being single – the ambiguity of whether or not they will ever meet the man of their choosing

"Of course, you have to make yourself into the best woman you can be and resolve old baggage from childhood and prior relationships," says Dr. Lewis. "You have to have a full and meaningful life – whether or not you ever meet a man of your choosing. You have to do all this so when or if you do meet this man, he will be the icing on the already wonderful cake of your life." She points out an advantage of being single: it allows you to focus more on your own personal growth.

Dr. Lewis has written a book called, *With or without a Man: Single Women Taking Control of Their Lives*, which defines affirmative choices for single women. A companion workbook offers strategies and tools to make being single easier and less stressful. One section offers guidance on how to deal with one's own feelings and biases about being single.

She helps her patients understand the distinction between their public persona and their private persona. The public persona may say: "I am content with being single. I want to be a modern woman. My life is great."

The private persona may feel a little differently about being single: "Sure, I would love to have a man in my life. I may or not want to get married, but I would never tell anyone that because they may see me as pathetic."

Lewis said women with that persona are reluctant to reveal their feelings because they're embarrassed. "It comes too close to being pitied."

"Where did you get the message that there's something wrong with you if you're single?" Dr. Lewis asks her patients. "Let's look at how much of this really is your fault. Tell me all the reasons why you think you're single. Tell me all these awful things about you. Tell me about the men you've been with.

"Women have this headset that it must be their fault. Women believe it is their job to make a relationship successful, or to find a relationship if they are not currently in one."

Your job as a female

Dr. Lewis asserts that this belief comes, in part, from what society defines as our core identities. What it means to be a good man and a good woman.

"The man's core identity is to be a man, be successful in the work role. To make money. Some men don't care about that. Most men either meet that standard or don't meet that standard. Once they retire, they don't have to worry about that any more.

"For women, the core identity is relationships. Your job as a female is to take care of relationships. And if there is a problem in relationships, it's your job to fix the problem."

The fallacy of that kind of thinking is: Where are the men? Are they working on their own personal growth?

"The women come in trying to make themselves emotionally healthy so that men are going to want them more but the men are not making themselves emotionally healthy, because far fewer men come in to therapy.

"So as women get more emotionally healthy, they are more appropriately choosey. So of course, they are going to find even fewer men that they're going to want to be with."

Dr. Lewis said that women who have done growth work on themselves tend to rule out potential partners faster because they can tell when men haven't done growth work and don't know how to have a relationship.

Consequently – and ironically – the chances of women getting married decrease as they get psychologically healthy – until men retire. At that point, according to Dr. Lewis, a shift occurs. Prior to retirement, men focus their energy on their work. Relationships may be important, but for most men, they are still secondary to work. Once men retire, though, they have the energy for relationships – which opens up lots of interesting possibilities for always single women of a certain age.

"Men are not as threatened at that point to be with a woman," says Dr. Lewis.

She conducts weekend-long Unique Retreats for single women in which she does *not* teach them how and where to meet eligible men, how to make themselves more attractive to men or how to flirt. Instead, the retreats focus on:

- getting women to stop blaming themselves for being single
- helping them cope with bias from society, family and friends
- showing them how to get support and understanding from other single women

American women aren't the only ones who grapple with the emotional issues of singledom. Although Dr. Lewis' practice is based in Boston, Massachusetts and Silver Spring and Bethesda, Maryland, she finds herself working with patients all over the U.S. and in countries like Saudi Arabia, Turkey and Scandinavia via Skype or phone.

"Never Married" versus "Always Single"

In addition to changing the way unmarried women feel about themselves, Dr. Lewis is on a crusade to change the way society thinks about them. For starters, she wants to establish a new term for us because the phrase "never married" is negative, and puts the focus on what we *haven't* done – we haven't gotten married.

"I refuse to use the word unmarried, because that's like saying you are talking to an unman who is untall," says Lewis. "Our language hasn't caught up with what is happening in the world today. We only have language for young singles. Date. Unmarried. Boyfriend, girlfriend. "

These terms were useful many years ago, when most people got married in their teens or 20s, but new ones are needed now, especially to apply to women who have always been single. "There is such a huge percentage of women now who are not married, and we don't have a language for that."

In keeping with her preference for the positive, Lewis calls Baby Boomer women who have never married "always single" – a term I've opted to use in this book. She calls those who are single after a divorce or the death of a husband "single again."

A family life cycle developed by therapists Betty Carter and Monica Goldrick in 1980 deals with the nuclear family. It identifies three stages which encompass the unmarried state. First is the family of origin experiences; leaving home and the premarriage stage. After that, it's on to childless couple stage; family with young children; family with adolescents; launching children and then, late family life. That's a useful model for families, but what about for the always single people?

Lewis has devised a life stage model which, after childhood and adolescence, hits an adult divide – a fork in the road, if you will – and defines a new paradigm.

"The two pathways are single and married – or partnered. Many people go back and forth between the two pathways, and almost everyone ends up single. It's a whole new way of looking at singlehood as a life stage in adulthood, as opposed to a deviance that you haven't yet married."

The odd woman out

Although some of the women that I interviewed for this book had expected or hoped to get married, none of them said they were chronically unhappy over the fact that they are single. This may be because it a self-selecting group comprised of women who were willing to talk to me because they are ok with being single. Or, it could be because many women *are* ok with being single.

Still, there are times when it's difficult not to feel like the odd woman out when you're surrounded by couples. There are also activities we may be inclined to avoid if we don't have a regular partner. I didn't travel as much as I wanted to when I was younger because I was always waiting for the right guy to come along and go with me on my adventures. I also wanted him to join me in taking ballroom dancing classes (why bother learning if you'll have no one to dance with?).

"That's the only drawback"

Debbie, the one-time band manager, expressed a similar sentiment.

"There are some things like, tomorrow night I want to go downtown for a concert. If I had that partner, I'd already have that built-in person, for concerts and weddings and things. That's the only thing, not having that person who would just go with you on occasions like that. Like on a cruise, or vacations."

She's taken many solo vacations and always had a great time, but now that she's in her 50s, she'd really like to have someone to go with.

"I used to go by myself but there were always people I knew, where I was going. But now, it's not always like that. Going someplace by yourself, you're on your own the whole time. But that's the only drawback of being single, especially when you get older."

If she invites a girlfriend to do something it's likely to be someone who's single or divorced. The married ones tend to want to bring their husbands along, which makes Debbie a third wheel.

Do single women get lonely? In my admittedly unscientific sampling, I found that the answer is: sometimes.

"I don't have time to be lonely"

Joan White is a stylish 40-something fashion designer from Winston-Salem, North Carolina (you can find her Voluptuous Diva Inc. brand on Facebook). A plus-sized woman with a vivacious, plus-sized personality, Joan says she occasionally feels lonely.

"Every now and then it might hit me for a brief moment. But alone does not mean lonely. I have a full life. I have a wonderful family. I have some very good friends and family. I don't have time to be lonely, really, because I have so much to do. My dream and my vision and my purpose are so full and they are what drive me towards greatness daily."

Ellen's loneliness is also fleeting. The 60-something retired businesswoman stays busy with volunteer work at a local hospital and outings with her friends, and so rarely has the time to feel lonely. However, the Arizona resident had to navigate an enormous midlife change when she left her career to care for her ailing parents – and ended up living with her mother for ten years. Now, after her mother's passing, the house feels empty without her. Ellen also has had to adjust to being free from her mother's rules – some of which negatively affected Ellen's love life.

"She wouldn't let me have a guy come in past the front door, so I haven't really had a chance to date. That's worked out ok, I mean, because I feel like my parents did a lot for me and I'm happy that I was able to do things for them."

Travel business owner Stephanie enjoys being alone in some ways. "I'm happy having my own time. I'm alone but I don't really feel lonely. I don't feel this yearning inside." Still, she thinks it's possible to be too independent. "You have to allow people in," she acknowledges, "to say, let me help you or let me share that burden" - although she once shied away from that kind of obligation. "For instance, if I had to move, I'd hire a mover. I would never ask a friend to help me move," she remembers. "I've learned to let people do things for me and feel nice about it and be very thankful and grateful, too."

She feels as if she needs to teach herself that it's ok to let other people help her, "because I'm quite accustomed to doing the things myself."

Beyond loneliness, do always single women suffer an emotional toll because society seems to value single women less than married women? In a way, this is a loaded question. I think *mothers* are, mostly, amazing, and should be greatly appreciated. They have the toughest, most challenging, multi-layered and consequential mission in the world: to raise children to adulthood, to protect them, guide them and help them learn how to be happy and productive. That's HUGE.

But leaving mothers aside, should a woman get a big fat nod of approval from society simply because she's snagged a husband? Or, to reverse that: should a woman be thought of as inferior simply because she hasn't?

"It kind of just slapped me in the face"

Educator and coach Jo-Sue, for whom religion is very important, has felt the sting of being treated differently in church.

"I feel less valued sometimes. And I hate to say that. But some things that have happened in churches, like, 'Ok, we're going to have communion today, we're going to have you take it with your family.' Well, *I'm* the only person in my family at that church. But there've always been people in the church who say, 'Hey, Jo-Sue, come join with us.' But still, it felt like I was a little bit isolated at that moment."

Once, her church announced that they were looking for a couple to serve as youth pastors – a role Jo-Sue had performed by herself. "It kind of just slapped me in the face, them saying they wanted a couple." She understood the point of having a husband and wife to deal with both boys and girls, but she couldn't help but feel "a little bit less valued" by this decision.

In her broader community, though, among people who have known her for a long time, she feels generally accepted for who she is. "I haven't really had a whole lot of problems with them saying, 'You're not good enough because you're not with somebody.'"

"So I didn't contribute to the gene pool – so what?"

For university administrator Andrea, being single has sometimes made a difference in the workplace.

"There have been times when I have felt it, in the earlier stages of my career. The other women I was working with were mothers, and they would say, 'Oh, it's 4:30, I have to go pick my kid up from day care. I can't stay. I can't work late. I can't go on the out of town business trip."

Consequently, Andrea was the one who invariably ended up working late, or traveling on business. "Yes, there were times when I felt put upon."

Andrea talks a lot about being a useful member of society, making a difference, giving back. "So I didn't contribute to the gene pool – so what? There are people who know me who still think I'm valuable. They've told me so in any number of ways, by telling me they're glad I moved here. At the risk of sounding kind of full of myself, within a matter of being just two or three years in this community, I have gotten recognition by way of different community awards that some people who've lived here all their lives never receive. That's not why I do it, but it's recognition that in some way I am giving back to the community, by the way I spend my time – in ways other than contributing to the gene pool or getting married."

Ellen, the retired businesswoman living in Arizona, has experienced similar work-related differences from employers who expected single people to put in more overtime and be more available than women with children. "They could call in sick and say, 'Hey, I've got a problem with the kids' and things like that. And when I worked at the bank, women with families were given higher raises than women without children."

"There are times when I would sell my soul for a man in the house"

Leanne, the high school teacher and actor, isn't sure if single women are valued less, but she does get annoyed with the *assumption* that women of a certain age are married.

"I get tired of unraveling that for people. Like when I'm doing business anywhere, over the phone, or at a mall or something, it's always 'Mrs. ---.' I say, 'No. That's my Mom.'

"Or I'll go to the doctor and the doctor will ask, 'Do you snore?' Well hell if I know! Ask my dog. I mean, who would know that? Or, if you're going to need some sort of minor assistance after some surgery, they just assume that you share a home with someone and that there'll be someone to take care of you. And oftentimes I have to explain to people; 'I live alone, so no, I'm not capable of doing that.'"

When she drops her car off at the dealership for repairs that will take several days, she has to request a loaner, because she doesn't have a husband who can give her rides in the interim.

"So it's not so much devaluing, it's just not considering the plight of a woman by herself and what that might entail in terms of assistance."

For Leanne, the times when she doesn't necessarily enjoy being single are the social events that are organized for couples, like weddings. "You sit there at the table with the assorted other 'spares' and then it comes time to dance and there you sit. And New Year's Eve. The things that sort of *assume* a date are where I feel like, 'Shoot. I guess I'll just stay home.'"

Leanne brings up a subject that I can empathize with: the pitfalls of being a single woman homeowner. I am not naturally "handy," nor have I been able to acquire any significant DIY skill sets since I stopped renting and actually made the commitment to buy a house. When I attempt to repair something in said house I usually make the problem worse. Additionally, my ignorance is such that I'm pretty sure

I am routinely overcharged by workmen. When a furnace technician charged me $500 for a fix that turned out to take 20 minutes and require a small, uncomplicated-looking part, I knew I was being ripped off. I also knew that he wouldn't have done that to a man. However, it was the coldest day of the year and late in the afternoon. By the time I called another company, I'd be paying for nighttime rates which would cancel out part of the difference between the ripoff price and an honest one. And, I'd still have to pay the ripoff tech for the cost of a house call. And did I mention that this was the coldest day of the year and my teeth were chattering and my fingertips were turning blue? This was one of those rare times when I really wished I had a husband to deal with the situation. In any case, I bit the bullet and paid the price. I needed heat.

Leanne knows what that's like. "I despise being a single woman homeowner. Holy God! Things break around here and I do my best, but there are times when I would sell my soul for a man in the house right then. The feminist in me is like, 'Yeah….' But I do hate being alone when things like that happen, because I feel like this is one time when I could really use a champion."

"If I had a partner, that would make me feel safer"

Are there things we single women don't do, or put off, because we're single? Because we are still hoping that the right man will come along and join us in our adventures – or at least, make them look the way we think they're supposed to look?

Being single didn't curtail Atheria's activities until she developed a serious health issue. Then, flying solo was suddenly not as fun for the 49-year-old psychic medium who lives in New Mexico. A large personality in a tiny, 5' tall frame, Atheria is youthful-looking and pretty, with hazel eyes, auburn hair and cheekbones reminiscent of Hollywood's gilded age movie stars.

Her marital status became a problem when she was diagnosed with hypoglycemia and had such severe low blood sugar attacks that several times, she was afraid she was going to die.

"Because I lived alone that health issue triggered an anxiety panic disorder which has becoming increasingly debilitating," Atheria says. "Remote locations trigger me. I have to know where hospitals are at all times."

She is managing her anxiety better these days, but still can't handle being too far from home. "I think if I had a partner, that would make me feel safer. I'm actually debating right now, trying to force myself to go back to Costa Rica to see if I could handle it. I actually want to move there. I'm thinking of finally taking a chance and leaving the country and seeing how I do. Just flying to Rochester, New York for my high school reunion was extremely scary and I had to take Adivan.

"But if I had a partner in life that was traveling with me, I'd be more willing to travel, and not be afraid that I'm going to get sick and die in Italy or something."

"If I'm feeling lonely, I'll get out there"

Speaking of traveling, fifty-something retired firefighter Suzanne has not taken a very specific trip she's had in mind for a long time: a honeymoon in Venice. "I want to do the romantic thing in Venice," she says, with a big smile. "I want the gondola, the champagne, the violinist. It's something I've always wanted to do. That would be the perfect honeymoon. Is that weird?"

Suzanne, who is tall, vivacious and relentlessly positive, is described by friends as the person who'll come to your house early to chop vegetables for the party you're giving; help you paint your living room or go with you to the vet and hold your hand when you need to have your sick, elderly dog euthanized.

She admits to sometimes feeling lonely but points out, quite logically, that everyone does at one time or another.

"Even when you're in a relationship, sometimes you can feel lonely. But I don't let that stop me from anything. It doesn't stagnate me or immobilize me. If I'm feeling lonely, I'll get out there. I'll go to a bar, I'll meet somebody. Go on a trip." She laughs. "I've gotten more marriage proposals on trips than I've gotten any place else!"

"I wanted to be in a marriage relationship"

North Carolina fashion designer Joan put off buying a house and didn't purchase one until she was 37, because she thought a woman should buy a house with her husband. She also didn't adopt children because she kept thinking she'd get married.

"Those are things I just waited on. I always wanted to travel, but I was, I don't know, hesitant, fearful. When you have someone that's always in your ear with a lot of hurt and a lot of fear, you can be bound by that. I'm not bound by that anymore. If I've got the money and I want to go, I'll go."

"I wanted to be in a marriage relationship. I wanted to be in a Christian family that went to church, that led a Christian-guided life.

And I wanted it to be with a black man, so I could be an example for a quality African-American family. But it never happened that way."

"I'm just meant to be with somebody"

Pat Jones, a writer/director/producer in Detroit (writing under the name P.J. Edghill), always wanted to travel to exotic places, but didn't because she hated going alone. Now, she is hampered by a disability resulting from neurological symptoms that she attributes to Ground Zero exposure when she lived in New York City.

Petite and voluptuous, with long locs framing her face, a huge smile and a warm, humorous manner, Pat describes herself in sets of contradictions: spiritual and wild, assertive and sweet, high maintenance and easy going.

Does she every feel lonely? "Oh, God, yes. Yes. Yes. Yes."

Sunday is the worst day of the week for Pat, who lives with her sister, brother-in-law and young niece. They all go to 10:30 Mass together. Then Sunday afternoons loom empty in front of her – although not for her family members. "They seem to know what they're about and I don't know what I'm about," she says. "I'm just meant to be with somebody. I need a partner. I just do."

However, Pat has developed strategies for dealing with the feeling. When loneliness hits, she'll write (stage plays and fiction, among other things) or call friends, so that she does not isolate. "I'm not a wallflower. I do know what to do when I feel that way and it's not to hide it or mask it. It's to actually dissipate it. Get rid of it. Because you *can* get rid of it. The crippling pain of loneliness? You've got to work on getting out of that, because isolation is the devil's playground."

What Other People Think of Us and What We Think of Ourselves

Or, is it better to be a has been than a never was?

In an article[1] in *Boston Magazine*'s January 2012 issue entitled, "Single by Choice," writer Janelle Nanos profiles some happily unmarried people living in the Boston area. And in the online comments section which follows the article, we find: *"Don't talk to these people; they turned me into a newt!"*

Ah, the sophisticated humor of online commenters. At least these days, people only *joke* about old maids being witches. They're no longer burning us at the stake. At the risk of reading too much into an anonymously posted wisecrack, its reference to an age-old stereotype draws from a familiar well: that there's something fundamentally wrong with women who remain single. We're *weird*. Our reasons for not entering into this basic social compact *must* be negative, right? Maybe we can't attract men because we're ugly or overweight or have abrasive personalities (or all of the above). Maybe we're man-haters. And of course, there's the ever-popular: maybe we're lesbians. Many women who are single *are* lesbians. Many women who are single are straight. And here's a news flash: ever since the U.S. Supreme Court's landmark ruling on same-sex marriages, many lesbians have tied the knot. Drawing conclusions about someone's sexual orientation from their marital status makes about as much sense as giving your bank account number to a stranger who emails you to ask for help in moving six million dollars out of Nigeria.

Single women who are over a certain age are well aware of the general assumption that being married is the norm and being single is *ab*normal because people - even people we've just met – often feel quite free to discuss this unnatural deviance on our part with us. Otherwise well-mannered folk who would almost never consider prying into the private lives of a brand new acquaintance have no reluctance in doing so when they find out that she's an old maid. I've experienced this with bosses, co-workers, a man at a class reunion whom I hadn't seen in 30 years, dental hygienists, a stranger sitting next to me on an airplane, manicurists, a woman waiting at an auto dealership for her car to be fixed and various random strangers at parties. Wherever one is expected to strike up a polite conversation and reveal a few facts about oneself, a woman can expect to come under scrutiny if she lets slip that she has never been married. (I did recently have a different experience with a hair stylist who is divorced and struggling to raise two kids with no financial help from her ex. Upon finding out that I had never gotten married, she said, "How'd you get so lucky?" – but that reaction is the exception.)

People want an explanation. A story. Something that makes you make sense to them.

I look normal

I try to be compassionate rather than annoyed. After all, these friendly, unsuspecting people have struck up a conversation with someone who *appears* normal. It's natural for them to expect the usual exchange of banal details. Where do you live? What do you do for a living? How long have you been married? Oh, you're not married? So you're divorced? You're not…divorced. But…if you're not divorced, and you're not currently married, that means…you've *never been married?*

This dissonant cognition is so startling to some people that it stops them cold. After all (they think) isn't everybody supposed to grow up and get married? And a woman who doesn't share this world view with them might deviate from what they are convinced is the natural order of things in other ways as well! Who knows what dark secrets lurk beneath the ordinary-looking exteriors of old maids?!

Aside from challenging a pervasive value system, a happily unmarried woman might also serve – unwittingly – as a sort of mirror, reflecting back an image of an alternate reality. On occasion, I've had the sneaking suspicion that the person asking *how-is-it-that-you've-never-been-married* (HIITYNBM) is someone who is stuck in an unsatisfying marriage and questioning their own choices, rather than mine.

What's interesting about all this is that as a society, our ideas about marriage and family have undergone profound changes in recent years. While there's still considerable resistance from some quarters to anything other than traditional social constructs, a great many Americans are embracing, or at least tolerating, same-sex couples and their raising of children together. It may have taken Aunt Vivian awhile to accept the fact that her niece Carolyn will be exchanging vows with someone named *Diane*, but Viv wouldn't think of missing the wedding. All of the relatives will be there, and she's determined to demonstrate that she's as open-minded as the next person. (Besides, she's just dying to see which woman will wear the big white gown. Or will they both do that? Or neither!)

But what about people who don't get married to anyone? Now *that's* radical.

"They're putting it all on me"

"The reaction that I get that pisses me off – I get really mad now – and it mostly comes from men – the reaction is always; 'but you're attractive and you've got so much going for you, I don't understand it. How could you be single?' In other words, they're putting it all on me."

This comes from Atheria, the psychic medium. In addition to being quite pretty, Atheria is zany, extroverted and spiritual. She owns a handgun. She's a writer and an indie filmmaker. She was once abducted by aliens; now she channels them at paranormal forums. (Find her online information in the About the Women in this Book section.)

Atheria is many things, but what she is *not* is a man-hater – although she's come to hate the conversations about her marital status that she often has with the men she encounters.

"The snotty response I give them, especially in New Mexico, where the men are just…the man situation here is *so* bad, I say, 'I know I'm good-looking. I've got a great bod. I'm intelligent. I have this house. I'm financially secure. The problem is, the men here are gross, boring and have no ambition. It's not me, it's them. I don't find them attractive.'"

"Just go for that fat, bald one."

Atheria also gets irritated when she's told that at her age, she should "settle" for whatever man she can get.

"I've actually had women say to me that I shouldn't even try to look for an attractive guy. That I'm being shallow. Just go for that fat, bald one. Be desperate and take whatever. And I say, 'I'm sorry, no. I'd rather be alone.'"

There's nothing wrong with us.

Jo-Sue – the high school assistant principal – has also learned to deal with disbelief from new acquaintances. "When people find out that I'm not married, they're shocked because I have a great personality," she says. "I get: 'You're good-looking, blah blah blah.' They don't understand why I haven't found that right person yet."

And what does she tell them?

"That there are slim pickings where I live! And I'm very choosy. And I've seen too many marriages that…just to settle for something? I say, 'I'm not going to settle. I'd rather be single and make my own decisions than be miserable and married.'

"I'm not single by choice. Well it *is* by choice, because I chose not to go with the people who pursued me a few times. But I'm single. I'm not going to lie down in a ditch and cry and moan about it. Only weak people do that, really. You have to have enough confidence. I think sometimes people think that maybe there's something wrong with single people. There's nothing wrong with us. Just because we didn't get married it does not mean there's something wrong with us. We're just enjoying our life and building with what we have, and if marriage happens, it happens. But if it doesn't, that's not going to be the end of us. We're still going to have an impact on the world. There are a lot of single people out there. A lot, both guys and girls, that are still single. We contribute a huge amount to society. So I don't feel less of a person because I'm single."

Sheryl, a 50-something Southern Californian who works in the fashion industry, gets the kind of response from strangers that we old maids know all too well. "They're kind of surprised, because I think they see me as sort of an attractive woman who has my stuff together and I seem pleasant and friendly enough, so why wouldn't a man have wanted me? That's the reaction I get."

Sheryl is tall and slim, with shoulder-length dark hair, a fair complexion, grey-blue eyes and a fondness for hats. She lives in a home decorated with an eclectic mix of contemporary, Art Deco and mid-century modern furniture, and accessorized with dog toys and dog beds. Bookcases teeming with books and altars holding crystals reflect her love of reading and her interest in the metaphysical. "I do my best to keep it tidy; however I've released the need to live in an immaculate home that I held onto in my younger years, so it could be classified as 'lived in,'" she says with a laugh.

Sheryl's friends describe her as mellow, quiet and caring. She describes herself as introverted and thoughtful and believes that people often underestimate her because of her cool exterior. Nonetheless; "I am very resilient, strong plus hopeful, and I believe there is always a way."

"Oh, the poor thing, she never found anyone."

In her fashion industry career, Sheryl interacts with many associates who come from very traditional cultures. Those are the people who tend to be most mystified by her single status.

"You know, California is so racially diverse and since I'm in the apparel business, I've worked with a lot of companies where I'm the only one of European descent. Right now the owners of the company I work for are Cambodian and Chinese. The Chinese culture in general is very family-oriented. A lot of Latino cultures are very family-oriented. So I think sometimes they look at me and they can't figure me out, or they think I'm sort of suspect or there's got to be something really unusual about me. Sometimes they'll ask me questions. Latinos – a lot of people I've worked with have had children at 14 or 15 years old, so for them it's really unusual and I think they think, 'Oh, the poor thing, she never found anyone.'"

Many times, HIITYNBM is followed by compliments, presumably to lessen the sting of what that question implies: *something must be wrong with you.* "I'm just surprised you've never been married because you're nice looking and you have such a great personality" is something I've heard more than a few times. I appreciate the sentiment, but it still leaves me with the burden of explaining myself to someone who can't think outside of society's box.

Lucy has been on the receiving end of HIITYNBM many times. The blue-eyed, 47-year-old Denver stockbroker is petite and, by her own admission, very pretty – a characteristic which seems to confound people who learn that she's single.

"I get very strange reactions"

"I'm fairly attractive – especially when I was younger, I was really attractive," she says, matter-of-factly. "I've kind of faded a little bit. Women and guys, they just can't figure it out. They're like, 'What's wrong with you? How could you possibly be single?' I get very strange reactions, especially on a first date. It's a warning flag to them that something's wrong with you, but I think I'm the most well balanced person I know."

Like Jo-Sue with her "slim pickings" and Atheria with her "I'd rather be alone than settle," Lucy has developed a response – "a little story-line," she calls it – that's designed to placate the curious. She does *not* tell them the truth, which is that she wanted to avoid having a life like her mother's – one based on serving her family and coping with financial hardship after a divorce (more on Lucy's story in the chapter on attitudes toward marriage).

"What I say is, 'I'm not married because I didn't want kids and all the guys that I was meeting wanted children.' So that's been my tag-line, my excuse 'why' for my 20s and 30s. Now, in my 40s, that's really not working anymore, because the men are older and they're over the kid thing or they're already done with it and they have adult children."

I walk away as quickly as possible

Lucy's first date experiences are very familiar to me. I've been on my fair share of first dates. (The worst ones – like the time my date and I almost got kicked out of a movie theatre because he wouldn't stop talking loudly – have at least provided me with material for the plays I've written.). The revelation that I've never been married seems to send up a big red flag to whatever man I'm with – more so than if I said I'd been married and divorced a couple of times.

Multiple divorces are certainly a big red flag to *me*. When I meet a man who tells me he's been through three divorces – and *none* of them were his fault – I walk away as quickly as possible. Someone with a track record like that (and the excessive amount of baggage that usually accompanies it) is not someone I need in my life. He's either a serial cheater or a genuine jerk. Most likely a serial cheater. Why men who aren't able or willing to be monogamous marry again and again is something I will never understand. Perhaps they enjoy the idea of being married but not the reality of being committed to one woman. Or maybe they keep getting married *because they think that's what's expected of them*.

Perfectly nice people get divorced. It happens. But when you find yourself doing it again and again, it's possible that, on some level, you don't really want to be married. Just sayin'.

So back to the first date dilemma. I've considered lying and saying that I'm divorced, just to avoid the inevitable HIITYNBM question. I've never done it, though. Whether it's because I have too much integrity to lie or because I'm too lazy to come up with all of the details that lying would entail is up for debate. For one thing, I'm bad with numbers. He'd probably ask, "How long were you married?" followed by, "How long have you been divorced?" These are common first date questions. They presumably help establish your level of bitterness toward the opposite sex. The thinking goes that if you've been divorced for a long time, relative to the number of years you were married, you probably aren't still brimming over with anger and mistrust. Probably.

If we'd also established how old I was when I walked down the aisle to (temporary) wedded bliss, the entire line of questioning would require me to do math in my head – something of which I'm incapable (see the "bad with numbers" comment).

On the other hand, if I've already decided that I don't want to spend more time with the man sitting across the table from me in the Italian/Thai/Mediterranean restaurant and telling me how his ex-wife and her lawyer screwed him in the divorce, dropping the *I've-never-been-married* bomb is a convenient way to increase the likelihood that he won't call me again.

Being an aberration has its advantages.

I try to have empathy for those who are truly perplexed by the lack of an obvious explanation for why a woman of a certain age is not and has never been married. Their belief in normalcy shaken, their curiosity left raw and unsatisfied, I must make them feel as if the earth is suddenly tilting on its axis at the wrong angle.

"Who wants to settle down? I want to keep going!"

Stephanie – the travel entrepreneur – takes it all with a grain of salt. "People compliment me, saying, you're a really nice lady and you're attractive and intelligent – why haven't you ever gotten married? They're kind of saying I'm a catch. Why haven't I been caught yet?"

Marcy – the ski instructor – is also used to the strange reactions. "In the beginning, when you meet people they're like, 'Wow, you have so much on the ball, you have so much going for you, you've never settled down and gotten married?' Who wants to settle down?" she asks. "I want to keep going!" Like most of us, she, too, has developed a standard explanation, which she keeps at the ready. Hers is simple: "There hasn't been the right one."

That's the answer retired businesswoman Ellen gives as well. "I have a lot of people ask me why I'm not married, because I actually look pretty young for my age," said the slender, toned Arizona resident, who wears her blonde hair in a short bob and has unlined skin and perfectly sculpted eyebrows. "Most people would never guess my age. All I tell people is, 'I just never found that right person at the right time.'" Ellen's family history has a lot to do with her not being married; more on that in the chapter on attitudes toward marriage and where they come from.

"What is wrong with these men?"

Forty-something Lavender Moon, a petite, physically fit African-American woman with large, expressive eyes and the kind of smile that immediately puts you at ease, said many people are shocked when they discover that she's never been married. A single mom who spends her free time with family and friends, Lavender Moon says the typical response is, "'Oh, wow, you're not married? You're the marrying type. You carry yourself well, like a lady.' People always say, 'What is wrong with these men?' It's never anything on my end."

When she moved back to her home state of Indiana, Andrea – the corporate exec turned higher education administrator – soon found herself on the receiving end of the kind of interrogations to which we always single women are accustomed. For example, one day she arrived at church shortly before the service was to begin and introduced herself to the older woman sitting next to her.

"She asked me whether I was married or had any kids and I said, no, I'd never been married and I had no children. And she said something on the order of, 'Well I can't believe that somebody as lovely as you, that nobody ever wanted to marry you.' And I just smiled. I wasn't nasty about it. I just smiled and said, 'Don't assume that it was because nobody wanted to marry me. It was my choice.' And that was kind of the end of it. It was clearly a generational difference. In her generation, an unmarried woman was a spinster that nobody wanted. And I knew that she didn't mean anything negative. It was kind of a back-handed compliment. We were sitting in church and I wasn't going to be nasty to her. She was very nice to me from that point on."

She's not married but she has money?

It's mystifying enough (to some people) that Andrea is single. As a result of her successful corporate career, she is also well-to-do – something which made her an even greater object of curiosity in her new community. After all, how was it possible that a woman without a husband is wealthy?

"I entertain a lot and have a lot of open houses," she said. "The first couple I had, the church was so small I just invited anybody and everybody from the church who wanted to come. Well of course my parents were here, too, and my Mom told me afterwards that all the little old church ladies were asking her a lot of questions about me. They wouldn't ask me, but they would ask her because she was kind of their contemporary. They wanted to know where I worked. The point was: where did I get so much money to build a house like that? That was kind of what they were trying to get at. As in, did I get a lot of money from divorcing men? That kind of thing. And of course, my mother's even cagier than I am, and all she would say was that I had had a lot of good jobs. Where other mothers will brag about their grandkids, my mother will brag about my jobs. So it's been kind of interesting to watch her over the years. She really doesn't have to bug me about getting married and having kids, because I've given her plenty to talk about."

At 60, Kay – the singer and dancer turned vegan educator - doesn't hear HIITYNBM as much these days, but it came up many times in the past. Kay laughs when she recalls the reactions.

"People were incredulous: 'You're so great, how could you not have found a guy?' Well I didn't find the right guy *for me*. You don't just get married to get married if you don't cross paths with the right person, someone that you feel compelled to spend your life with. There are plenty of women who compromised and got married. That's why they ended up divorced, eventually."

"People always come up with the wrong conclusions"

Michelle, the poet/writer/director and real estate agent (among other things), has encountered the same sort of disbelief. "They think that something must be wrong with you," she said. "Or you may be a difficult person. Or if you're an accomplished person, they may think that you're too arrogant or something like that. Never that you're really a spiritually grounded person who knows exactly what you want in your life. You never get accused of that. But, yeah, I think people always question why you're not married and come up with wrong conclusions. I have to follow my own process."

Because she participates in spoken word performances and has strutted the stage in beauty pageants, people don't believe Michelle when she tells them that she's somewhat solitary in nature. "I can't connect with just anybody. People look at me and think that I must be this outgoing person because when I'm involved with something I'm pretty outgoing, but for the most part, I'm more of an introvert. I like to have my moments and my time. I like to spend that time in a quiet place, in a peaceful place, so I often do things to make sure that I have peace in my world."

"I don't wake up every day and think, I'm single."

Debbie the gypsy has her explanation ready. "Usually I'll say, 'I did a lot of traveling, I did a lot of partying, I just didn't want to get tied down, I didn't want to have kids.' No one's ever been rude enough to keep asking me questions. If some people don't know anyone who's never gotten married, it's a bizarre thing to them, yet I know so many people who haven't gotten married.

"I don't even really think about it a lot until somebody asks. It doesn't faze me until it's brought up. I don't wake up every day and think, *I'm single*.

"I think I've gone for so long without it, without having to depend on a man for anything – my happiness, or my financial security. It would be great to find somebody else to help pay the bills, but then there's all that other stuff that goes with it, and I don't want all that."

"Who's going to marry you? I mean, look at you."

These days, Joan - the designer of plus-size fashions - doesn't pay much attention to what people think of her single status, but she did when she was younger. Today she is confident and full of charisma, but it took her a long time to get there. Joan suffered from low self-esteem for many years.

"I've been told most of my life that because of my weight, I would never have a husband, I would never accomplish much in my life. One of my uncles said to me, 'Who's going to marry you? I mean, look at you,'" she recalls. "I think in a lot of ways I am a self fulfilling prophecy in that regard."

However, Joan says she's glad she didn't marry when her morale was low and her attitude one of hopelessness. "I'm kind of glad I never got anybody then, because I don't think I would have picked someone that would have known the value of my worth."

A deeply religious woman, Joan credits a spiritual awakening with restoring her self-confidence.

"I remember feeling so bad. I said, 'Lord, if I could just lose the weight. I knew all my life if I could just lose the weight, my life would be better. If I could just lose the weight, I'd have a family, I'd have kids, I'd have a husband. But I couldn't lose it. I would lose it, and I would gain it back."

God, she said, responded and told her to change her thinking – and she did. "He delivered my heart from feeling like I was unworthy or inadequate. He set me on a different path and a different mindset."

"It no longer validates me as a woman of worth"

Joan overcame her self-doubt, got a college degree and headed to Washington D.C. with $47 to her name. She found work with the largest grantor of faculty research grants and Ph.D scholarships in the world, bought a house and went to grad school. "Everything people said I couldn't do, I did."

After four and a half years, her mother became seriously ill and Joan returned to North Carolina to help care for her. She started her own Medicaid contracting company providing short and long term care for people with developmental disabilities and mental illness and grew it into a business with more than 150 clients and a sizeable staff. After eight years, Joan "got worn down by it" and was relieved when the state didn't renew her company's contract.

"It was one of the most bittersweet days of my life," she remembers. "I shouted and I screamed, 'Thank you, Jesus!' Because I'd gotten to the point where I felt like I was enslaved to something that I no longer enjoyed."

Joan then decided to turn her love of clothes and her message of empowerment into a lifestyle blog for women over 35 and fashion line for plus-sized women. She says building a brand is difficult, but...

"I honestly believe that once this all goes forward, the fruition of everything I've worked for is going to be worth it. All the hard work, all the struggle, the culmination of everything."

Joan says she's now comfortable in the skin she's in. "I have this wonderful vision and purpose that drives me and keeps me moving forward."

She has learned to be content with being a single. "If it happens, great. If it doesn't happen, ok. But it no longer validates me as a woman of worth nor determines whether or not I can have a great life – and for many, many years, it did. I felt like maybe there was something wrong with me because that was not something that had manifested. We're taught, as women, 'You're supposed to get married. And if you don't get married, what's wrong with you? What did you do wrong, that you didn't get a husband?' I'm just not bound by that anymore.

"I continue to work daily towards my health by eating right. I don't always do it the way I should but when I get off, I get back on and keep on moving. Nothing is going to deter me from what I am called to be and what I am called to do. Nothing."

Joan may have been self-conscious about not being married when she was in her 20s and early 30s, but she isn't now that she is approaching 50. "Honestly, in the African-American community, unmarried women my age are not that uncommon. I would say the majority of my friends around my age or in their 40s are not married, which I find very interesting. It's not because they don't want to be. They just aren't. According to statistics, however, only 13% of black women have never been married by age 53, so I still have a few years left to get there and I am very optimistic that I will."

Tish, a feisty, funny and fierce 70-year-old who lives in eastern Pennsylvania, is not concerned about being a lifelong singleton. After breaking off an engagement to a troubled man when she was young, she never found a suitable replacement, and so has lived her life as an always single woman – and with relish. Having retired from a career as a nurse anesthetist, she has the money and the freedom to indulge in the things she loves, like traveling and buying expensive cars.

"I want to marry because I love."

When people meet Tish and find out she's never been married, she says their reaction is: 'What the hell happened there?'

"I know this is going to sound terrible, but I'm still, at this age, attractive. I'm blue-eyed, dark-haired, light skinned, kind of ruddy. Irish. And I'm in decent shape. People think, 'what happened there?' Her usual response: 'Well, I was smart enough to make the right decision.' And that brings laughter, and that's the end of that subject."

Tish doesn't feel as if she has to explain herself to the curious. "No, not at all. Listen - I have two Audis, you know what I mean? People go, 'Wow, you have two Audis!' I want to marry because I love." She is still, she adds, open to that possibility.

Tish scoffs at any suggestion that women who don't get married are unhappy and unfulfilled.

"Oh, my God! I think that is the most ridiculous thing. I have such a circle of friends. It's to the point that, at this time I'm meeting this one for dinner, that one for something else. Do you know what I mean? I have a full life!"

The lesbian assumption

Like many always single women, Tish has, at times, been thought to be a lesbian.

"I've lived with this for a lifetime. At least once a decade, I've had to face this thing: 'Are you gay?' Noooo. Just smart! They don't understand. I'm attractive, had a wonderful job, and yet: 'What's wrong with you?' No, there's nothing wrong. It's just being smart. But tomorrow I would marry, if I thought I could love. And that's the most important thing here."

Eleanore, the Spinsterlicious marketing professional, has encountered the lesbian assumption as well. "I remember when I was in my 30s, and poppin' it and droppin' it and having fun and being interesting, but one co-worker was so sure I was gay. And I said to him, 'Do you think Lynn is gay?' Lynn was a woman we worked with who was single, too. And he said, 'No.' And I said, 'Why not?' He said, 'Well, look at her. She's not that attractive. She's not interesting. She's weird. But you are attractive, you're fun, you're interesting. You're all these things.'

"So that finally explained to me that you can't be interesting and exciting, because if you were really all those things, someone would have snatched you up."

On one memorable occasion, a close friend tried – in the nicest way possible – to get Eleanore to admit that she was a lesbian. "She wanted so much to make me comfortable. And she's a social worker, so she had the script and everything, you know, how to do it. How to make someone comfortable with coming out in front of you and letting them know that you love them and you don't care? And she had the script down pat. But my point is: how do you defend yourself against something that you didn't do? It's like a double negative there. So if I laughed it off – which I tried to do – she was thinking: 'This is a nervous laughter and she's not comfortable.' But then, when she kept pushing, I *was* starting to get annoyed."

If Eleanore had shown her annoyance, her friend would have thought that she'd pushed a button, that she'd been accurate in her assumption.

"So in my mind, no matter how I responded, my 'No' was going to be taken as: 'She's just not ready.'"

Sheryl, the L.A. resident who works in the fashion industry, says she always felt like an "odd duck" when she was growing up. "Now that I'm older I'm suspect. There's nothing wrong with being homosexual but I'm not a lesbian. I've had plenty of men. I've not lived a nun's life."

"There's been nobody interested in you in all this time?"

At least the lesbian assumption gives people a tangible – if often erroneous – explanation for why a woman might be a singleton. If that one doesn't occur to them, their struggle to understand how an attractive woman could not be coupled up with a man continues.

Leanne – the teacher/actress who long ago shed the "divorced" label and now checks the box next to "single" – says that strangers who meet her and learn that she she's been divorced for 16 years and doesn't have a boyfriend "certainly are quick to judge and produce completely unhelpful comments, but people who know me *get it* and they would support me no matter what I chose."

One of those unhelpful comments she gets is: 'There's nobody interested? There's been nobody interested in you in all this time?'" Leanne laughs. "Apparently not!"

However, she says that increasingly, she hears admiration and even a bit of envy from married women. "I know the grass is always greener, but there are a lot of married women that go, 'Atta girl. Go, you.'"

Leanne knows many fabulous women of a certain age who are single (more on that in the chapter on friendships). She tells me: "I want to applaud you for taking this topic on, because it is sort of the silent majority, in a sense, and nobody talks about it. No one has celebrated the state of the single, mature woman as being ok and cool on its own, so bravo to you for recognizing that we're all out there, and we're ok."

For her part, Leanne is fine with life as a singleton. "My mailbox fell over the other day and I was struggling to put it back up, and screaming and cursing at the sky and I thought: *Reason #7 why I need a man.*" She laughs. "After 16 years, that's pretty damn good.

"I do feel fulfilled. If I have something I want to do, I do it. If I want to change the color of paint in a room, I repaint it. When I don't have something I want, I go get it." All of these things are done without asking permission from or consulting a husband. She doesn't long for male companionship, but "it would be great to have it. If I had someone who was a true winner, yeah, that'd be cool."

"You're a freakin' leper here."

Pat – the Detroit writer/editor/director - thinks location plays a large part in how single women are perceived. She lived for many years in New York City and had a successful career as a branding expert, an exciting night life, a closet full of high heels and a large circle of friends who didn't judge her. When health problems she attributes to exposure to Ground Zero toxins forced her to move back to the Midwest to live with her sister's family, she was suddenly made acutely aware of her singleton singularity.

"You're a freakin' leper here," she says wryly.

She is not anti-marriage. In fact, Pat intends to get married in the future (more on that in the chapter on attitudes toward marriage).

That expectation might tend to make the "leper" treatment especially galling, but Pat chooses to ignore it.

"I don't want her to end up pathetic and single"

Disapproval can come from some surprising sources. Eleanore, for instance, has a close friend who is married and has two kids.

"I remember one time telling her about how I'd gone out with my boyfriend – my ex, now. We had an amazing New Year's Eve. We went to three or four parties, got home at 5:00 in the morning. So I'm talking to her the next day and I'm telling her about this and she was being really bitchy to me. She admitted to me later that she was jealous."

During a different conversation, this friend talked about how much she wanted her 20-year-old to marry her boyfriend.

"I was surprised that this woman was really pushing her daughter to lock it down. To get married. And I said, 'Are you crazy? She's 20. Why in the world would she…?' And then she slipped and said, 'I don't want her to end up pathetic and single.' Something like that. And I said, 'For all these years, you think I'm pathetic? How do you reconcile all the times you've been envious of my situation with 'if she's single, she'll be pathetic and single.' It was astounding to me."

And yet, Eleanore – who prefers the term "spinster" over "old maid" – has other friends who admire her precisely for her single woman joie de vivre. "Lots of people just do sort of hear about something I did and say, 'Oh my God, I love your life.'"

"I do think society values single women less."

"Obviously, I am not the only spinster out there. I know – and I know you know – lots of fabulous women who are not wives or mothers. In fact, there's a whole world of similarly-situated women out there who just want to be acknowledged as the smart, attractive, fascinating people they are.

"I think there are more single women who've done amazing things because they *can*. They don't have other stuff to get in the way. They make their own decisions. All the things that slow you down with the husband and kids, they have the freedom to do. But I do think society values single women less. Still."

Eleanore is representative of what appears to be a growing trend among always single women to take ownership of that identify and celebrate it – or at least acknowledge it and not apologize for it. Women of previous generations? Not so much.

"I was stunned when she gave me that advice"

Eleanore recalls a conversation she had when she was in her late 20s or early 30s with an older unmarried woman whom she admired. The other woman advised her to find a man and marry him. "You don't even have to stay married long," she said. "You can divorce him."

"We worked together and I used to look up to her. I thought she was doing what I'm doing now. I was stunned when she gave me that advice, because on the outside, she seemed to be having the life I have now. A pretty amazing life. But in her mind and because she is from a different generation – I guess that's part of it – she felt like it's better to be a has-been than a never-was. I think that was certainly true of her generation, and I think it's still kind of true. The reason why it's ok to be married many times and divorced many times versus never is because people still think it's better to be a has-been than a never-was. 'Somebody wanted me' is the way they interpret it."

Surprisingly, Eleanore believes that we single women are responsible for making others feel comfortable about our unmarried or childfree state.

"For some reason, it is really ok for people to ask you about your single status or your unmother status, but if you put those questions back to them, it's seen as judgmental. I can't say to someone: 'So how's your marriage?' 'Why did you decide to have kids?' They can question our choices, but we can't question theirs. And when the conversation comes up, the onus is on the single woman to handle it somehow, in such a light-hearted way, that nobody is offended. Because if you don't, you are just sort of crazy and aggressive and angry – and that explains why you're single to begin with."

"I'm not going to pretend that most never-married women are excited and happy about their situation."

Through her popular blog and book (find information about them in the About the Women in This Book section), Eleanore has heard from many always single women, not all of whom enthusiastically embrace their singledom.

"I was a little disappointed, actually, because when I started the 'Spinsterlicious' thing, I thought most women who were never married were like me. And I really wish they were."

Based on responses to her blog as well as personal letters written to her by readers, Eleanore has come up with a way to categorize always single women.

"There are people like you and me, never got married, never cared about it one way or the other and have amazing lives. There's a group of women who are single, really wanted to get married and have kids and it didn't happen and now they have managed to build these lives that are amazing and they're happy with them. There's another group that really wanted to get married and have kids, didn't, and still are struggling with that because they still would like to. They're longing for it. And there're a lot of those out there that I have come across. I just wish they had found more peace with it.

"But I'm not going to pretend that most never-married women are excited and happy about their situation. Because I don't think most are. I'd say half are. The ones either who have always been there, or the ones who eventually got there."

A lot of women in their 20s and 30s write to her and tell her that they don't think they want to get married and have children, but they're afraid not to. "They ask: 'Is it going to be ok? Am I going to be ok? I'm getting pressure from my family. I don't know what to do.'"

She's also been stunned by the number of women who write and say, "I wish I had the courage that you do to not get married or have kids, because I don't like either one of these things very much, and I kind of always knew in the back of my mind that I wouldn't, but it never occurred to me that I could *not do it*."

"I don't need somebody else in my life to be whole."

Marcy, the ski instructor from Colorado, is not one of those always single women who are in the feel-like-something's missing category. "I'm happy with me right now, and I know I don't ever need to get married to feel complete," she says.

"I don't feel like a failure at all. Anywhere. In any capacity of my life. I don't need somebody else in my life to be whole. You are what you make of your life, and whatever you put out there. I get a lot of gratification from what I do with all aspects of my life."

"I'm not going to get married just to get married."

Suzannne, the retired firefighter, very much wanted to get married and have children, but none of the many long-term relationships she had led to marriage (more about her boyfriend sagas in the chapter on relationships). Suzanne's determination to tie the knot diminished once she aged out of the childbearing years.

"I don't care about getting married, at this point," she says. "I did care before. Very much. I always felt like I was a failure if I didn't get married. Not anymore. Since I can't have kids anymore, it became unimportant. I would like to get married, you know? I would like to meet the right guy. But if that doesn't happen, I'm not going to get married just to get married. I might have gotten married just to have kids, but I'm not going to make a mistake like that now."

"I'm actually very proud I've gotten this far on my own"

Vegan educator Kay takes pride in what she's been able to accomplish, sans a husband. "I know a lot of single women who are very independent like me, but I think probably every one of them is divorced. I'm actually very proud I've gotten this far on my own. I never expected anything different, but now, looking at others, I see that it isn't the norm and it's pretty cool that I've been that self sufficient, especially as someone who has always been self employed."

Making the most of your circumstances – whatever they are – is one thing, but in the long dark night of the soul when our lives are laid bare and we are forced to look closely at what we've done and what we will never do, will we old maids regret being…old maids?

Jo-Sue won't. The educator and youth pastor says, "I don't know if I'd regret anything in my life, if I feel like I'm doing everything that I'm supposed to be doing. Would I like to be married? I would love to be married, I think, but if it doesn't happen, my life will not be over. I'll continue with my life, and do everything that I can, and enjoy it as much as I can."

Leanne may wonder what she might have missed – "what gentlemen are out there that might have been really cool to have known – not necessarily married or been in any kind of committed relationship with."

Any sadness Leanne feels about being single comes from the total lack of interested parties.

"I know there are people out there that I would like to meet and get to know, but somehow we just haven't crossed paths. So I guess my deathbed regret would be, 'Who would I have met had circumstances been somehow different?' But regretting having a tombstone with just my name on it? No. I'm good with that."

"I don't see a lot of happy marriages"

The many tales of bad marriages she's heard keep psychic medium Atheria from yearning for a change in her marital status. "I'm also really leery to get financially tied to somebody where if they screw up you're held responsible for it. Because that's happened to people that I know. I don't see a lot of happy marriages. And I never have. I have no problem actually doing a little a commitment ceremony and even wearing a ring, maybe, but actually getting legally tied to somebody – I'm not real keen on that."

However...

"If I actually fell head over heels for somebody and he fell head over heels for me, and he actually asked me to marry him, I don't know what my reaction would be. Never say never. I think I would be so surprised that somebody loved me so much that they wanted to marry me that I might say yes, but I'd be very scared to do it. Because of the horror stories that I see."

As she gets older, she feels as if she's running out of time. "What does bother me is that I've never gotten to experience things that other people have been able to experience, in terms of a relationship. I'm really afraid that I'm going to go to my grave never knowing what it's like to have somebody love me. Never knowing what it's like to wake up with somebody and have breakfast in bed. Simple stuff. So that is affecting the quality of my life to a degree. I hate knowing that I'm never going to experience these things."

However appealing true love may be, Atheria's regrets do not specifically include the lack of a husband.

"It's more about purpose," she says. "Having fulfilling work and making a difference in the world. Also, my dream never came true. The only dream I ever had was to be a movie star. And I tried. I'm a Screen Actors Guild member. I tried in Los Angeles for many years to have a successful career. Talent has nothing to do with success in Los Angeles. That's very evident with the Kardashians. It just never worked out for me. So I'm not happy with my life because I'm working for the federal government, doing this work that's boring as hell, a total waste of my incarnation. It makes me very unhappy to not do fulfilling work. So that's the reason I'm unhappy with my life. Not men."

"I've always been ok being alone"

L.A. resident Sheryl also doesn't have any qualms about the path she's taken by staying single.

"I think that if you look at yourself when you get more mature, you hopefully get some wisdom from your life experiences.

"I could look back at my life and say, 'I could have made better choices. Wiser choices.' But I feel like I'm using the information, the wisdom I have now to reflect on my past. If I look at who I was and the choices I made at the time, those are the choices that were right for me then. I don't regret things in that sense. Maybe I feel like I could have been a little smarter. I shouldn't have bought those expensive shoes. I could have put the money in the bank." She laughs.

Growing up as an only child and with an alcoholic father had one advantage: Sheryl has always been ok with being by herself.

"I grew up being alone because my parents were doing their own thing." As a child she spent lots of time with her mom and grand-mother, but by junior high school, she was often left on her own. "My mom's not really a drinker, but she went through a period where she wanted to hang out with my dad and drink with him. An 'if you can't beat 'em, join 'em' type of thing. She'd go out and hang with him, so I stayed home by myself a lot.

"I've had to be self-sufficient and self-entertaining for a long time, so I don't mind doing things by myself. Sometimes I actually prefer it, which I think is detrimental to me, because I do like people, but I need a lot of solitude."

"I have a very full life."

The "no regret" living Tiffany practices really seems to pay off.

"I have a magnificent life, and I created it for myself," she says. "I didn't rely on somebody else to do that. I am the architect of my life. We can make our lives whatever we want it to be. I made mine very special. I have a very unique life: I'm a world traveler, I run several businesses. I do very fascinating things. I've been all over the world. I've been to every continent except Antarctica. I have a very full life."

Denver stockbroker Lucy says there are certain areas of her life that could be better, but overall, she is content. "I think one thing that I'm lacking is friendships. That is something that I would like to foster. Some really good female friendships, that I just haven't been able to attract that into my life, if you will."

However, she's pleased with the wisdom that she has acquired over time. "I'm comfortable now with who I am. I love me and I wouldn't want to be anybody else. So as to that part, I'm satisfied. There are areas that could be improved. But I am more confident in myself."

Single mom Lavender Moon also gets great satisfaction from what she's learned throughout the years. "I know exactly what I want now. And I know exactly where I went wrong. I sat down and I thought about it and I know life is beautiful now and life is what you make it. I've just got way more knowledge than I had before. I regret that it took me so long to awaken and open my eyes."

She would, she says, be disappointed if she never got married, because with her children grown and busy with her own lives, she does sometimes feel a bit lonely. Thank goodness for grandchildren. "Oh, yes, they love me!" she laughs. "They want to spend all the time in the world with me."

Tish, retired nurse anesthetist in Pennsylvania, doesn't dwell on what might have been because her nature is a naturally happy one. "I'm really a fun-filled person," she says. "I'm just unique. I'm not your average person. That's what life's about. You have to make yourself happy. You can't have other people making you happy. I'm a person of depth, and I really do think about things, and I have philosophies that I live by. You have to have that, or you're nothing."

Does Tish ever get lonely? "I like having a gentleman friend in my life (more on that in the chapter on relationships) and I have wonderful friends. And that's very important to me. So I'm not really alone. I'm very happy."

"You can't miss what you didn't have."

Former band manager Debbie sees life as an adventure, which drove her own nomadic story. "Look at the people who traveled across the country in covered wagons. You know? Everybody said, 'Oh there are mountains, you can't go around that.' I've always said I would have been one of those people who would have just said, 'You know what? Let's go and see if there's something on the other side – because I've done that so many times in my life. Sometimes I fly by the seat of my pants. Sometimes I kind of have a plan. I tell myself: if you don't do it, you're going to regret it.

"I've always said I don't want to get old and have regrets. I'm just going to do it. If it doesn't work out, you can always revert back. When I left to go to California, my mom told me, 'If it doesn't work out, you can always come back home. You always have a home.'

"I didn't ask to be born, you know, I didn't ask for this life, I'm just going to have to make the most of it. I'm going to do it the way I want to do it. I just never wanted to compromise. I think that's from growing up with too many rules: you can't do this, you can't do that. It wasn't for me."

Does Debbie feel as if she's missed out on something because she's never been married?

"No, because this is what my life has been. You can't miss what you didn't have. And I'm comfortable with myself. If I had to bring somebody in and explain myself to somebody, like how sometimes I just want to be quiet at home and watch the news and somebody wants to talk to me, that would piss me off."

At one time, she shared an apartment with her brother. "If he bothered me while the news was on, I would bark at him and he'd get really upset. I thought: this is what it would it would be like if I had a husband or a live-in boyfriend. I don't know if I would be a bitch or if it would just drive me crazy. I felt really bad and I apologized to him. I said, 'I'm sorry, I guess I'm just used to being by myself.'"

University administrator Andrea says that when she reached important milestone ages, she did wonder if she was going to regret the things she hadn't done. "When I was going through my 20s, I was thinking, 'Gosh, when I hit 30, will I wish I'd gotten married? When I hit 40 will I wish I'd had kids? Will I...?' Now, about to turn 60, I'm like, 'No, I'm good!'"

"You could just see the desperation."

A 40-something co-worker of hers who'd never been married and had no kids was a sad example of a woman who was *not* at peace with being single.

"She was always desperate to find a man. You know nothing shows more than that. And she told me once that her greatest regret in life was that she had never gotten married and had children. And that just broke my heart, because she was professionally successful. She was attractive. She had a lovely home. Such a great career. She did very well for herself, was well spoken. And when she told me that, it almost made me cry, because I thought she and I were basically in the same place, but for that one thing. And she had that regret. That showed in her relationships with men. You could just see the desperation, at age 45. And it just broke my heart. And there's nothing you can say or do."

Denver stockbroker Lucy estimates that aside from wanting children, 60 to 70 percent of women pursue men because that's what society tells them they should be doing. "They want to feel that they're doing what's expected of them. You know: you have to be with someone, you have this image of being a couple. I believe that I'm single for a reason. I'm exactly where I should be because it's happening. And I don't fight against it.

"I think that single women are more stable, more secure and even stronger, because it takes a lot to be single in this society and to be comfortable with it and content with it. I think that takes more strength. And to be able to support yourself financially, buy a home and do all those things – that's huge for women."

Lucy believes that both men and women are afraid of being single. "It's a fearful thing for them, so they won't give it a try. They won't even attempt it. But if they worked through that fear and stayed single for a year... Men can't do that, because they want sex, but let's pretend that they could. Stay single for a year, get over the fear, fight the fear of being alone. I bet after a year, a lot of them would keep it going. They'd be like, 'Oh my gosh, this is awesome. What was I so fearful of?' And they would just hang onto that. And just date here and there, maybe have a boyfriend or girlfriend, but never move in with them. Still keep your identity and be a separate entity from them."

"The single black mom is a mantra in our community."

Because we're regularly reminded that we're outliers, do we single women feel marginalized? Less appreciated for who we are and what we accomplish?

That may depend upon your culture, according to Joan. "I think society as a whole values single women less than married women but not in the black community," she says. "The single black mom is a mantra in our community. She is strong, loving and hard-working. We know the single woman is doing her thing. So I think it all depends on the culture."

Animal-rights activist and vegan educator Kay thinks married women are regarded as more valuable because they're more likely to produce children. "They're running a household. I would say it really depends on the culture and the religion. I don't identify with either. I don't have a religion. I'm Irish-Polish but I don't necessarily feel Irish-Polish. I feel like I'm just me. I love Latin music – that's not in my background, but I love it! It makes me want to dance!"

She meets people who are intent on marrying someone from their culture or religion, because they were raised to believe that having a spouse from the same background as theirs is important.

"They soak it in and they agree with it and accept it and live their life that way. They don't rebel and say, 'That's nice, but I met someone who's not in this circle and I love her and want to be with her.' They follow that narrow road, and that's their choice. I think those kind of people are very rigid in their vision of what is the norm. That a woman is to be a mother. A woman is to run the household. A woman is to be married. Whereas there are so many different pictures of what a woman or a man is. It's high time everybody accepted that and let everybody be themselves.

"I think that's starting to happen. It's way behind schedule, but I have hopes that we can turn things around in many directions in my lifetime. And if we don't, the human population simply isn't going to survive. And if it comes to that, it doesn't deserve to."

What Lives We Lead

There are, of course, some significant differences between the way married women and single women live their lives. I'd like to suggest what will be, to some, a subversive notion to people who think that being a wife and mother is the highest possible calling for *any* woman: that marriage might prevent some women from accomplishing the things they really want to do. From fulfilling their destinies, so to speak.

Would women today have the vote if Susan B. Anthony had had to balance her activism with putting dinner on the table for a husband every evening? As ruler of England for 44 years, would Elizabeth I have had to make sure her spouse didn't feel neglected while she was busy making decisions that affected an entire nation? If Dr. Condoleeza Rice had been married during her tenure as U.S. Secretary of State, would she have felt conflicted about the amount of travel she was required to do if there'd been a husband raising an eyebrow every time she pulled a suitcase out of the closet? Would Dr. Mae C. Jemison have had the time to gain the education and training she needed to have in order to fly into space as the first female African-American astronaut?

Would I have been able to write this book?

Yeah, I did that: snuck myself into a group of high achievers!

But what about the rest of us? We women who are not famous activists or astronauts, who will not be finding a cure for cancer or ruling a country anytime soon? Does being single make it easier for us to accomplish things on our own more modest level – or at least, to live our lives the way we want to?

Oh, the places she'll go

Andrea, the successful businesswoman from Indiana, loves to throw parties. It helps that she's got lots of money, some of which she's used to build a house that she estimates is three to four times the size she needs. The house is perfect for the scale of entertaining she prefers, which is large. The 60th wedding anniversary celebration she held for her parents included 100 guests.

Andrea also enjoys going to the symphony and Broadway shows and serves on a lot of boards that are associated with education, economic development and the arts.

She doesn't travel as much as she used to when she had to traverse the globe numerous times for business. Her jaunts these days tend to be stateside, and have a more personal meaning for her. "I do have a trip to Maine coming up," she says. "It's some place I've never been. I decided to get out of town for my birthday, so I'm giving myself a trip to Maine for a couple of weeks, just to explore it. I travel by myself. I love that, because I meet new people. That's a lot of fun. So there are lots of places I haven't been to yet that I will go to."

Although she could afford it, her practical, financially-savvy side has made her decide against doing things that will require her to pay a big upcharge for double occupancy just because she'd be going by herself.

But is there anything Andrea does *not* do because she's single?

"Not really," she says. "If I want to go out to dinner, I go out to dinner. Sometimes I go by myself, sometimes I call a friend. There are quite a few friends that I've made here."

She didn't know anyone when she moved back to Indiana eight years ago.

"I came here because I liked the location. I'm on a small body of water, and I live an hour from my parents and the rest of my family."

It didn't take her long to get into the swing of things because she quickly got involved in lots of activities and joined a church. She also met people through her job.

"I probably have more friends here now than anywhere I've ever lived, because I've lived here longer than anywhere else I've ever been in my entire adult life, which is kind of nice. I have friends who are married, friends who are divorced or widowed."

When I ask Andrea if she ever feels lonely, I get a response similar to answers I've heard from other single women I've talked to: that in some ways, they *like* being alone. (I do, too. As much as I love doing things with my friends and am very close to my family, I want and need a certain amount of time by myself.)

"As outgoing as I am, I'm a strange dichotomy," Andrea says. "I'm actually a loner. And I always have been. When I was a little kid, I was fine playing by myself and I always did the Barbie thing. I never did the baby dolls. I always liked grown up dolls and their fancy houses and the clothes. That kind of stuff. I need my alone time. I'll be out with lots of people, lots of friends, but then I've got to get back home and have my alone time. And I've always been that way. The hardest thing in the world for me in college was having a roommate. It just drove me nuts, having somebody there all the time. So I'm fine, perfectly fine amusing myself."

However, now that she's back in her home state, Andrea loves to be near her family and among many people that she's known since she was a kid. "I'm just having the best time. It's so much fun. I fell into things I could not have planned in a million years and it's working out great. I'm so fortunate. I love it.

"You can take the girl out of the country but you can't take the country out of the girl. To think that I literally started out in the cornfields, and have been to some of the places I've been. My mom has this thing, I'll tell her some wild story and she'll just look at me and say, 'Not bad for a girl who went to high school in the middle of a cornfield.' I think she'd rather say that than, 'You're getting a little too big for your britches.'"

Colorado ski instructor Marcy's comfort level with being single also is also related to where she lives.

"If I'm invited to a wedding and it says bring a plus one, I don't feel as if I have to show up with a plus one. I feel confident on my own. And being single, I don't cook a lot, so I go out to eat a lot by myself. Fortunately I'm in a small community where I know most of the people at restaurants. I golf by myself. My friends say, 'You golf by yourself?' And I say, 'Yes, it's fun. You can golf pretty fast.'

"There are more single women out there now than in years past, and there's not as much of a stigma in being single."

"The loneliness is really hitting me hard"

Although psychic medium Atheria has always done many things by herself – such as traveling – she likes going solo less as she gets older.

"I am to the point where I'm getting tired of doing everything alone. When I was younger it didn't bother me so much, but it's starting to really bother me, that I do have to do everything alone. The loneliness is really hitting me hard the past year or so. The fact that I don't have a partner is starting to really depress me, actually."

Still, she has no desire to become dependent on a man, like a friend of hers who became engaged to a man three months after being widowed because she couldn't stand being alone.

"Being single has made me very independent and I do like to take care of myself," she says.

Poet and writer Michelle is also very self-sufficient, which she attributes, in part, to the fact that she was a single mother at a relatively young age.

"I became pregnant at the age of 20. That made me become very, very serious about life because I felt like I was going to be responsible for this little person, so I needed to have all my ducks in a row. I think that's what set me off into being more serious than most women my age at the time."

That attitude resulted in her getting a good job with the Internal Revenue Service and to buying her first house at the age of 21.

"Well, looks like I'm off to Colorado"

As discussed in the chapter on the benefits of being single, Debbie has been able to jump from job to job and city to city because she's free to do so. That has resulted in some wonderful adventures, but because of that lifestyle, she's also faced difficulties that she had to surmount all by herself. When friends tempted her to move from San Diego to L.A. in order to manage their band, their plan fell apart in about two weeks. The band members (and Debbie, their new manager) couldn't find affordable apartments in L.A. and were quickly running through their savings. One member had a sister who lived in Boulder, Colorado who was willing to put them up for awhile. "So they decided to go back to Boulder, hang out there, get their shit together and come back to L.A.," she remembers. "I said, 'Are you kidding? You haven't even given it a shot yet!' They offered to take me with them, or they'd take me back to San Diego in their van."

Although Debbie wasn't thrilled with the idea of going to Boulder, she'd given up her job and apartment in San Diego and felt that there was no point in returning there.

"I'm like, well, looks like I'm off to Colorado. It took me awhile to decide. I had to think about it for two days. I didn't have a car. Yes, I moved out to California without a car. There were four of us living in a van. We got motel rooms sometimes.

"My biggest thing about going to Colorado was that it snows in Colorado! I'd just moved away from snow (in Michigan) a year before that. But what was I going to do?"

Debbie was in Boulder for a year, until the band members finally decided they were ready to return to L.A. She was not particularly enamored with that city – its sprawl and freeways – but she went anyway. Debbie and the six members of the band shared an apartment, with the guys in one room and the girls in another. Debbie found a full-time job in a hotel while the others relied on their families to send them money – some of which they spent on going out and partying every night (they *were* a band, after all). Debbie, who had to be at work at 6 a.m. every morning, didn't join them, which angered the band leader. He felt that as their manager, she should be out with them, making connections at the venues they were going to.

"I said, 'If the band manager is going to make a paycheck then I'll quit my job. But there's no work for me yet as manager, so I have to have a real job. After about two months it got old, and there was a lot of fighting. One day we all came home from work and all the guys' stuff was gone. They had left. They'd gone to Louisiana. They'd met this chick and would party with her. She seemed cool. She had this ferret. We would all sit around and party. They wanted her to move in and we said, "No, there are already three girls in our bedroom.' So they said she could stay in their room. We thought cool, it'll be less rent, but they said, 'She's not working right now so she she'll just stay here for free.'"

Debbie stayed in L.A. for awhile and became a live-in nanny. She enjoyed it, until the family "got into her business" – such as questioning her when she went out late, on her own time.

Next came the move to Seattle, where she worked in the hospitality industry and traveled extensively.

"I had a blast. I loved Seattle." She loved it, that is, until tourism in the city bottomed out after the 9/11 terrorist attacks and she was laid off.

"All of a sudden I started getting that itch. Seattle didn't feel the same anymore. I couldn't do all the things I liked doing because I wasn't making the money I'd been making. At the time I felt that I had to get out of there, so I went to Vegas. That was a big mistake."

She considered returning to L.A. but didn't think she could get a job that paid enough to allow her to make car payments and afford an apartment.

As financially responsible as she was trying to be with her decision to move to Las Vegas instead of Los Angeles, it was at that point that Debbie experienced what can be one of the major disadvantages of being single: financial *in*security. You'll hear more about her money misadventures in the chapter on finances.

"Ah, who cares? I'm by myself."

Jo-Sue mainly travels within her state, to visit her sister. The high school assistant principal has not yet made it to the more far-flung destinations she'd like to visit: Europe, Prince Edward Island, the Bahamas, Hawaii.

"I'm not the kind of person who would enjoy going by myself," she says. "I want to go and see things with other people. One year I drove to Arizona by myself, and while the drive was interesting – I listened to books on tape the whole way out there – there were things I wanted to just peel off the road and go look at, and I'm like, 'Ah, who cares?

I'm by myself. I can't take pictures by myself. Now with selfies you can do that, but it just doesn't seem as fun without somebody else."

Now when she drives to Arizona, she takes some of her nieces or nephews with her. "It's fun to watch the excitement on their face, of seeing new things."

"If you're going to dream, dream big"

Lavender Moon hasn't had much opportunity to travel yet, but it's on her "to do" list, and she has an exotic destination in mind.

"Travel is something that I would do alone, but I would love to do it with a husband," she says. "But if I don't have one, I'm not going to let that stop me."

And the first place she'd go? "I want to visit Senegal." She laughs. "Maybe that's why I never reach my goals. I've got to make them more realistic. I can't remember who told me this but they said, 'If you're going to dream, dream big. If you're going to ask for a car, ask for a Cadillac, not a Pinto.'"

Until that dream trip happens, though, Lavender Moon's favorite pastime is indulging in a pleasure that is closer to home: dining out in restaurants. "I love to eat, so I go out to eat a lot. I don't eat pork. I don't eat red meat. Most of the time I eat healthy, organic food. I go to different places, for Thai food, other kinds of cuisines. I like sit down restaurants, nice, healthy food and people watching."

Business owner Tiffany is fine with dining in a restaurant or going to a movie solo, although she doesn't go to concerts or the theatre by herself. If there's an occasion that she really needs a date for and her boyfriend is not available, she practices something she calls, *rent-a-date*. "I have people who are friends. We're not quite the right fit but we do things together. And I think that's really special, to be able to find somebody of the opposite sex that you can do things with, as a companion."

Southern Californian Sheryl loves salsa dancing, yoga and hanging out with her dogs. "Now just staying at home is fun for me, because lately I've been working 12-, 13-hour days," she says. "I'm working way too much."

She's gotten certified for Reiki, a healing technique in which a therapist channels energy into a patient through touch in order to restore physical and emotional well-being. "That's a side of me that has always been there and I just haven't developed it. I was actually thinking of what I could do, honestly, as an elder. Maybe shifting into doing more healing work."

"Alone does not mean lonely"

Joan has found some healing for herself through her participation in the Miss Plus America Pageant, which saw her crowned Miss North Carolina in 2014. After spending a considerable portion of her life suffering from low self-esteem due to her weight, it took her several years to work up the nerve to enter the competition, but she's glad she did it.

"The pageant was very educational. It was about celebrating plus size women in a positive manner. It was very liberating. There were a lot of beautiful, caring, loving people there, as well as a lot of catty people, too. When you've got a lot of women together, it's going to be that way. But I left feeling very empowered.

"Plus size pageants are just magnificent. It was wonderful experience and my self-esteem went to a whole other level as a result of that process."

"I definitely go into fantasy mode"

Leanne describes herself as a "narrative junkie" who is drawn to stories in many forms: books, movies and plays. She is an accomplished actress and has performed in dozens of stage plays in local theatres.

"I like to enact the stories," she says. "It's the escapism. It's the fantasy, the once-upon-a-time that attracts me to all of these things, so when I have free time, I definitely go into fantasy mode in some capacity and explore worlds outside of my own, whether it's me physically doing it as an actress or imagination through art or something."

When she retires from teaching – not too many years down the road – what will Leanne be doing? She is considering many different possibilities, including working as an archivist or training dogs for Leader Dogs for the Blind or Paws with a Cause. She will seek "something else that interests me, that taps into another talent or another ability that I have that isn't a health or human services kind of thing. I'm tired of giving to humanity at great peril to myself. That's why the dog thing is so appealing. I love teaching. I don't like, necessarily, teaching unwilling students. I don't like teaching willing students with dim-witted parents. I'm kind of done with people, on a grand scale, which is why something like a library or voiceover work or animals is appealing. I'm ready to kind of draw back in a little bit."

In keeping with her love of fantasy and make-believe, she's also thought about working for the Walt Disney Company. "I'm a huge Disney fan. I love Disney. I used to go to Walt Disney World many times a year. I like the idea of providing – fictitious as it is – entertainment and indeed, an entire resort or travel experience that is geared toward the pleasant and happy and whimsical. I would love to work at Walt Disney World in a capacity that wasn't customer service, necessarily, but developing ideas for a show, or developing ideas for an attraction. Something creative but also very much rooted in the idea of whimsy and magic."

Single women and dogs

I'd like to conduct a poll sometime to find out if a higher percentage of single people than married people have dogs. Certainly canine companions have been a constant in *my* life, and it didn't surprise me to hear that that was true of many of the women featured in this book.

Leanne's take on her dogs is typical: "They are my family. If you are looking at traditional – I come home and who do I deal with? It's my dogs. I love having dogs. I *get* dogs. I have an infinite amount of patience with dogs. I put up with dogs far better than I put up with people, even if dogs behave badly."

The only drawback is that dog ownership does tie one down. If Leanne is going to make a career change/life swap in a few years, will she still have her two very large dogs to consider? It does limit her options.

"If I don't have them, then I'm freed up to really do whatever I want to do," she says. "Then I can get dogs once I re-settle again. So they're very important to me. They're members of my family. The two I have right now *are* my family, but would I replace them? I might not, at this point in my life, until I figure out where I'm going to land."

Attitudes Toward Marriage and Where They Come From

Would Nancy Drew marry and have babies?

When I was young, I assumed that someday I'd get married and have a family. After all, doesn't everybody do that? I didn't have a clear picture of what that would look like, although I was definite about *not* wanting to do a lot of housework, like my mother did. (I still don't; I pay someone to clean my house). I had no interest in cooking – another of her daily chores – and I usually managed to burn the simple dishes we were taught to make in classes at the local community center. (I've gotten a little better at cooking but still burn things, although now I regard that as a useful way of testing smoke detector batteries.) As for motherhood aspirations, I preferred Barbies to baby dolls. My Barbie had mod dresses and tiny plastic shoes and a boyfriend named Ken. Baby dolls were nice, but boring. They pretty much just lay there, wearing the same thing day after day. They didn't live in a Dream House and have a wardrobe with its own carrying case.

My childhood idol was Nancy Drew. I devoured every book about the famous girl detective that I could get my hands on, often while sitting up in the tart cherry tree in our backyard in what we grandly referred to as "the tree house" – several planks my father had nailed across adjoining branches. In my leafy retreat, while eating peanut butter and jelly sandwiches, the neat rows of solid brick houses, white painted garages and tidy yards below me faded away as I became lost in Nancy's exciting stories. I envied everything about her life: her handsome, football player boyfriend Ned Nickerson; her best friends Bess and George; her excellent wardrobe; her convertible; her quiet, reasonable father (who never yelled like mine) and her trips to everywhere – even though they invariably landed her in danger. Nancy Drew always kept her cool, though, reasoning her way out of trouble and solving the mystery at hand with her keen intellect and persistent questions.

I wanted an existence just like hers, instead of the rather quotidian, humdrum one I actually had: school, homework, dinner every evening at 6 p.m., playing with the other kids in the neighborhood every night until the streetlights came on (the curfew all the parents agreed upon). My family's travels consisted of camping trips to state parks, not the exotic locales visited by Nancy and her friends. Later on, of course, I realized that all that predictability was a good thing. It provided me with the kind of security that many children don't have. I grew up safe and supported.

I don't believe I ever speculated on the kind of life my fictional heroine would have as an adult. Would Nancy Drew marry and have babies? Settle into a suburban split-level as Mrs. Nickerson? And if did, would her sleuthing days be over? Saddled with a spouse and kids, she certainly wouldn't be as free to travel as a single woman, so she'd miss out on all of the mysteries she came across on her frequent trips. Would she even be able to tackle mysteries close to home, if she had to pick up the kids from school (in the family-friendly vehicle she'd traded the convertible for, no doubt) and get dinner on the table on time for when Ned came home from work?

It's noteworthy that another famous fictional female detective, Jessica Fletcher of the *Murder She Wrote* TV series, was free to engage in mystery solving because she was a widow and had no children (she and her late husband "just weren't blessed that way," she explained once).

My life was nothing like Nancy Drew's. I rarely had adventures. The only mysteries I encountered were in math class – and I never did solve those. My wardrobe consisted mainly of hand-me-downs from my older sister, Kathy. (My younger Tina had it worse; she would get those clothes third-hand, after *I* outgrew them.)

While it didn't compare with my imaginary, book-inspired life, it was actually a wonderful way to grow up. I'm grateful to have been raised in a close-knit, loving family. However, all that tradition had a downside, at least as far as I was concerned. My father was the boss and my stay-at-home mother *asked for permission* to do things – like spend money. I decided early on that I would *never* live that way. I vowed that when I was grown, I would never, ever, ever ask a man for permission to do anything.

My parents were mostly content with their arrangement but it didn't appeal to me, a child of the 60s and 70s who saw new doors swinging open for women, offering us opportunities that had not been available to my mother when she was coming of age. In between unending housework, making lunches and cooking dinners, going to PTA meetings and running school bake sales, my mother got to have fun in a Wednesday night bowling league and at euchre parties and dinner dances. I was too ambitious – or perhaps arrogant –for a life like that. Besides, I'm a lousy bowler.

I wanted excitement and something outside of the mainstream, and I knew that marriage would restrict my options. My youthful aspiration to be an international spy never came to fruition, which is just as well for America because I can't keep a secret. I also wanted to star on Broadway. Didn't do that, but I do act and sing in local theatre productions, which is a lot like being in Broadway shows except for the money, the fame and audiences that mostly consist of your family and friends. I wanted to be a writer and I have done that. I was able to get out of the Midwest and live elsewhere – lots of elsewheres – although, like Dorothy in "The Wizard of Oz," I eventually decided that there's no place like home and returned to my roots. I haven't always had a lot of money, but what I do have is mine to do with as I wish, as is my time. Whatever actions I take or choices I make, I do it all without having to consult with, negotiate with or ask permission from anybody, and I enjoy the hell out of that.

My parents' relationship did evolve over time. They were married for more than 60 years, until my mother died of Alzheimer's in 2013. Even in the last stages of her illness, my father remained a devoted husband. He went to my mother's nursing home every morning to feed her breakfast. Although dinner was my usual shift with her, I sometimes went with Dad in the morning, and it was kind of funny to see that if my dad tried to get Mom to eat too fast, she would make an angry noise and shake her head, her expression defiant. She was confined to a wheelchair by this time and could no longer remember either his name or her own, but it was clear that she was still determined to assert her right to eat at her own pace, and not at the speed set by my notoriously impatient father.

My mother and father grew up during the Depression, in adjoining small towns in eastern Pennsylvania. They were products of their time and of the circumstances which shaped their values. Fortunately for me and my siblings, my parents regarded the welfare of their family as their top priority. Each felt that their most important role in life was that of parent. I benefited greatly from that.

The reasons I didn't want to emulate them may be because I'm also a product of my time and of the circumstances which shaped my values.

An iron fist

Following World War II, my parents moved to Detroit. Bustling with economic growth, the city offered job opportunities for my father - who'd gotten a college degree in business thanks to the G.I. Bill - that were unavailable at that time in Wilkes-Barre, Pennsylvania.

I was raised in a predominantly Catholic, close-knit neighborhood where moms stayed home and dads went off to work every day.

There were no career women there at that time to provide me with role models.

My father ruled the household finances with an iron fist. Later, I came to understand why he had to do that: he was caring for a family of six on one salary. During the depths of the Depression, his own father – an Italian immigrant who worked as a coal miner, when there was work – had had to shoot pigeons in order to feed *his* family. Memories like that, I'm sure, helped fuel my Dad's anxiety over money.

In contrast, Mom's family had been a little better off than my father's, so she had a greater sense of financial security. As an adult, *her* main goal was to see that her children had what they needed.

That dynamic set the stage for a decades-long struggle for control over the family's purse strings. I used to cringe when I heard my mother ask if she could buy us things – especially when my father's answer was "No." When Mom really felt the item in question was needed, though, she was willing to use wily tactics in order to circumvent Dad's authority. For instance, she would take us shopping for new clothes and hide the bags in the trunk of the car until she could sneak them into the house without my father seeing them.

Usually, though, Mom gave in to my father on money matters. To some extent, that was probably due to her tendency to be a peacemaker and her desire to avoid unpleasant confrontations.

"Now you can bitch at me for spending money"

There's a locally famous story about our next-door-neighbors at the time that demonstrated a different approach to a tight budget. That family – whom we'll call the Smiths – was similar to ours, except Mrs. Smith was much more formidable than my mother. On one occasion, Mrs. Smith bought shoes for their three young children and also took one to a doctor for the treatment of some ailment. When Mr. Smith complained about the amount of money she'd spent that day, Mrs. Smith went to a department store and bought herself an entire outfit: a dress, purse, gloves, shoes and hat. For someone in our working class neighborhood, it represented an extravagant outlay of cash. She laid all of the items out on their bed in front of her astonished husband, pointed to them and said, "*Now* you can bitch at me for spending money."

Mr. Smith, the story goes, never said another word about money. Like my parents, the Smiths were married for decades, a close union that only ended with death.

When my mother was coming of age, financial dependence on a husband was inevitable. Like many young women in the 1940s, she worked after high school and in the early years of her marriage, but stopped working outside the home once she had children. When her youngest child was in middle school, my mother found work as a receptionist, getting positions through a temp agency. Even though such work added stress to her schedule – she still had to do laundry for a family of six, after all – she *loved* it. Every weekday she got to wear something other than a cotton housedress and go to work in a professional environment where people respected her abilities and acknowledged her competence and intelligence. She wasn't just the maker of casseroles, the finder of lost socks, a referee who settled arguments among squabbling siblings. She was a professional woman, valued for her work ethic and cheerful demeanor wherever she went. Because of those qualities, the receptionist duties in various work-places always expanded to include more complex responsibilities, which my mother accepted eagerly and learned quickly. When she was offered a permanent position at an engineering association, she took it with pleasure.

Occasionally, I'd pop in at her workplace, and I was always struck by how her co-workers treated her better than her own children did. My mother's determination to do every task well – in addition to her kindness and friendly personality – had a tangible effect on the people around her. They appreciated her. It made me see her in a different light. It made her see herself in a different light. She blossomed.

From housewife to working woman

As her confidence grew, so too did her willingness to voice her opinions and challenge my father when she felt strongly about something. Mom's transformation from housewife to working woman was not entirely welcomed by my Dad, who was, for a long time, unpleasantly surprised that his own wife would disagree with him about *anything*. Their discussions about politics, in particular, were heated. (Given the social and political divisions in the U.S. in the '60s and '70s, I'm sure ours weren't the only family dinners enlivened by loud debates.) We children joked that the two of them went to the polls each election for years and canceled out each other's votes.

In addition to confidence, my mother had, for the first time, something palpable: money of her own. She contributed to household expenses but she also kept a little for her own discretionary spending. She loved being able to slip me a $20 bill and say, "Here- go buy that blouse you were talking about." But there was always an air of secrecy about the gesture: we were putting one over on my father. I hated the secrecy.

Are my Mom and Dad responsible for my not marrying?

I love my parents and am incredibly grateful for the love and support I got from them, so I feel guilty for citing their marriage as one reason why I'm *not* married. It sounds as if I'm blaming them. That's not my intention, although my ideas about marriage were formed, at least in part, by what I saw of theirs.

That was true for many of the women I spoke to for this book. Some of the themes which emerged were negative: dominant, intimidating fathers or dysfunctional relationships among parents that set a bad example of marriage for their children. In other instances, though, the parents had healthy, loving unions and their daughters formed a very positive opinion of marriage.

"I didn't want anyone telling me what to do."

Debbie is one of those who chafed under the rigid control of an authoritarian father. "My Dad was a cop. He laid down the law and there was no getting out of order. There were so many rules: 'You don't talk out of line. You don't question what I say, you just do it.'"

With eight children being raised on one salary, money was tight in Debbie's house. As soon as they were old enough to do some kind of work, the kids got jobs, and their cash-strapped parents sometimes had to borrow money from *them*. Debbie, for instance, earned 75 cents an hour busing tables at a Knights of Columbus hall. With those jobs, Debbie and her siblings were expected to buy the things they wanted, beyond basic necessities. Debbie learned a valuable lesson early on: that she was responsible for herself. "If I wanted anything I knew I was going to have to make money for it."

Her mother tried to prepare Debbie for the future she expected her to have. "My mother would tell stories about what I could or couldn't do when I got married: 'You have to give this up and give that up.' I don't think that she was trying to make me think one way or another about marriage. She was just stating the facts. But I don't know what it is in me that doesn't want somebody telling me, 'You can't do it' or 'You can't reach that.' From a young age I wanted to do my own thing. I didn't want anyone telling me what to do."

When Debbie started high school, her mother advised her to take typing and sewing classes, so that she'd have the skills to become a secretary and to make clothing for her family.

"She tried to groom me for the life *she* had," Debbie says. "These were things *she* had to do, and that she did. My Mom was thinking that life was going to continue the way it was. This was the mold we were in and this was the way it was going to be. It's not going to change. We're not rich people. You're not going to live differently from the way everybody in our family has always lived. So she figured I'd get out of school and get a secretarial job. I'd meet somebody, get married, start having kids and that would be it.

"That was how she lived. That was how her mother lived. So she figured that was the way it was going to go."

Despite the family's limited finances, her mom thought it was very important that Debbie go on her high school senior class trip to Hawaii, because once her daughter got married and had children, she would never again be able to take a trip like that.

"And I was like, 'Oh, hell no,'" recalls Debbie, who would spend the following decades making trips just like that.

Debbie's friends and siblings began getting married and having babies, but she knew she wasn't ready to settle down. She also was certain that she didn't want children.

"At a young age I was nervous thinking that I was going to have to have kids. Everybody around me was getting married, but then a lot of them were getting divorced. Then my parents got divorced. And I thought: why get married? Why do all that and probably end up divorced, because those are the odds."

Debbie thought she wouldn't beat those odds herself because she didn't want a husband telling her to do, where to live, or that she had to have children.

"I went to San Diego for one year, then Boulder for a year, then back to LA. And I thought: I can just move whenever I want to. I just say I want to move and I move. There's no, 'Can I move? Do you think we should move? Do you think this is the right thing?' No. I just do it.

"And I thought: No, no, no, it ain't going to work for me. And I used to always tell my friends, 'Yeah, when I'm like 60 and I need a husband, I'll get married.' I'm almost 60 and I can't even see it. I can't even see it."

"I knew I did not want that life"

Lucy's mother and, in particular, what her mother went through after a divorce, provided her daughter with an anti-role model.

"What inspired me being single is that I didn't want my mother's life," says the Denver stockbroker. "I had it really ingrained in my psyche. As a teenager, watching my mother's life, I would just repeat to myself, 'I do not want this life. I do not want this life.' And it really stuck. She had five children. She stayed at home, raising her kids and serving others. She didn't work."

After her parents divorced, Lucy saw her 45-year-old mother (who had no work skills or experience) struggle to support herself and the children who still lived at home.

"When I saw that happen to her, I knew I did not want that life. I did not want to depend on a man. I don't want to serve anyone, take care of anyone. I didn't want kids. So that really kept me single in my 20s and 30s because that thought was so ingrained in my head.

"I held onto that thought – I don't want to be my mother, I don't want to live that life – and I defended that thought fiercely."

Has Lucy had any second thoughts about her decision to remain unmarried?

"I honestly feel that I'm missing nothing," she says. "I haven't missed a thing."

"Why would women volunteer for this?"

Sheryl was an only child whose parents eloped to Vegas to get married when they were both only 18. She remembers an unconventional childhood with an alcoholic father.

"I was brought to a lot of adult parties when I was young," says the LA resident. I was bartending for my Dad at ten. Playing poker with his friends men when I was 12. I was a good kid in school, but I had this odd childhood. Now I know it's really odd, but when you're growing up, you don't really know that."

Her father was not affectionate even when sober, and he was a mean drunk. "He got meaner when I was in high school. So when I was growing up, I guess I used to think: 'Why do women do this to themselves? Why do they voluntarily get married?'

"He drank so much he's lucky he didn't kill himself. He would drink screwdrivers. He would drink a full tumbler of vodka with a splash of orange juice. My Dad was a large man, 6'2", about 220 pounds. He was a tall, strong man. He worked as a mechanic on construction equipment. He was actually very brilliant. He fixed all his friends' cars. He could have had his own business. He could take anything apart and put it together. He built two race cars in our garage from scratch. He's a mechanical genius, but I guess he had some demons, maybe because he was abandoned by his parents."

Her father was extremely controlling. "He really ruled the roost," Sheryl recalls. He dictated what television shows they watched, for example, and refused to give birthday or Christmas gifts to his wife and daughter. His philosophy was, she said: "You've got a roof over your head, you've got food on the table, shut up and toe the line."

Her mother was a stay-at-home mom – literally. Because her father used the family's only car to get to and from work, her mother had no form of transportation. Although her own limits were sharply circumscribed by her husband, Sheryl's mom foresaw an unlimited horizon for her daughter – especially if she got an education.

"She always told me, 'You can do whatever you want in life,' which was really, for a traditional-type mom, actually quite revolutionary. And she was always an explorer. She was open to other things, other cultures and religions."

She let Sheryl know that she could do and be what she wanted, that she didn't have to get married young, or have children. It was a surprising message, given her mother's very traditional path and what Sheryl describes as her "passive-aggressive" response to her husband.

It was Sheryl's grandmother, a widowed nurse, who provided her with the role model of a working woman. "She was very strong and independent," and taught Sheryl that woman can work and earn a living without a husband.

Surprisingly, Sheryl said her parents appeared to outsiders to have a good marriage, because they didn't argue in public.

"A lot of the people that my parents socialized with, the moms were screaming at their kids. My mother was never like that. The husbands and wives would bicker and I used to think, 'Why would women volunteer for this?'"

Sheryl inwardly rebelled against her father's authoritarian ways.

"My Dad would always say, 'It's my way or the highway.' And I would think: 'When I get older, I'm going to take care of myself. I will put my own roof over my head. I will feed myself. And if I have a man, he can never hold that against me.' You know what I mean? If I ever do decide to get married, I know I can take care of myself. I guess that's one of the ways I got the message that it wasn't necessary to be married."

Sheryl's father used to criticize her for not helping her mother enough in the kitchen, and for not learning the skills she'd need to take care of her own family some day.

"He would say; 'What are you going to do when you raise your kids? How are you going to feed your kids? How are you going to take care of your husband?' I'd say, 'I'm not going to get married. I'm not going to have children or a husband. He'd say, 'That's going to change when you get older.' I'd say, 'No, I don't think it is.'

"From a very young age, I never felt the need to do those things and I never felt unfulfilled because I didn't. This sounds really awful, but my childhood was not that supportive and I felt like I had some damage from that. When I was in my 20s and I became more aware of it. I thought: I need to look at these things, in my relationships with men."

"I felt like I had this secret life."

Having an alcoholic father had a significant impact on Sheryl's social development.

"Growing up in the 70s, everyone was smoking weed and drinking. I didn't want to do any of that. Not because I thought I was so pure. People saw me as this conservative, pure girl, but I knew I had this darker side to me, because I descended from my father. This man could party like nobody's business. And I had a lot of anger inside of me. So I thought: if I go down that road - this is going to be very vulgar - I'm going to be one of these women who's going to party hard, end up doing heroin or some hard core drugs, and end up sucking some guy's dick for a fix. I had this sense of myself and I did not want to go down that dark path."

That's why Sheryl made the decision to not indulge in the substances so popular at the time. It caused people to perceive her as being "uptight." She knew they had no idea what she was really about. "I'm thinking, inside: they don't really know, because I felt like I had this secret life."

High school parties didn't interest her because her father had been taking her to adult parties since she was very young. She hadn't been drinking at them; mainly she'd dance, or serve as bartender. Still those experiences made the parties friends had during her high school years look juvenile by comparison. "I'd been partying with adults, in that environment, when I was a kid. I had already been there, done that."

Apart from being a no-show at parties, Sheryl seemed to be having a fairly normal high school experience. She was voted most likely to succeed and was active in student politics. "The only thing kind of weird was I didn't date, because I was afraid of men. My dad was so intimidating, I was kind of scared of boys, in a sense."

She was also shy. "I felt awkward around boys and didn't think I was pretty."

Dating also meant running the risk of pregnancy.

"In my neighborhood there were some girls who got pregnant at 15, 16. And in those days, it was really a stigma. They made you go to a school for unwed moms. They kicked you out of high school. It was a real stigma and people looked at you funny."

"You're dad's leaving us and I don't know what I'm going to do."

When Sheryl was 14, her father had an affair and threatened to leave her mother.

"She was terrified because she didn't know how she was going to support herself. I thought I was probably going to have to lie and say I was older and go to work to help support my mother, because I didn't see her as very strong.

"My mom looked so ethereal. She'd woken up and she was in this nightgown. She looked so fragile and she says; 'You're dad's leaving us and I don't know what I'm going to do. I haven't worked since I was 15.'

"I went to school thinking: 'I'm going to have to be the adult. To parent my mother. I don't know how we're going to stay in the house and keep the dog, but we'll figure it out.'"

Her father stayed, but his threat served a purpose. It motivated her mother to go back to school, get a job and become more independent. "It shifted the dynamic, and my dad didn't like it. He used to tell her she was too weak and then he was complaining she was too strong." Sheryl laughs bitterly. "You can't win sometimes."

Even applying for financial aid for college became an ordeal for her, because of her father's refusal to provide her with information about his income and his attempts to undermine her confidence.

"His comment was that it wasn't the government's goddamn business how much money he made. He refused to volunteer any information to help me, to see if I could get a grant or any kind of financial aid to go to school. He wasn't going to waste his money on my education or help me in any way. We actually ended up having a week of arguments because he was drunk every night and wouldn't listen to me. The gist of that was that he was comparing me to one of his friend's children, saying that I was too dumb, that I would fail at school, and he would never support my education."

In spite of her father's opposition, Sheryl did end up going to a local college, paying some of the costs by working at a restaurant. That, she says, is when she started getting involved with men.

"I was 18 and really dumb. I had a lot of these older men hitting on me. The first guy that I was seeing, I was so dumb, I didn't know he was married. One of the people I was working with said, 'Don't you realize he's married?' I said, 'No, I didn't.' I was more or less fooling around with him and experimenting with him, trying more things sexually."

"He starts ripping off my clothes and I started screaming, 'Take me home!'"

"Then after that, there was another guy hitting on me at the restaurant. He actually kidnapped me, came by my house and picked me up late. My parents weren't home yet. I said, 'Ok, let's just go around the block and get a soda or something and come back, because it's late.'"

Once he got Sheryl in his car, the man insisted on taking her to his apartment. Sheryl said she didn't want to go there – she hadn't left a note for her parents, telling them where she was going. Her "date" ignored her wishes.

"He takes me to his place. He didn't really force me into his apartment but I said, 'I'll go in for awhile.' Then he starts ripping off my clothes and I started screaming, 'Take me home!'"

In an attempt to quiet her, he gave her what he said was an aspirin. She believes it was something else.

"I think he gave me a Quaalude or something. In any case, I consider it a date rape, even though he didn't really force me, per se. But I remember being hallucinatory, like his face was changing, a devil's face, then a kid's face. It was just really horrible and he wouldn't take me home."

To make matters worse, Sheryl had left her house without any money or ID, because she hadn't expected to go anywhere. The thought of fleeing his apartment ran headlong into the reality she'd face being by herself at night in a bad neighborhood with no money for a cab. This was the pre-cell phone era, which meant that calling her parents for help would require finding a telephone to use.

"I was thinking, can I go out at night in this neighborhood? And walk down the street and ask somebody for money to make a phone call? It was a little sketchy, because I wasn't sure if I could get out of his apartment. I remember thinking, 'If I go out on the street at 3:00 or 4:00 in the morning by myself, is that going to be worse?'"

It was a moot point. Her captor prevented her from physically going anywhere. He told her he was going to turn her into a woman and raped her.

The following day, the rapist agreed to drive her home. He even allowed her to call her parents first, although he stood close to her so that he could listen to what she said. It was a painful conversation. Her father answered and asked where she was and if she was all right.

"And I said, 'I'm with this guy. I spent the night with this guy.' Because what can I say? And he says, 'Well I thought-' He was going to say, 'Well I thought you were better than that.' And then he said, 'Talk to your mother.'

"So my dad thinks I was just out running the streets, because I can't say anything because this guy is monitoring me. My mom said, 'Are you coming home?' and I said, 'Yeah, he's driving me home.'"

When they reached Sheryl's house, a bizarre scene unfolded. The rapist walked Sheryl to her door and told her mother that she'd been in good hands – and that nothing had happened.

"I walked in the house and I took a shower for – I don't know – about 2½, 3 hours, because I felt like I could never get clean again. And my Mom never said anything. She just said, 'Are you ok?'"

It wasn't until six years later that her mother asked her if she'd been raped. Why didn't Sheryl tell them at the time it happened? "I felt like my parents didn't really care," she says.

"I was also ashamed because there was a part of my body that responded to it"

Why didn't Sheryl report the rape to the police?

"I guess because I felt like he didn't really force me, in a sense. I didn't think of it as being drug-related, because I didn't do drugs. I guess I was also ashamed because there was a part of my body that responded to it, even though it wasn't what I wanted to do. I felt like how could you say it was against your will when your body kind of kicked into gear? But I think that was because of the drugs."

Sheryl says she gained weight following the rape. "I got a little chubby after that. I guess I wanted to put on some weight, to be more protected or something. I wanted to become very ugly. I didn't want male attention."

"We were told what we could NOT do."

While Sheryl's mother encouraged her to spread her wings, Elizabeth got a different message from hers – and, she says, from the era in which she came of age. The Washington state resident has lived with her boyfriend for 23 years without benefit of marriage, despite the priority placed on matrimony when she was growing up.

"I am still from that generation where that was the be all and end all, and if somebody wanted to marry you, that was sealing the deal," says Elizabeth. "You know: they really did love you. And a lot of that is from lack of self-confidence."

In her early 60s, Elizabeth is still slim and supple, like the professional dancer she once was (she still takes dance classes). Smart and a bit sarcastic, Elizabeth says she works every day at being kind, loving and forgiving. She's a talented seamstress and a jigsaw puzzle enthusiast – both of which make her feel, she says with a laugh, *geriatric*. She's also a binge watcher of BBC shows (who isn't?).

Elizabeth says that women in her age group were not encouraged to explore their potential when they were young.

"We were told what we could *not* do. I told my mother when I was five years old that I wanted to be a policeman on horseback and she said, 'No, you can't do that. You're a girl.' I wanted to be a farmer. She said; 'No you can't that. You'll have to marry one.'"

Her parents' marriage appeared to be normal when she was young, but when she was grown and out of the house they separated because her father was having an affair. Elizabeth ultimately discovered that he'd had multiple extra-marital affairs.

"But I didn't learn any of that until my mom died, so I can't use it for why I never got married," she says. "They did seem to have a stable marriage the whole time. You know, it's complicated – and I'm sure people tell you that – but there is no one reason why I never got married."

"I am not picky. It's not about that."

Poet and real estate agent Michelle was raised by a single mom – in a close-knit, loving family like my own – but with strict adherence to religious principles. This was something decided upon not by Michelle's mother, but by the children themselves.

"It's something that we chose as young girls. My sisters and I chose to live in the Church of God in Christ lifestyle." That included not wearing makeup or pants and not participating in activities that were considered worldly, like going to the movies.

"When you grow up in a strict church, you often are not taught about how to love, and relationships. We were basically taught to wait on God for our husbands or our mates. We were not taught how to really accept love or identify with love when it comes to you. We weren't taught how to have an actual relationship. We were just taught that if there's a man in the church who says that God sent him and both of you are in church and have the same religion, then it must be that God is saying, 'well this is your husband.'"

Is she describing an arranged marriage?

"Not so much as arranged, because no one actually picked someone for you and said, 'This is your husband.' But they encourage that if a male figure in the church comes to you and says, 'God said that you're my wife,' more people were accepting of a process like that. But I don't necessarily view that process as the most accurate way or 100% way to meet your partner, because you're already under the influence by being in the church. Our mindsets have been influenced to believe that, he's from the church then he must be of God, and that's not necessarily the truth."

Despite her exposure to this belief system, when Michelle was a young girl, she expected to be single when she grew up, because even then she had unique views about marriage. Those ideas have continued to evolve over time.

"The more I've been researching some things myself and kind of being on a self-discovery of love, my views changed about how the church taught us about those things, about love and marriage," she says. "It would be surprising to many to hear my views with regard to marriage. I don't feel that a woman should wait in a church for a person from the church to come and say, 'You're my wife.' I think that it happens in many different ways. A person could be in another country and you guys come into this beautiful place and the universe kind of guides people to be together – you know, that perfect timing. I don't think it has anything necessarily to do with religion, or cultural differences. I've seen that if something is divinely meant to be, and it is of God, it doesn't have to be something that is geared by a religious connection – more of a spiritual one. I've learned that being spiritual and being religious are two different things."

Michelle does not have a negative opinion of marriage. In fact, she deems it as "sacred." When an acquaintance asked her if she was jealous of her two younger sisters because they're both married, Michelle said she wasn't.

"For me, marriage is something totally different. I need more of a spiritual connection rather than a religious connection or that I find somebody attractive and then we decide that we want to be together. I think that most people who connect with people like that often end up in divorce because they don't really know their partner. For me, I need somebody to be spiritually connected to in order for me to say that this can be my partner."

Unlike many always single women, Michelle has never gotten pressure from family members to get married, nor has she been accused of being too demanding in terms of the qualities she wants in a potential mate.

"I am not picky," she says. "It's not about that. I don't feel like a man has to be perfect, because he will not be perfect. But he will be the right person for me. My views have been very clear. I need to definitely connect with the person on a spiritual level rather than any other level, because I know it won't work otherwise. But now I am at a point where I want to be connected with my life partner and consider marriage on a spiritual basis."

And if that doesn't happen? How will Michelle feel if she never marries?

"I do want a partner in my life. It would not be the end of the world for me if I didn't have a partner, but I do desire a partnership."

"I just wish you would find somebody to be with so that you're not alone."

In a union that has lasted more than 60 years, university administrator Andrea's parents have shown her what a strong and mutually supportive marriage looks like.

"They had their ups and downs, but there was never any indication that they wouldn't stay together," she says. "There was never any doubt in my mind that they weren't solid. They love each other dearly. You can tell they're just extremely devoted to each other, but they drive each other nuts."

With that kind of positive example in front of her, why does Andrea think she has never married?

"I just never wanted kids, and that seemed to be, in my mind, the main reason people got married. Either that, or you needed somebody to support you and I never needed that, either."

This is surprising, given the fact that Andrea's childhood in central Indiana sounds more likely to foster very traditional ideas about marriage and children than to produce the jet-setting corporate executive that she ultimately became.

"It was very normal, if there is such a thing," she says of her growing up. "We were very solidly blue collar. My father was a state trooper. Mom worked part-time secretarial jobs and in a ladies dress shop. It was a very rural upbringing. We were literally surrounded by cornfields. Most of my friends were farmers or worked in a nearby auto factory. I went to a very small, rural high school – also out in the cornfields."

Her family lived in a small enclave of homes. "There was a pack of maybe 20 kids all within five years of my age. We all grew up together. If your parents weren't looking out for you, somebody else's parents were, so it was a very salt of the earth, Midwestern upbringing. Almost every family had both parents."

Andrea's mother and father made it clear that they expected her to go to college, but not necessarily to get married.

"Mom typically expressed the opinion that the guys I dated were not right for me or not good enough for me, so she kind of went in the other direction. And throughout my life, she never mentioned my having children, although she lived in inordinate fear that I would get pregnant out of wedlock. That was never a really big risk for me in my younger days, because she put such a fear of God in me that I was a pretty straight arrow."

Her mother did mention marriage to her once in a way that surprised her. Andrea was 27 and buying her first home, a condo. By this time, she'd had been out of college and on her own for five years.

She invited her parents to have a look at her new home just before she closed on it.

"She said, 'Andrea, I just have one thing to say' – and I thought for sure it was going to be, 'Why don't you wait until you're married to buy a house.' And what she actually said was, 'If and when you get married, make sure you keep this in your name only, so nobody can ever take it away from you.' That totally shocked me.

"My mother at that point had been married 30 years, and never – I don't think – had ever had *anything* in just her name. That blew me away.

"And then shortly after my brother died a couple of years ago, she said, 'I just wish you would find somebody to be with so that you're not alone.' And those are the only things she's ever said."

"I'm never going to be in a position where I can't walk away."

Psychic medium Atheria's parents have been "miserably married" for more than 50 years.

"It was difficult," she recalls. "When I was really young things were fine. At least they seemed fine. But it was when I got a little older that my parents' fighting got really, really bad and that did severely affect me, actually."

She remembers a defining moment in her life when she was around 12 years old.

"All I ever did was listen to my mother talk about how my father had ruined her life, and how her life sucked because of Dad. If I'd listened to her, I would never have had anything to do with men ever in my life. But I stood there one day and she was crying and going on about how her life was so miserable because of Dad." (Atheria realized later that her mother was partly to blame for her unhappy marriage.)

"I remember saying to myself, mentally, that I will never, ever become financially dependent on a man so that I can't walk away. Because she was financially dependent on my father. She's never wanted to work. She just wants to obsess about her health and her jewelry and watch television. She sold her soul because of money, really."

Atheria vowed that she would never be in a position where she couldn't walk away from a relationship. "I'm always going to be independent. I'm always going to take care of myself.' I made a conscious decision, standing in the kitchen that day. I do think that probably has affected things.

"But the basic issue is: I just never wanted to be with a guy who's wanted to be with me. That's the main problem."

"Now we have freedom of choice."

Travel company owner Stephanie is not anti-marriage, but… "There's nothing wrong with marriage and there's nothing wrong with families – they're wonderful institutions." Having said that, she's seen enough dysfunctional marriages to be wary of the arrangement. "I think the really, really good, wonderful marriages – not even wonderful, but respectful, kind, considerate relationships - are few and far between. Being stuck and being absorbed in a bad relationship has got to be just really awful."

Stephanie's parents impressed upon her the need for both an education and a strong work ethic – values which have served her well and established the basis for her independence.

"There was a period where women got married for social and economic reasons," she says. "They went from mom and dad to their spouses. But that's not freedom. Now we have freedom of choice."

When she was in grad school, Stephanie heard a speaker who made a great impression on her – a businesswoman who sat on several corporate boards.

"She said something I thought was very interesting. She said, 'Ok, ladies, here you are, you're about to get a masters degree in business. And some of you may feel trapped, that now you have to go be big executives in business. Now you have the *choice* (to do that).'"

The takeaway, for Stephanie: women could get married and raise families if they wanted to, but not because they had no other choice.

"I feel like sometimes women, when their kids are grown and their husbands have these jobs, they may have a crisis at a certain age and say, 'Who am I?' It's a legitimate question. 'Who are we, independent of those other elements, which in most cases means family?'"

Stephanie has no desire to get married in the future, but she wouldn't mind having a partner. "In some ways I have no idea what that would look like because I do travel a lot, but that's why I get back to saying it would be something where we both kind of have our lives. I don't see myself just all of a sudden absorbing into someone else's life, but I do see sharing each other's lives."

"I was meant to marry"

Tish describes her childhood in the early 1950s as idyllic. "I don't mean to sound like Mr. Rogers, but I had lovely parents," asserts the retired nurse anesthetist. "I'm the oldest of three children. We had a middle class life. I had the best possible thing – which I later thanked my father for – an at-home mom."

Her parents were married for nearly 50 years, until her mother's death.

"They traveled, they went to the store together. They did everything together. The only difference was, my father was a non-Catholic and my mother raised us in the Irish Catholic way, my brother and sister and I. We were like little chicks, going over to church every Sunday. But I had a wonderful childhood. I had nothing to complain about."

As a young girl, did Tish dream about the big white dress and the walk down the aisle with an organ playing in the background and friends and family looking on?

"Actually, I'm extremely shy and a very small get together would have been a better wedding for me. An elaborate wedding is something I would have done at one time, when I was young. But I have no desire to do that now. A nice quiet ceremony would have been great with me. And may still be."

When Tish was grown, she planned to marry her high school boyfriend Bob – until he went to serve in Vietnam. "After his return from Vietnam, he suddenly was very, very different. I had the sense to know it was not the way I wanted life to be and we broke up. So I went on to date other people, and it's not like marriage was not an option. But I never felt it was quite right."

Tish believes she was meant to marry and meant to have children. "Both of them. But it didn't work out. So my point is this: why just marry to marry?"

Her siblings have had mixed marital experiences. Her brother married and divorced – a rancorous split after which he was largely prevented from seeing his daughter. Her sister, after being married for 27 years, made a big change in her life.

"I had a dear friend – I am not gay, I am straight – but this wonderful woman and I were good friends," Tish says. "And she came to our house, my sister's house, swam in the pool, with the kids and everything else. Well here, suddenly, my sister leaves and goes off with her and they now have a gay relationship. And to a certain degree, I held myself responsible for bringing her around the house, but I mean, I had no idea. She had four children. That's like Jerry Springer, isn't it?"

Tish's objection was not to her sister being a lesbian, but to the affair that caused the breakup of her marriage.

As for Tish's long stretch as a single woman; "If it's not meant to be, then you don't get married. You don't use somebody for money, looking good, this and that, no. It should be love. Love is the answer, and if it's not that, it's not worth doing. No matter how corny that sounds.

"I hope I have helped you realize another woman's perspective. I am not a needy woman, and I think a lot of times there are a lot of needy women who are afraid to be alone. Well, it's not always easy. Sure, I have a couple of minutes where I might think, 'Oh, I'm lonely.' It doesn't last. It's what you make of it."

Tish has a boyfriend that she sees every weekend. At 70, she is still open to the prospect of marriage.

"I would marry tomorrow if I loved, and that's the theme here. And I think so often people do it because it's what they think they have to do and, years later, people change. I've changed. You have to think of that."

"When asked, I would say: not right now. And not right now became never."

Australian transplant Eleanore's parents have what she calls a "fine" marriage, one that did not influence her attitude toward matrimony in a negative way.

"I didn't think marriage was bad. I think, as long as I can remember, I always thought marriage was boring," recalls the marketing professional. What I always remember is feeling that women got the short end of the stick." Despite this, there were no divorces among her parents and neighbors and aunts and uncles. "They all seemed to have pretty – in quotes – 'decent' marriages. I guess they would probably be considered traditional."

It did seem to Eleanore, though, as if the women did all the "grunt" work.

"We would go visit relatives and the women would be in the kitchen, cooking food damn near all day long while the men were hanging out in the backyard, smoking cigars, laughing, having a good time. My parents' and the marriages around me all seemed fine *enough*, but not very interesting or exciting, and I think I need interesting and exciting."

Eleanore never consciously made the choice to *not* get married. "More likely, when asked, I would say: not right now. And not right now became never. But I always knew, as long as I can remember, that marriage and kids – I have to say marriage and kids because as a kid I thought they just sort of went together – just never seemed that interesting to me."

She remembers, as a very young child, playing house with other children. Most of the girls would fight over who got to be the mother, although children were needed to play all of the roles; mother, father, children.

"I was happy to be anybody," Eleanore says. "I was never fighting to be the mother, and I certainly don't think I knew why then, but when I look back at that, I remember thinking: I don't know what the big deal is here. I can be anybody.

"So as long as I can remember, I know that I've never felt that burning desire for marriage and kids that I guess most little girls do. I don't think I ever consciously said, 'I don't ever, ever, ever want to get married.' I just always felt like, this is not the time. You know, maybe some other time, but not right now.' And, you know, here we are."

Some of Eleanore's six siblings are in long-term marriages. One is divorced and remarried. One sister is divorced and is staying divorced.

"She thought she wanted to remarry, but now she thinks she likes the freedom," says Eleanore. Of the divorces, she says; "Neither of their marriages was horrific. It was one of those, you just sort of outgrow each other or you don't have anything in common anymore."

Through her book and blog, Eleanore has heard from many single women in the U.S. and abroad who are miserable, but not necessarily because they are unmarried.

"I get a lot of letters from women in small towns in the south and small towns in other places who say: 'I'm the only single woman in town and I hate it because everybody makes me feel weird.' It's not that they hate so much being single. They hate the way they are treated because they're single. It's fascinating to me, actually."

Many unmarried women – especially young girls – who read Eleanore's blog or follow her via Twitter regard her as a role model. "I *feel* like I'm a role model," she says. "I think most women would be lucky to have the life that I have. Whether they're married or not."

"I always felt that if I fell for a guy, I'd be cheating on my Dad, in a way"

Kay's parents' marriage fell into the not-so-good column, to put it mildly.

"In my opinion, my parents had the worst kind of marriage," says the actor-turned-animal rights activist. "It was never a good example to me. They weren't loving. They weren't affectionate. There was a lot of arguing. And that really turned me off to marriage."

She often thought that her parents should get divorced and yet was perversely relieved that they stayed together, because she had friends from broken homes who had to split their time between their parents.

"So I was grateful we had that consistency, that balance. But I wonder what it could have been like if there wasn't always the arguing. If we spent time with Dad and then spent time with Mom. Being that they were Catholic, that was never going to happen. They stayed together simply because they were Catholic. Which to me is a horrible reason, but again, my father taught me the meaning of commitment."

When, as an adult, she asked her father why he never left her mother, he admitted that he'd thought about doing so many times, but didn't because he'd made a commitment to her. "How could she have survived without me?" he asked her.

She understood.

"She was not an independent woman. She was not a woman who could have figured out what to do to survive, and he knew that. I thought it was admirable of my Dad but I often wondered how fair it was to him, what a different life he could have had if he would have been willing to leave. Because I felt like he was not treated well, as a husband. He deserved better. And it would have been nice to see him at least, if not with another woman, then it would have been better without all that verbal abuse."

Nonetheless, her parents remained married for five decades. During a phone call Kay had with her father when he was terminally ill, he said something that took her by surprise.

"I called him on the phone a few days before he died and mentioned how convenient it was that he and Mom got sick at different times so that they were able to take care of each other, and it was wonderful how attentive they both were to each other. And he said, 'Oh, yes, we have a great love.' I was so shocked to hear him say that, because I'd never heard him say 'I love you' to her. He would sign 'love' on a card, but they never *said* it.

"It made me realize, you can't be with someone 50 years and not have some kind of love for them. You can't share life with them for that long. And that just because their type of love didn't fit my description of what I would want or would accept in my life, it didn't mean they didn't love each other. They have their own brand of love. That was very eye-opening for me, that everybody's definition of love can be different. And nobody has to follow anyone else's, or approve of yours or theirs. Everyone needs to find what works for them. So that was very shocking to me."

Kay's feelings toward her father complicated her attitude toward marriage.

"I did have a very close relationship with my father and I think I always felt that if I fell for a guy, I'd be cheating on my Dad, in a way. I'd be hurting his feelings, because he wants his little girl to stay a little girl and not grow up and be with a man. So I think there was that kind of feeling of staying a little girl."

As the baby of the family, Kay felt very sheltered growing up and yet, conversely, quite self-sufficient. Her two sisters were close in age to each other and she was quite a bit younger than them, so she spent most of her time on her own. "Because I didn't have a sibling that I hung out with, to do things with, from childhood on, I always felt very OK by myself, and very independent. I just felt like that was already set out."

Kay speculates that being an only child or a child who's much younger or older than her siblings could have a bearing on the ability of someone to be happily alone when grown. Kay's sisters grew up to be the kind of women who could never be alone, who went from one relationship right into the next one, or from one marriage into another.

"They're five and six years older than me but they're only 20 months apart from each other, so they were buds. In their teens, they did everything together and I was the bratty little sister. *I'm* not calling myself bratty," she laughs. "They did."

One sister has been divorced once, the other twice. "I saw them stay for the kids, stay because they weren't sure what else to do. They were afraid. They didn't have confidence. And eventually, at long last, they left. You've got to wonder."

Unlike her sisters, when she was grown Kay focused on her career rather than on finding Mr. Right. "Not that there really were opportunities to get married, because I wasn't really developing relationships," she says. "I wasn't looking for a man to take care of me. That just wasn't in my DNA. I think I learned early on how to live economically and be able to survive on what I made. And even once I started making a little more, I still was smart about how I spent my money. The independence has just been the through line, where I would rather struggle a little on my own than be with someone that I feel trapped with or I feel dependent upon. I don't want to feel that I'm stuck here, I can't get out of this even if I don't want to be here. Sometimes people will stay in relationships when they really don't want to."

"I didn't see anybody who was loving and affectionate and happy"

Marriage was never a goal for Kay because it didn't look attractive to her, based on the relationship she saw between her father and mother. "You know, that's your first and primary example: your parents. And certainly along the way you can meet other people who have good examples. I think I had aunts and uncles who were divorced. So I got off right away thinking that marriage wasn't beautiful. I didn't see anybody who was loving and affectionate and happy. I didn't have any imagination of it being so."

Kay believes a lot of people get married too quickly, before they really know the person they're marrying.

"I think that's a big mistake, that people don't see each other through every season, every holiday, preferably twice." She believes that a couple should live together and really get to know each other, so that there aren't any surprises.

"There can always be surprises later. People change or they go through things that put them into a depression that you never saw before. But I have a girlfriend who married a guy after four months. And she's now been in a miserable marriage for 11 years. She feels trapped but can't leave."

Her own parents married when her mother was 29 and her father was 35, making them older-than-average newlyweds for their era.

"They just married so late, but I think he thought it was his last shot. He was the perpetual bachelor. She lured him in and probably shouldn't have. But, you know, if she hadn't, I wouldn't be here!"

Kay has come to have a more positive view of marriage in recent years, mainly because she's gotten to know some married couples who have healthy, mutually nurturing relationships.

"I guess before, all I was noticing were the breakups, all the fighting, the unhappy relationships. I was like, 'Oh, God. Why do people do this? Just live your own life and have a great dog who loves you. You have your career. Why have all the turmoil of a relationship? It just takes so much time and energy and too much pain.' And that was always my experience in the past."

In recent years, though, her observation of some happy couples who respect and value each other has given her a fresh perspective on marriage.

"They really like being with each other. It's not just an obligation. It wasn't just, 'Oh, I have to be with somebody.' It was genuine. And I finally recognized that *is* possible. There are people who have that. All marriages aren't miserable compromises."

"I wouldn't have wanted any of my sisters' marriages."

Retired businesswoman Ellen's parents had a close, loving relationship, but her family's difficult financial circumstances led her to focus on getting an education and having a successful career, rather than following their example. The Arizona resident grew up in Montana, the daughter of a teenage mother who dropped out of high school and a father who had to forgo a college education in order to marry his pregnant girlfriend.

"My Mom was barely 17 when she had me and my Dad was 21. He had to give up a football scholarship. They had to get married because of me. Back then, that was just what you did. And they were madly in love with each other, too."

The hardships began well before Ellen was born. Nonetheless, her parents' determination made a strong impression on her. Their resolve was not something that originated with their marriage, but a quality that developed much earlier in their lives. She tells of her father living in an abandoned boxcar by the side of the railroad as a child, retrieving frozen cowpies from a nearby field to burn for heat, wearing cardboard in his shoes.

"His dad forced him to work in the fields and took all the money he made. He also delivered newspapers." A scholarship to college looked like the key to a better future, until his girlfriend – Ellen's mother – got pregnant. After Ellen was born, three more children followed in quick succession. Her father worked two and three jobs at a time to support the family. Despite the difficulties, Ellen said her parents tried hard to try to make their children's lives as nice as possible.

Additionally, they demonstrated the value of hard work and perseverance. Ellen's mother eventually went back to school and got her GED, then went on to obtain a teaching degree, graduating with honors. Her father, meanwhile, transitioned from being an oil company roughneck to having his own insurance business.

They made it clear to Ellen and her sisters that they wanted them to go to college. They also let them know of the consequences of sex. "They each had their little talk with us: 'Make sure it's someone you really care about and use proper protection.'"

She considers herself lucky. "I had wonderful parents who taught me to get an education; work hard, treat others well, be independent, be thankful for what you have and give back when you can. They were supportive of all of my sisters and me; treated us well and tried to be very fair no matter what direction we went in – which turned out to be all over the map between us!"

Ellen and her sisters, who were raised to be very independent and think for themselves, pursued different careers. They also pursued different lifestyles. All three of her sisters got married, one to a man who was abusive (something her sister knew prior to the wedding). Another sister is a deeply religious stay-at-home mom who regards her husband as the king of the household.

"In their home, her husband brings in the income and he basically controls everything," says Ellen. "There is no way I'd want to live in a marriage like that. I'm pretty independent. I wouldn't have wanted any of my sisters' marriages."

Ellen, armed with B.A.s in business administration and information systems, embarked upon a successful career and owned her own home and a fully paid for car by the time she was 25. She left Montana and spent ten years in Orange County, California as a bank manager in charge of data processing.

"I was in charge of all their computer operations. I was responsible for about $20 million a day in transactions. I had very little time for a social life. I later found out that I was actually making half of what someone else would make in that position but I felt like, 'Well, they gave me this opportunity.' I made many improvements and changed procedures that saved the company thousands of dollars. I did so much for that company."

Unfortunately, sexual harassment by her boss at the bank caused Ellen to resign and file a lawsuit, which was eventually settled.

Was marriage on her radar at this time, as it is for many young women?

"I tended to date guys that were older than I was because I was mature for my age," Ellen remembers. "I would have gotten married if I'd met the right person at the right time. I had several proposals of marriage but I always knew it wasn't the right person at the right time. One of my goals was to make sure that if I got married and if anything ever happened with the family, that I would able to support them."

In her 20s, she found out that she would not be able to have children. It was something she didn't tell her own family for decades.

Ellen focused on work, getting a masters degree in computer information systems and amassing a lengthy resume whose credits include market research, project manager and technical manager. Her career required her to travel extensively and to move to Denver, Washington D.C. and Virginia.

Family responsibilities beckoned, though. When her father was diagnosed with terminal cancer, Ellen headed to her parents' condo in Arizona with one suitcase, intending to stay for awhile and help take care of him. That plan changed when her mother was diagnosed with chronic obstructive pulmonary disease.

"I took care of him for a year – basically took care of both of them. I decided that since I didn't have a family and hadn't gotten married, I was going to focus on helping my family, treating my parents well and showing them how much I appreciated everything they did for me."

After her father passed away, Ellen was offered a terrific career opportunity at a major healthcare company. She turned it down in order to continue caring for her mother.

"She was so sweet. I was able to make her wish to pass away in her home come true."

Ellen is now living alone in the condo she inherited from her mother

"If you wanted to boil down the main reason why I never got married, it is just that I never met the right person at the right time. You never know, the right time for marriage or living with someone again could be a few years from now…or never."

"I always said, I will get married, but not until I'm in my 40s."

Dreamer Lavender Moon grew up with a mother and stepfather who never married, despite being together for 40 years. Her mother was the parent who called the shots.

"My mother was very bossy," she says, with a laugh. "She was one of those people where she did what she wanted, whenever she wanted, how she wanted. She wasn't very good with taking orders. My father – well I call him my father, because that's who raised me – my father was humble. He would just go with the flow. He didn't care. He would just let her handle everything."

The two met when her mother was only 20, and there was a 20 year difference between them.

"As with any relationship, they went through their ups and downs," she says. "They went through infidelity, arguments and whatever. My mother was young. Her thing was just getting out and having fun. My mother never worked, either. When she got together with (my stepfather), it was more for stability. She already had two children by my biological father. He wasn't a provider and he wasn't a father. My mother's parents died when she and her sisters and brothers were very young, so they kind of were scattered. They really raised themselves. I think that's another reason why she didn't get married."

Lavender Moon, however, fully expected *her* future to include marriage. "I think it builds a stronger foundation for both people, especially if it's healthy and if you have children. I think it has a better impact on the children. And then you only have one person to deal with instead of being out there, dating. It's easier if you decide to live together, because you've invested all your time in this person, so you can combine what you have and just build."

She also had a lot of career goals. "I saw me as living in this big old house, with lots of money, and traveling."

The murder of her brother when he was only 14 had a traumatic effect on her. The two were very close. The case was never resolved. "I was very angry," she says. "We never knew who did it. There was all type of speculation."

Having a too-restrictive mother led Lavender Moon to rebel. She became pregnant and had her first child, a daughter, when she was only 16.

"That was something that I was doing, maybe, to get out of the house. I really didn't know much. I didn't have a good relationship with my mother. She was bossy, kind of mean, and she kept us locked up in the house, really. We couldn't really go anywhere, do anything. She was very strict and her motto was, 'Just do what I say.' So when I got out there on the streets, I broke loose. I got tired of being in the house, not being able to go anywhere, not being able to go outside."

She has four children by three different men, but never wanted to marry any of them.

"I always said – and you should be careful what you say, maybe the universe heard me – I always said, 'I will get married, but not until I'm in my 40s.'"

Lavender Moon's daughter, who is now grown, is a single mother herself.

"I tried to stop her. She did it once. She just has one child and she says she will not have another one until she is married, and she's being careful about what type of man she's choosing. She had that one time when she got pregnant by him – it only took her one time, and she actually has been in a pretty good relationship since then. It ended well, they're still friends. But I think really, she's *gotten* it."

Lavender Moon would like to get married, but has very definite ideas about the type of union she wants.

"I want a marriage where the guy is open and willing to help around the house. Some guys are like, 'Oh, I go to work.' The woman works, too, but still, he comes in, opens up a beer and sits there in front of the TV while she has to cook and clean. I don't want that. I want us to share the duties, the responsibilities of keeping the house clean and things like that. You cook sometimes, I'll cook sometimes."

The passage of time has increased her desire to be in a relationship with someone.

"I don't want to grow old and be lonely, just be by myself. And I don't want to give up my independence. It has to be somebody who has the same or similar interests as I do. I don't want to deal with somebody who's not into what I'm into. I don't."

"It's not something I'm afraid of or against."

Jo-Sue's parents' five-decades-long marriage is solid, but…

"My parents weren't really affectionate in their marriage – we didn't see that in front of us very often. So I didn't see that aspect of it. My Dad would make the decisions most often, but as I grew older I saw that my Mom kind of pushed which directions the decisions went in, unless my Dad felt strongly about it. Then he would say, 'No, this is what we're doing.' But my Mom was kind of a take charge person too.

"So I guess I didn't really think, 'I don't want to get married because of what I saw of their relationship - but if I did get married, I would want a more affectionate marriage," asserts the high school assistant principal and youth pastor.

Jo-Sue recalls a stable and supportive childhood. She's the middle of five siblings.

"I came from a pretty good family. It was a Christian home. My Dad was a pastor. He was also a high school math teacher. My mom was an elementary school secretary, but she was at home the entire time, when we were growing up, until we were all in school. Then she went back to work."

When Jo-Sue was a young girl, what were her expectations about her future?

"To be honest, I don't think I really thought about marriage until my teenage years. I actually didn't really want to get a job and work. I guess I thought that I was going to go to college and meet the person that I was going to marry, get married and have kids, but it just never turned out that way. But it never stopped me. I was like, 'Ok, I guess that's not the direction I'm going in right now.' So I started my career and just kept going."

But although she always assumed she would get married, she doesn't remember ever having had what she calls "a normal girl's dreams" about the kind of wedding she wanted. "I never really thought about those kinds of things."

All four of her siblings are married.

"I think they all have great marriages, so it's not something I'm afraid of or against. There just hasn't really been anyone in my life that I was interested in marrying."

Jo-Sue has had an independent nature ever since she was a baby.

"My Mom told me that I was the only one of the kids who didn't want to be held and rocked to sleep. I would cry and cry until I was put in my bed by myself. And then I would fall asleep. She didn't like that, because she liked to rock the kids to sleep, and I was the only one who didn't want to be rocked to sleep. I wanted to be put in the crib and left alone."

If she were to marry, what would that look like?

"I want a relationship with someone that I consider a friend first. Someone that I'm able to talk to. I want to be deeply in love with him, but I want to have a friendship first, because at this point in my life, if I can't be friends with him and share everything that's going on in my life, for me, that would not even be worth getting into.

"And I've seen relationships where they're sometimes afraid of sharing too much. I've seen marriages where people are unequally yoked. My relationship with Jesus is very important to me. I've seen marriages where someone's gotten married to a non-Christian, and I've seen how tough it has been for them." Although some of those marriages have lasted, she has observed bitter arguments among husbands and wives – especially concerning how the children will be raised. "If I'm going to get married, they have to be a Christian. They have to be a friend first."

As to whether she is still open to the idea of getting married, she responds: "Yes. I think so. I think I am."

After a pause, however, she adds: "I'm glad I'm not married."

"They loved each other but they fought all the time."

Suzanne was one of those little girls who was positive she'd have both a husband and children (a dozen of them, she figured!). She had grand plans for a magnificent, fairytale-like wedding, with twelve attendants on both sides and a number of flower girls.

"The whole deal," recalls the retired firefighter. "A Cinderella wedding, of course. I've been thinking about it since I was a little girl."

These elaborate fantasies may have helped her deal with the unpleasant realities she faced in her own family. Her father was rarely home. Her mother was intelligent, creative, and mentally ill, which rendered her unable to effectively care for her children. Suzanne and her two brothers were forced to fend for themselves. She remembers making "soup" out of ketchup and whatever random items could be found in the kitchen cupboards, which were usually bare.

"Oh, that was sad," she says. "I don't know how to describe it. My dad was a workaholic. My mom was incapable of finishing anything, so she didn't do housecleaning, she didn't do any kind of… She kind of became stagnant. Maybe it was a type of depression. She screamed all the time. It was *not* fun."

Her mother didn't allow any visitors in the house, which meant that Suzanne and her brothers couldn't have any of their friends over. Suzanne also didn't date in high school.

"I think I had one date and one prom date. Because my Mom swore so much, I couldn't bring anybody home. I'm wasn't going to have her screaming and swearing. It just wasn't worth it. I wasn't going to be embarrassed like that."

As for the marriage Suzanne saw play out every day…

"My parents loved each other. It was complicated. They loved each other but they fought all the time."

Did those experiences undermine Suzanne's desire to get married? Possibly. It's also possible that the independent spirit she had to develop in order to survive having a neglectful, emotionally volatile mother may also be a contributing factor, because it's a personality trait some of her boyfriends have resented (more on that in the chapter on relationships).

"Just because you are married doesn't mean you were meant to be married"

Joan's parents had a turbulent marriage.

"I grew up a southern Christian – a preacher's kid. A PK," says the fashion designer from Winston-Salem, NC. "My father was not always a good example of a pastor. Between alcohol and women, he basically ruined our home. A lot of hurts and scars there, but you know, you grow up and you heal and you move on. My mom never married again but he did. There were good memories but there were also a lot of painful ones, because he, the alcohol and the womanizing wreaked a lot of havoc in our household."

Joan remembers sitting in the bathtub when she was 12 years old and vowing that she would never let a man do to her what her father had done to her mother.

"And I haven't. I think my mom knows that all of this kind of damaged me and maybe subconsciously it stopped me from being married. Sometimes she'll make mention of it. I'm not going to lie: I may have put up with some stupid foolishness from men for a little while, but I have never had a man do to me what my dad did to her and I never will. I will remain alone before I will allow a man to ridicule me, cheat on me, put me down and devalue my worth the way my father did my mom. So in a way, her life made me strong."

Her mother has been alone since she was 45 and is vehement about not wanting another man in her life.

"Her mindset is she doesn't believe there are any good men out there for her to have a happy life with. I would love to see her have a companion that she could travel with and just enjoy herself with. But she doesn't believe a man like that is out there. I think that's sad, because whatever you think about, you bring about."

Joan has witnessed plenty of troubled unions. "So many women have such unhappy marriages. While I don't judge someone else's marriage by my ability to be happy, I pay attention to the fact that just because you are married doesn't mean you were meant to be married. It doesn't mean God ordained for you to have (a husband); it's just what you settled for. And that makes a big difference."

Joan's ability to form healthy relationships was hindered by low self-esteem, which started when she was very young. She began loathing herself at the age of ten.

"I was always told; 'you're too fat, you've got to diet, you can't eat this, you can't eat that.' You grow up hearing your father saying, 'You got that fat from your Mama's side and you got your brains from my side.'

"My Mama's the one with two degrees, but she's stupid and you're smart? Just crazy stuff! It damages you and it's hard to move on, but God healed me."

The healing took a long time, but Joan finally arrived at a place of peace, self-acceptance and confidence.

"I am a fabulous woman, not because of what other people tell me, but because of what God revealed to me about who I am," she says. "Voluptuous Diva (her line of clothing for plus-sized women) is a *calling*, because there are so many women who are like me. I couldn't understand for years why I went through the things that I did, but my pastor's mom helped me to understand. She said, 'Joan, you are called for a time such as this, because so many women are going to be blessed by the power of your testimony, by the light of your life and the vision that you have.' And that's the thing that holds me."

"Nothing is going to deter me from what I am called to be and what I am called to do, nothing."

In spite of everything – her father's philandering, her parents' divorce – Joan is still open to the idea of marriage. "I want to be married very much, I really do. I believe with all my heart there is a man out there who has a mindset to be with me, to love me. And if he never shows, I'm going to travel and enjoy my life.

"For me, marriage is probably a plus. It doesn't *have* to happen, even though I would love for it to happen.

"However, I look at the mindset of people concerning marriage in this country, and the state of the African-American family. Unfortunately, as a black woman, I've had to realize: it may not happen for me. And that's okay."

"I was scared of my Dad a lot growing up."

Sally believes that a lot of women get married just to get out of their parents' house. "Or because no one's ever told them that they *can* take care of themselves. I don't think that a lot of women are told – even now – that they can do that. Or that they're expected to take care of themselves."

Both of Sally's parents were college graduates – an unusual circumstance in her neighborhood when she was a child. Being equally educated, though, did not mean that their relationship was one of equals.

"In spite of how smart she was, my mom was very subservient to my father," says the outspoken redhead. "I don't know if it got any better over time, but she accepted it, so I also blame her for it, because he could not treat her that way if she did not allow him to. My one brother and I actually got into an argument over that once. I said, 'I don't like the way he treats her either, but it's in her power to change it, and she never did.' Of course, in her era, women didn't."

Despite her father's "very dominant, Type A personality," Sally's parents were best friends who were married for more than five decades, until her mother's death from breast cancer.

"I did not like the way my dad talked to my mom. I was scared of my dad a lot growing up." When it came time to discipline his children, her father would "get the belt out." Although he didn't usually hit Sally with it, she did find herself on the receiving end of the belt when she was five years old. She and her brothers had been roasting marshmallows in the backyard – something they weren't supposed to do.

"My father asked me who started it and I said I didn't know – right up until he hit me. He probably just tapped me but it didn't matter. I gave my brother Kevin up in a heartbeat. And I probably would have told him anything else he wanted to know at that particular moment," she says, with a wry laugh.

She wasn't always afraid of her father, but his unpredictability kept her in a state of uncertainty. "If he was in a good mood, it was great. You just didn't know which mood was going to be the one that you saw."

A show of affection on her part – like sitting next to him, hugging him and calling him "Daddy," could produce two wildly different reactions. "If he was in a good mood, that was a fun thing. If he was in a bad mood, he'd tell me to get the hell away from him and grow up."

"I actually told him once, when I was in high school. 'You know, if you're in a good mood, you think this is cute. If you're in a bad mood, you tell me to grow up. Well you have to pick one or the other.'"

While he generally didn't hit Sally when she did something wrong, she was always fearful that he might. "For the most part, he never followed up. He would say things like he would break your arm, but he never did."

He never had to threaten Sally's older sister, Sharon, who was a rule-follower. Sally learned from Sharon that being compliant has its disadvantages, which came, in her household, in the form of additional responsibilities. Because Sally was a reluctant eater, Sharon was assigned the responsibility of making sure that her younger sister finished her dinner every night.

"I didn't like eating. Anything. I wish they'd left me with that concept. And Sharon had to sit with me at the table. She couldn't get up until I finished and I couldn't get up until I finished. If she'd had any freaking sense she'd have thrown my food away and told my parents I'd finished, but Sharon was a good girl, and she didn't. I think that's how I figured out how NOT to be like that.

"I was more like my brothers in terms of tempers, athletics, craziness, wildness, but very much a big ass baby inside."

Sally's mother had had a job until she became pregnant with her first child. When Sally was in the sixth grade, she observed her mother asking permission to go back to work. It made a strong impression on the girl who would grow up to be a successful career woman.

"She convinced my Dad – he had to approve – that she was going to go back to work. She was actually going to take over my sister's job, as a cashier in a little grocery store."

Sally's father set the rules for his wife's employment: she couldn't leave for work until the two youngest children had left for school for the day, and had to be home before they got home.

"She had brilliance and a career and she had to stay home and be a mother – and I'm thankful for that," Sally says. "Don't get me wrong. I think it's awesome. I can't image the ones who, when they got sick, couldn't go home from school. If I got sick, I called my Mom and she came and picked me up. I didn't have to sit in the principal's office like some kids did. Not many, because with most of us, our mothers stayed home, unless it was a divorce. That was rare."

"I'm going to find somebody like my Dad, who I lord over."

Ironically, although her father brought home (most of) the bacon, Sally's mother had complete charge of the finances.

"My Dad actually couldn't cash his own check because it didn't match the signatures, or when he would go into the bank – because people knew who you were then – they didn't know who he was. And they never asked my Mom for her ID, even though it was *his* check."

Her mother handled the family budget and paid all of the bills. Sally remembers that her mother would never buy anything for herself.

"I remember one time we were in J.C. Penney's and there was a blouse on sale. I said; 'Buy it!' She said; 'I don't really need it.' I'm like, 'Who cares? It's two dollars.' So she ran the household, but I think she put stricter controls on herself financially than my Dad did."

Does Sally think that her parents' marriage influenced her own decision to not get married?

"I always expected that I *would* get married. It's not that I didn't want to. And I actually thought that if I got married, I'd have several kids, because I thought growing up in a big family was awesome."

However, she had very definite ideas about dominance in a relationship. A conversation she had with her uncle when she was a teenager is telling.

"I said to him; 'I'm going to find somebody like my Dad, who *I* lord over. He said, 'No, no, that's not the way to go.' So I figured, maybe I didn't want the one that I could lord over, but I wasn't going to let somebody lord over *me*."

She did not have the dream of walking down the aisle in a big white dress. She did know that she was going to get an education, but beyond that…

"I thought I'd get married. I didn't plan anything. I didn't even plan going to school, for the most part. I just knew I was going to. And my mother or father never did insinuate that I was getting married. They never said anything about that. They definitely didn't direct me toward *dating* in any way shape or form."

"That, combined with the earlier childhood experience, just didn't make me think too highly of men in general."

When Sally was only five years old, she was sexually molested by a teenage neighbor. That crime – and her parents' response to it – had a long-lasting effect on her.

"I don't know how long it actually was going on. He actually had me in his parents' house – which was right across the street from *my* parents' house, so he wasn't too smart a person. And he didn't have a back door, so he had to let me out the side door, and my parents were always on the porch in the summertime. So one night, my Mom asked me why I was over there and I told her."

The next morning, Sally came down the stairs in her home and saw the predator's parents standing in the vestibule.

"His mother hadn't seen me yet, but I heard her say, 'She's lying.' And my mother said, 'Well where would she get that idea, of what he was doing?' So they moved. I don't know all the other stuff that happened. I'm sure my Dad threatened them."

What did *not* happen was a phone call to the police, followed by an arrest. The pedophile had been forced to leave the neighborhood – so the danger to Sally was eliminated – but the crime was quietly swept under the rug. As Sally grew up, she found herself thinking a great deal about what had happened to her. As for her parents' failure to press charges against the molester, she says: "That's what you did back then. But who knows what else he did, to other people?"

An episode that occurred when she was in her early 20s also left Sally with some trust issues. She was out with a friend one night when she met a man in a bar who asked her for a date. This was the pre-cell phone era. Sally gave him her phone number but she didn't get his, so when she got very ill just prior to the date, she was unable to call him and tell him not to come.

"So when he got there, I said, 'I just feel awful.' Well he still wanted me to go out. So now I'm pissed. I go out with him, but I don't want anything to do with this person because he could care less about how I felt."

They went to the movies and then he took her home. In the days that followed, she admits that she didn't do "the most mature thing." She refused to answer the phone when he called.

That prompted a barrage of unwanted attention from him. He began calling her house every hour, well into the night. "He'd call eight times in a row. I'd pick it up and he'd hang up and then call back. Then I'd finally unplug the phone."

Sally actually had to have her phone tapped in order to document the harassment, so that she'd have evidence to take to the police and hopefully, have it stopped. The police did follow up on the information. Whatever they did worked: she did not hear from her pursuer again.

"So that combined with the earlier childhood experience just didn't make me think too highly of men in general. I don't think I actively thought of that, but maybe on a subconscious level."

"Long-term marriages were what I grew up around."

Leanne was born when her mother was 40 and her father 42. For that era, she was considered a late-in-life baby. Because her only sibling, a sister, was 20 years older than her, Leanne was virtually raised as an only child.

"So my parents' marriage was a mature one by the time I came on the scene," says the teacher and actor. "They'd been married 20 years before I ever showed up, so there was a whole lot of history there that I was born into. That tended to give me a lot of privileges that many children don't have when their parents are 20-somethings. I was very well looked after. I was very cared for. My Mom was almost too much in my life."

Her parents, who were married for 65 years, had "huge" fights, according to Leanne, but those arguments never had long-lasting effects. "There was never any undercurrent of resentment or hostility. There was no major threat of divorce or anything like that. It was really a very put-together family."

Her mother was a stay-at-home mom until Leanne was in middle school, when she got a part-time job, "just to make sure that she got her own life."

Her father was in charge of finances, but her mother was in charge of the family.

"It was very much like a 1940s, 50s lifestyle. It was affectionate. I mean, they were mid- to late 40s – in their 50s – by the time I really paid attention to the dynamics of men and women and their relationship – but there was a tremendous respect for each other. But I think after 40, 50 years of marriage, they're roommates at this point."

Very few people in Leanne's family are divorced. "My sister's been married for 47 years. Most of my aunts and uncles were in long-term marriages except for one, and he was sort of the black sheep of the family, because he got married several times. My grandparents were married forever. Long-term marriages were what I grew up around."

Did that make it harder for Leanne when she got divorced?

"In a sense, yes. I didn't feel that I failed, but I felt like I was part of a failed *something*. I could see where the problems were and it wasn't anything that I had control over or could prevent, but I did feel like I blew it in the sense that my marriage did not make it and everybody else's did.

"I think we've set these incredibly ridiculous standards and these narratives and these stories, and the second either side disappoints, it's a downward spiral because people aren't seeing each other as human beings. As individuals. 'And the two shall become one.' God, I hope not! That was the problem. And I feel like the young'uns for generations have been told, 'You will form this union and this new world.' Well, what happens to *me*, that I brought to the party?"

When she divorced, Leanne found herself examining other people's long-term marriages and trying to determine what they did right and what she did wrong.

"Now, as a single person, I'm like, 'Oh my God, I'd forgotten how much trouble all that is.' Look at these guys. They're having to negotiate times and who gets the car and all of this *stuff* that I don't have to think about. I thought about it – when I got divorced – as a bummer, but since then, nope!" She laughs. "Nope!"

Of her own divorce and her parents' long-lasting marriage, Leanne says: "'Thank God, whatever happens in my life, I will *not* be married 65 years. Holy God. I don't know that people are cut out to be together that long. Not like it went south, but just, *what do you say?* What could you possibly have to talk about?"

She believes after many years, marriage becomes a habit, like doing laundry or emptying the dishwasher. "I'm seeing it with my sister as well. I'm watching – that's not really a marriage anymore. That's a co-habitation. And I feel like, looking at some of these really long-term marriages, people stay to stay. I don't know how many people are still passionately in love with their partner."

Longevity aside, would she ever consider getting married again?

"I don't know. I'm not opposed to it. I'm not swearing off, 'Never again,' but it would have to be somebody who adds something to the life that I have. It would have to be somebody who brings something that I can't provide for myself. I don't feel lonely. I don't feel the need for companionship. I don't pine away. But if somebody were to come into my life that was interesting and challenged me and had kindness and all the cool things that you would want in any partner, then I would certainly consider getting married again."

"It made me make sure that I didn't want their marriage."

Pat was not one of those women who wanted to be single. That was not her plan. "But in saying that, I will also say that I had a lot of self-esteem issues, which people don't always believe because I know how to behave like a confident person," admits the writer.

She wanted to be married for all the wrong reasons. "I wanted someone to rescue me. I don't feel that way anymore by a long shot, but that's who I was, as someone who wanted to be married back in the day."

Pat always found her parents' marriage challenging. "I saw a lot of frustration with each other. A lot of exasperation. Miscommunication. When divorce became popular in the 70s, I started asking my mother every year, 'Would you divorce Daddy?' And it was always, 'No.' And one year it was finally, 'I don't know.' I remember being like, 'Really?' I told a therapist that and she said, 'Oh my God, I can't believe you were a child asking your mother that question!' It was just because there was so much tension in the house."

Pat's mother died from cancer when she was 16 and her father later remarried.

She has an older brother and sister whose perceptions of their parents' relationship differ considerably from hers, because things were not the same by the time Pat came along. "I didn't see that love affair, or that they were enamored with each other. "I'm always thinking, wow, we did not have the same experience."

Did her parents' marriage affect her own ideas about matrimony? "Yes," she says. "It made me make sure that I didn't want *their* marriage."

Her sister's marriage, though, is one she'd gladly emulate. "One of the things I admire about my sister's marriage is that she has not fallen into those traps," Pat says. "She and her husband have very open communication. They discuss things. I'm always surprised at the things they discuss. They communicate well, and I love that."

As a young girl looking ahead to her future, Pat faced a double whammy: crippling insecurities coupled with intense pressure to achieve that came from her highly accomplished parents.

"Because of my insecurities, I didn't really have expectations about my future. I had dreams about my future, but there was always this gulf in between. You know, here's this idea of what I want, and here's my reality and the gulf in between was: I don't know if I'm worthy of that."

She was fascinated by Hollywood and dreamed of being an actor, but didn't know how she would achieve that.

"My parents are educated African-Americans who came into their being and their education before civil rights, to a certain extent," so their reaction to her acting aspirations tended to be, 'That's nice, but it's a hobby. Get a degree in business or law.' My dreams were not actually supported because I'm an artist in my soul. It was really hard for me because I was thinking, 'I don't want to do that. I want a different life.' I didn't know how to express it. I didn't know if I could expect it, if I could have it."

Pat's self-esteem problem was rooted, at least in part, in her childhood.

"You know, it was weird to be growing up in the 60s and the 70s in Detroit, which was one of the most racially polarized places on earth. It was weird to be educated and African-American. People didn't expect that of you in Detroit. If we'd lived in New York, it'd be different. New York is classist, not racist."

She and her siblings went to a private school in a wealthy suburb with very few African-American students.

"I think there were issues about us getting accepted into the school, and my father put lawyers on them. I think that was the basis of my self-esteem issues. My parents were educated. I had a lot of white friends. I just didn't understand all of that. I grew up around white society, so that was what was confusing to me. I didn't have any black friends. I had all white friends, because of where I went to school."

"My father was puritanical. He was very funny about sex, and boys."

When Pat did begin to date, she primarily dated white men, although that kind of socializing didn't happen until she was of a certain age.

"My dad was an uber Catholic, so dating was not even on the horizon. Boys were off limits. Never discussed. We were never even allowed to think about it. My father was puritanical. He was very funny about sex, and boys. It was something that was feared. We weren't allowed the attentions – I was scared of the attentions from men."

Attending an all-girls boarding school in the north of England from the ages of ten to 18 didn't bring Pat into contact with many prospective boyfriends. "Boys were just a completely foreign thing to me."

She was sent there not to keep her from dating boys, but because her father had been a Fulbright scholar who'd fallen in love with the area while studying at the University of Leeds.

"It was amazing. I loved it. I tell people, 'It was Harry Potter, without the magic.' I was head of my house, deputy head girl. It was in my identity." She believes her time there had an enormous impact on the person she became. "I can't get away from it. You deny it and eventually it just becomes you and you stop fighting it."

She still keeps in contact via Skype with the close friends she made in England, and confesses to being very particular about the kinds of tea she'll drink.

"I'm horrible about my tea. I'm like, 'Do *not* stick it in the micro-wave.' I bring my own teabags because I don't like anybody else's tea. It's a British brand." She laughs. "I'm awful about my tea."

And will there someday be a Mr. Pat, with whom to share that tea?

"I want to be married," she says firmly. "I will be married."

The Mommy Gene

When I made my elementary school basketball team in the 6th grade, I spent most of each game sitting on the bench, watching the 7th and 8th graders play. Through the din of the school gym I could periodically hear my father yell, "Put Paraventi in!" Sometimes I *did* get to play, usually in the last five minutes of the game. I ran around the court excitedly, if not always effectively, but I didn't care. I was getting to be a real basketball player! In a bright blue uniform! With the older girls!

Did my father's loud suggestions motivate my coach to put me in the game? Probably not; she had her own game plan. But that wasn't important. What was important is that I knew he would be at every game, cheering me on (or *hoping* for the chance to cheer me on). I knew he would fix my bike when it broke, teach me how to play tennis and take our family camping every summer just like I knew my mother would sew my costume for the school play (even if I told her about it the night before), bake me a cake for my birthday and bring my lunch to school when I forgot it. I had the thing that's most important to children: certainty, which creates a feeling of security.

I had the best parents in the world. My mother and my father considered being parents their most important roles in life. The funny thing is, they had some difficulty getting cast in those roles. After they tied the knot, they tried to get pregnant for eight long years, but were unable to. They finally initiated the process of adoption and were almost through with the inspections, interviews and paperwork required when my mother found out that she was pregnant. She gave birth to my sister Kathy – and later, to three more of us.

It's interesting that with loving, attentive role models like these, I didn't grow up wanting to be a parent. There's an assumption out there that all women want to – or should want to – bear children, but is there a Mommy gene that some women just don't have?

The fact that my parents put so much time and energy into raising us was wonderful for our development. It also demonstrated to me that that's what parents must do – and I was never sure that I could give the level of attention to a child that they gave to my siblings and me. I planned to put time and energy into my aspirations and ambitions. Additionally, the responsibilities that go along with being a parent *terrified* me.

Despite all of this, I still assumed that I would someday be a mother – that my attitude toward parenthood would magically be transformed once I met Mr. Right and became a Mrs. Lots of people assured me that this would happen.

I was absolutely certain I didn't want to be a single mother. Some women can do it, but I knew that I was not one of them. If I was intimidated by the idea of raising a child with the help of a husband, I knew I couldn't do it all by myself.

As my fertile years went by, I was torn, conflicted about the fact that I didn't really want children, but… I knew I would be missing out on one of the greatest experiences of life. And I wasn't really making the deliberate decision to forego children; I was letting time do the deciding for me.

Most of the always single women I spoke with for this book knew from an early age that they absolutely did not want children. A few of them did – and regret not being mothers. A few of them have kids.

"It would be planned, it wouldn't just happen"

Because she loved growing up in a large family, Sally – the redhead who works in telecommunications - used to think she'd have four or five kids. She told her mother that if she wasn't married by the age of 30, she'd have a baby anyway.

"And I *thought* maybe I meant it. But in reality, it wasn't fair to me or to them, because it's a lot of work and a child's not going to get 100 percent from me. I'm not saying it can't be done, but I truly don't believe it's the right thing for people to do. Single parenting by choice is, in my opinion, a bad choice. So I didn't go there."

Like me, Sally experienced some anxiety over the ticking of her biological clock.

"I loved turning 30," she says. "At 30, I was at the top of my game. Forty was hard for me, because I think that's where it sort of sunk in: I'm not having kids. At 30, I was still possibly having kids. By the time I had my mastectomies (more on that in the chapter on relationships)… it wasn't a complete impossibility at 43. My Mom had my brother at 44. I was not afraid of being an older parent, by any stretch."

She was in a committed relationship with her boyfriend Frank by that time, so why didn't she go ahead and get pregnant?

"One, we weren't married. Two, dumb luck! To me, marriage was going to come first, if we were going to have a child. And it would be planned, it wouldn't just happen."

Frank is a great guy and a loving companion, but she knew he wouldn't be the kind of father she'd need him to be.

"He'd be the friend, not the father. I'd be my dad. My mom always backed my father, but Frank wouldn't do that, and I remember families that were like that. It's horrible when the parents aren't a united front. And we wouldn't be. He'd be helping kids keep stuff from me, and I'd be bitter and mad. That's just not the right way to go."

She concedes that she'll never be as mature as her friends who have kids. "No matter how responsible I am about other things, I can't touch that."

Girls take care of their parents

Retired nurse anesthetist Tish has a very specific regret when it comes to motherhood: she's sorry that she didn't have a daughter, because she believes that girls take care of their parents as they age and boys separate from them as adults and don't look back.

"It's just how we treat our parents and how we care in later life. And I'm the oldest daughter in an Irish family. What does that tell you? Girls are always concerned with their parents' welfare. To me, a son, once they go off to college and have a girlfriend, it's over."

If she'd had a relationship that resulted in marriage, Tish says she probably would have had a child.

"If you're not going to do it wholeheartedly, don't do it"

Kay "never, ever, ever" wanted kids, and thinks for those who do, it's a terrible reason to get married. "Your relationship is not automatically going to be good just because you're parenting."

She knew at a fairly young age that she wouldn't make a good mother.

"I wish everyone knew it early on, because so many people don't figure it out until they have kids, and then they realize they're not really good at it. They don't have the patience."

Kay has friends who are single and childless yet are considering having a baby. If they can't tell her that it's a burning desire – that it's something they absolutely can't live without – she tries to talk them out of it.

"This is too important a job! You're not buying a car. You're bringing a human being into the world. And if you're not going to do it wholeheartedly, don't do it," says the vegan educator.

She was asked by friends what she'd do if she fell in love with a man who really wanted kids. Her answer: "I'm not the gal for him. He needs to go find someone else who has the same burning desire.

I am not going to have children just because he wants them. I'll be a terrible mom. It's not my desire. It takes over your life, and I have other things I want to do with my life – things that are important to me. It's not my drive and desire to be a mom. That's a lifelong job."

Her very Catholic parents didn't pressure her to have children but they did badger her about not getting pregnant before getting married, mainly because both of her sisters were in that state going down the aisle.

"It was horrifying for my father," she says. "It was humiliating for him. But I left the church at age 22, so it wasn't a factor either way for me."

She now appreciates other people's kids more than she ever did before. When a niece of hers had a baby, Kay uncharacteristically got involved with planning birthday and christening parties – something that drew her back into the family circle and made her appreciate "that cute stage and how fast they grow." However, she is fine with seeing the baby every few months. "I have no burning desire to be there every day."

"That chip was already in me"

Elizabeth, the Washington state resident who's been in a committed relationship with a man named Stephen for more than two decades, would probably have had children if she'd been with somebody who really wanted them.

"But I was sort of on the fence and I didn't meet him until I was 36. Who knows if I could have even gotten pregnant? But it wasn't a big goal of mine."

She didn't play with dolls when she was a kid; all of her toys were stuffed animals. "So that chip was already in me."

There are times she regrets not having a child, but not very often. She pours her love into dogs.

"I think puppies are just the best thing in the world, but babies are like, yeah, they're ok. They all look the same to me," she laughs.

Now that her nieces and nephews are college age, she loves hanging out with them, but when they were young, she didn't know what to do with them: what to say, or how to act. It was awkward.

Elizabeth's experiences with her own mother may well have affected her attitudes about being a parent. "My mother was not very affectionate," she says. "Neither was my father. My mother never told me she loved me. My father is only now doing it because *I* tell *him*. We're late in life here, right?

"I probably had an exceptionally uncaring childhood. My brothers used to beat up on me and I'd complain and my mom would say, 'Just ignore them.' She would never turn around and say, 'Cut it out. Leave her alone. She's smaller than you. What the hell are you doing?' You know, none of that. No one had my back."

"It would drive me crazy"

A key reason for her avoidance of motherhood, though, was a practical one: she knew that financially, she couldn't swing it. "I thought; I can't afford to have a kid. Because I've always understood that I have to pay my way. I'm guessing if Stephen and I had a kid together, it'd still be same thing. I don't think it'd be any different. I'd still have to pay for that, too. I heard on NPR the average child from the age of birth to the age of 18 is going to cost you $250,000."

Elizabeth realizes that part of her money anxiety comes from a perception of how spoiled children are these days.

"I see the way kids are treated now and all the things they get and I think, Jesus! I'm so glad I don't have a kid. It would drive me crazy. You know, they have to have the best shoes --that cost $150 – and they have to have all this electrical equipment, and the phone. You have to be walking them to school and if it rains out you have to drive them to school. I never had any of that. I just think they're so pampered."

Elizabeth has two brothers. One has never been married and the other has been married twice. Neither has any children, which means that her parents have no grandchildren.

"Someone once asked me if I had kids, and when I didn't, she said something about my parents being disappointed. I said to her, 'You know, my parents are smart enough that if it does bother them, they've never said anything.'"

She remembers attending a class about having goals when one is middle-aged, and one of the goals the instructor mentioned was having grandchildren.

"I thought, 'You can't have that as a goal. It's not *your* life.'"

Jo-Sue, the 40-something educator, says it's probably well past her time of having kids – and she sounds relieved about that.

"I'll be honest: after the last three weeks, I really don't think I want toddlers. My family was around, and toddlers are a *lot* of work. Oh my goodness! And noisy. I don't know if I could handle it, at my age, having patience with the kids. I'm more of a teenager person. I like to talk to teenagers."

"You don't have any babies?"

Pat thinks she'd be a good mother now, but she wouldn't have been when she was younger. The writer and director had a pregnancy scare years ago, when she was engaged, and sometimes thinks about how that child would have turned out if she'd actually been pregnant ("how much therapy I would have paid for," she jokes).

"Dear God, that poor child. I wouldn't have been consistent. I wouldn't have trusted my instincts as a mother, because I was so insecure. I think I would have been a disastrous mother. Now, I'd be a good mother, but I don't have a great desire to become one."

Instead, she loves being "Auntie Mame" to everybody's kids – especially her young niece, who was adopted and arrived at Pat's sister's house two weeks before Pat did.

"She's a gift from God," Pat says. "She affects everybody. She is an ambassadress of joy and goodwill. We call her Joybug."

Her niece really lives up to her name at the rare times when Pat feels herself spiraling into a blue mood. It happened recently, and Pat coped with it by inviting her niece to join her in a giggle contest.

"The energy shift was palpable. It was a wonderful exercise. It sandblasted my energy. I'm done with the funk. The funk is over."

Pat has felt the procreation pressure from people she meets, and not necessarily from her family members. "Older black women will kind of give you a run for your money on that one," she says. "They ask, 'You don't have any babies? No kids?' But that's cultural."

She says: "In all honesty, God knew what he was doing."

"Do I need to put another person on the planet just to pass on my DNA?"

Sheryl, an ardent environmentalist, cites the planet's overpopulation crisis as a big reason to not have children.

"To just pump out kids would not be beneficial to society. So many people have children and they can't parent well. Why have another generation of people that has issues? And then, also, the world's resources are really stressed. I think children are wonderful and I always say, 'Congratulations,' to my friends that have babies, but there are billions of people on this planet and resources are tight. What's going to happen to those kids?"

If Sheryl had ever decided to become a parent, she would have adopted, because there are so many unwanted children in need of good homes.

"As humans, we're already exploding on this planet, and we don't have a lot of value for the life forms that aren't human. As a general rule, we think we're the dominant species here. Because of that, we're really blasting through resources and they're not utilized evenly. I don't know what's going to happen. It's a mathematical progression: where is it all going to go? So I had that idea when I was in high school: 'Do I need to put another person on the planet just to pass on my DNA? Is that selfish of me?' And yet people think you're selfish when you *don't* have children. I felt the reverse. To have a bunch of kids and not care what the ramifications are for anyone else and possibly limited resources is selfish."

However, when Sheryl thought once that she was pregnant by an on-again, off-again boyfriend, she was very excited. She hadn't been using use birth control at the time because she was going through menopause and didn't think she could get pregnant.

"I didn't tell anybody else – only him."

An acupuncturist she went to because her energy was low said she felt a "quickening" in Sheryl, and asked her when her last period was. Her neighbor remarked that Sheryl looked as if she was "glowing."

Sheryl was terrified. "How in the heck was I going to have a kid at 50? What was going to happen?"

She did feel as though her body was changing, but the result of a home pregnancy test was negative. She didn't go to a doctor for a more formal test because she was deeply conflicted about the prospect of motherhood.

"There was a part of me that felt that this would be really cool, and a part of me that was terrified and felt like I really couldn't do it. I guess I didn't really want to know. I was kind of nutty. I couldn't settle down. I just couldn't deal with it. It felt overwhelming to me."

Her fears were alleviated somewhat when her boyfriend reacted positively to the news that he might soon be a father. "I didn't tell anybody else – only him."

Three weeks later, when she had a period, she cried. The period had some substance to it, so she suspected that she'd miscarried. She was eventually able to come to terms with the episode and to decide that due to her age and the circumstances, it had worked out for the best.

"I had my brother's children to love on"

If Joan doesn't get married within the next few years, she intends to adopt children by herself.

"I should have adopted a long time ago," says the North Carolinian. "I would start the process and then I would get scared and wonder, 'Am I really ready for this?' I liked my freedom and at that time I had my brother's children to love on. Any time I wanted to get those babies, I could. So if I wanted to mother something and spoil it, I would get them. So I never really missed having children because I always had my brother's."

When they became teenagers, though, and were busy with their own lives, Joan revisited the idea of adoption. She teased her nieces and nephews about it.

"They would always respond that *they* were the babies and I did not need to adopt anyone because I had them. To this day we are very close. They call me. They come over to my house and curl up in the bed beside me. They say, 'Auntie, I love you.'"

In that way, Joan considers herself a mother. However, she knows there are children out there who need to be adopted and loved.

"So, if and when I decide I want to adopt, then I will. And if I don't, I'm going to travel the world and enjoy my life, because you only get one."

"God help me if I were to give birth to something that had half of you in it"

Leanne never longed to have children. "I don't know if it's selfishness, or I just realize I have too much living to do yet, and I'm not willing to kind of bank that," says the high school teacher.

When she and her husband got married, they agreed that they weren't really interested in having children. Then he had a change of heart.

"Part of the whole decay of his mind was suddenly, 'Well you never wanted children and I do.' That got laid on me and I thought, 'God help me if I were to give birth to something that had half of you in it.'"

As the marriage deteriorated and came to an end, she was especially glad that she'd stuck to her decision.

"When it became a danger to know him, I was so grateful that we didn't have a child," which would have kept their lives intertwined. "So, during the marriage, 'No way.' After the divorce, 'Thank God.' And now, as a woman on my own, I am *still* glad, because again, I relish the freedom of not having to consider, constantly, the needs of others in making my life choices."

Leanne doesn't appreciate it when people who meet her assume that she must be sad about having had no children with her ex-husband. "I just think; 'Do you even have a clue what that would have been like?'"

She is not looking forward to ten years down the road, when she'll likely hear "granny comments" like; "You don't have any grandchildren?"

She's already decided not to let it bother her. "I figure, this is somebody who doesn't know, who hasn't walked my walk and doesn't understand."

(Not) Marrying for Money

Being single means that you don't have the financial safety net that an additional income offers. Being single also means that you don't have the financial stress that an irresponsible spouse offers.

The well-documented gender gap means that single women, in general, are at a definite economic disadvantage in our society, right? Despite that, a surprising number of women I spoke with mentioned finances as a reason to *not* get married. They've worked hard at demanding careers, invested wisely, scrimped and saved if they've had to and they worry that a free-spending husband could threaten the stability they've established for themselves. They are the opposite of gold diggers.

However, it is true that being single – whether you're a man or a woman – means you are on your own, without someone else's paycheck to carry you through tough times. Losing my job during the recession threw me into a financial panic. I was in my late 40s. I had aged out of the broadcasting industry and the skills I'd developed as a radio personality weren't easily transferable to other industries (although I tried hard on my resume to make the case that they were). Unemployment checks didn't cover all of my expenses. I watched my savings ebb away as I took classes that would enable me – I hoped – to switch careers, despite my age and the grim state of the economy. I joked about moving into the attic of my sister and brother-in-law's house, without finding it particularly funny. They didn't laugh.

It would have been so much easier if I'd been married to a rich man who could take care of my mortgage payments, pay for my groceries and car repairs and make sure I had health insurance. I fantasized about it. This wealthy illusory husband of mine – who looked a lot like George Clooney, by the way – would say to me (in a sexy growl that sounded a lot like George Clooney's sexy growl): "Honey, don't bother trying to find another job. I'm so incredibly rich that you don't ever have to work again – and I won't lose respect for you if you don't. You just spend your days writing your next novel. You're an artist. You shouldn't have to waste your time slaving away at a day job."

(This was a fantasy husband, after all!)

I did, eventually, get back on my feet. I found a new job in a new field. I continue to pay my own bills, without the help of a wealthy husband. However, anxiety over money remains a constant in my life, one which I may never shake. Would I feel this way if I were married? It's hard to say. I am, literally, on my own – by my own choice.

"They can crush your financial security in the blink of an eye"

Lucy, the Denver stockbroker who's done extremely well for herself, concedes that some women do marry for money. "It's a huge reason, but it can go in the other direction," she says. "You can have a loser guy hook up with a financially strong woman and bring her down."

Lucy has created a substantial financial foundation for herself that includes a home that's nearly paid off and a retirement plan that is in perfect order.

"I'm afraid of someone ruining that for me," she says. "If I brought a man into my life, you know, they can crush your financial security in the blink of an eye. So I have a little bit of fear with that. I'm very protective of my financial well-being, and I don't want anyone else to screw that up. There is fear based on not wanting to comingle lives to that extent of living together and sharing finances, because they can totally ruin that."

Lucy's anxiety is not free-floating; it's rooted in some of the experiences she's had with boyfriends. In her early 40s, she had back-to-back relationships with men who wanted to be taken care of. By her.

"They wanted me to quit my job, move in with them and take care of the house, cook their meals, provide sex. And this wasn't too many years ago that I was running into this! Not that they wanted to get married. They didn't want to get married. They had wealth and they wanted to protect that wealth. But they wanted me to walk away from *my* career, move in with them and, you know, serve them. I had three relationships in my early 40s that all wanted that."

Lucy pointed out each time that if she were to quit her job, she'd no longer be building her own wealth and establishing security for her retirement and her future – while the boyfriend was continuing to build his.

"I held onto that fiercely, you know: you need to continue to work. I had one guy offer to establish a trust for me so that I would have funds if we broke up – a fund of the so-called accumulated wealth that I would have attained during our relationship. I told him no. He was buying me. He was buying my being with him."

"I have that little shell of protection going on and I don't want it ever taken away or impacted by someone else. When I meet 'that guy,' he'll have more wealth than I do. That's a requirement."

"I was not going to risk anything."

Although Sally originally wanted to marry Frank, she's glad that never happened, and money is one of the reasons it didn't. She's got money and he doesn't. More than that, she's smart with money and he makes financial choices that she feels are foolish. Sally has done very well in her career, invested wisely and planned well.

"The longer we *weren't* married and the more I grew, the more I accumulated," she said. "I was not going to risk anything. I will *share* everything with him, but I'm sharing it. It's not his, just for the record."

If they were married – if it was going to be a real working marriage –Sally knows that she'd have to include Frank in all of the spending decisions she makes.

"At this point, I don't want to, because I've been on my own, my own boss, my own person my whole life."

Frank doesn't get angry about Sally's purchases. After all, as noted in the chapter on the benefits of being a single woman, that couch she's buying is for *her* house – which she's owned for 20+ years – not *their* house. Despite their decades-long relationship, at Sally's insistence they still live in separate houses.

"I try and include him, but if he shows disinterest, I'm done. And ultimately, it's still *my* decision."

"I have heard friends put price tags on their divorces."

Andrea's success in the corporate world has allowed her to create a very comfortable life for herself (and to build a really big house!). She is, understandably, wary of men who may be attracted to her for her money.

"I tend to pull back and pull away if I think anybody's looking at my money and my assets and house," she says. "The older I get, the more I get that way. That sounds very self-centered, and like I think a little too much of myself, but that's a fact."

Where does that suspicion come from? Has she actually been taken for a financial ride by a former boyfriend?

"I've seen it happen to my friends and – this sounds harsh – I have heard friends put price tags on their divorces; 'It cost me X to get rid of him.'"

"If I need money I go out and I work hard and I get it."

Stephanie got her strong work ethic from her father, who also stressed the value of education. Even though he paid for her college education, Stephanie spent her undergrad years getting up at 4:30 a.m.to work in the dorm cafeteria so that she could pay for her expenses and graduate from college without being in debt.

"I feel like I got the best of both worlds," she says. "I got a dad who said, 'You know what? If you get an education you're going to be able to do whatever you need to do. And if you learn and understand that, there's no one who's going to stop you. If you go to work and have the desire –the work ethic – then you're going to be fine and you don't need to depend on anybody."

Stephanie, a successful entrepreneur, calls herself a survivor. "If I need money I go out and I work hard and I get it. I've always had that sense about things."

"I'm disabled and poor yet I feel like I'm richer than I've ever been in my life."

Pat's financial security has been affected by her disability. She was a successful marketing professional living large in New York City when the recession claimed her job, and neurological symptoms that she attributes to Ground Zero exposure escalated and hampered her ability to physically function and to find another job.

"I've been through the ringer," she says. It's been a crazy ride."

When she got laid off, did she wish that she weren't single? That she had a husband to help her pay the bills?

"It was between that and winning the lottery," she laughs. "A husband or the lottery."

Losing her job made her feel like a failure, although she admits that she was burnt out by that time on what had initially been a deeply satisfying career and had been looking for a way to return to the creative pursuits that made her happy.

"I was at an emotional point where I thought, I cannot go back to corporate America or I'll die," she says. "I knew in my soul that I wouldn't make it. I'll die. I'll get cancer, something will happen, because I can't do this to myself anymore. I am not this person."

Nonetheless, Pat tried to find another corporate job, with little success. She ran through her savings – easy to do in one of the most expensive cities in the world. Her landlord began eviction proceedings against her. She eventually had to file for bankruptcy.

She did, though, manage to find work that was in the creative sphere, even if her particular position wasn't creative. As managing director of a small theatre space, she earned a salary that was much smaller than she'd been used to.

"It was a fascinating experience," she remembers."It was frustrating, though. I'm in theatre, but I'm not being a creative. I'm being the businesswoman. It was like, this is my compromise for my Dad. I'm going to be a businesswoman inside creativity so everybody will be happy."

Her health worsened, though, and after awhile she was no longer able to perform the duties required of her in her theatre job. She had to resign her position. Then her younger sister got married and pregnant all in the same year – two developments that made Pat take a hard look at her own life.

"I kind of lost my mind. I'm thinking; 'I'm 46 years old. What the hell happened to my life? I'm not doing anything I want to do. What the hell happened?'"

Her health continued to decline. She moved back to Detroit, where she lives with her sister, brother-in-law and niece. She is now officially disabled and unable to work, although she writes fiction and plays, records podcasts of her work and participates in a local playwrights group. Although her physical resources are not what they used to be, she is finally able to indulge in her passion for creative pursuits. She also gets strength from her faith and spirituality.

"I'm on this reset button part of my life. That's what I really feel this is. I used to pray that I wanted a second chance in life. I've been back in Michigan four years now. Within this time period, there's been tremendous inner healing, tremendous growth and experiences. This has been the re-set button.

"People think I'm insane!" she laughs. "I should tell you that."

Pat walks slowly and uses a wheelchair for anything other than short distances. Walking up stairs or down stairs takes her a long time. One hand is curled into a useless position. She needs help with basic tasks. Despite her physical limitations, she's vivacious, articulate and hilarious. She laughs often, revels in her writing activity and enjoys being with friends and family.

And, she says, if someone had told her that she'd be disabled and totally dependent on others but be incredibly happy, she would have told them that they're crazy.

"But you know what? I am really happy. I love my community. I love my life. I love my friends. I love where life has taken me. I'm so incredibly blessed."

Through therapy and prayer, she's experienced a profound healing of her self-esteem and has – astoundingly – reached the point of being really grateful for everything that's happened to her.

"I was that woman who relied on her high heels and her makeup to feel confident in any situation," she recalls. After a time, she couldn't even walk in high heels. "When that all gets taken away from you, you have to rely on yourself. Just you. That's an amazing experience because I am who I am and I completely love myself. But it took a long time."

When she reached the point of gratitude, that's when her self-esteem healed. "I'm disabled and poor yet I feel like I'm richer than I've ever been in my life."

"I'm not suffering. I make it work."

Elizabeth – the Washington State resident - is single, but has one of the disadvantages of being married. Her long-time partner Stephen calls the shots when it comes to money, and she must go along with his decisions.

Theirs is a long-term, committed relationship between financial unequals. Because her partner Stephen earns considerably more money than she does and has much different ideas about the way they should live, she often feels under financial pressure.

"He doesn't support me financially," she says. "He does a little bit, but I pay all my own expenses. My health insurance, my car insurance. No one's ever bought me a car. I paid for half the house we live in. All my clothing. We have a dog – I pay for half of that."

Elizabeth gives Stephen money every month that is supposed to cover food and insurance, but he claims that those costs exceed what she pays him. They have a joint checking account and a mutual credit card. She goes through the credit card bill every month and highlights everything she owes and pays that amount. Other financial assets, likes stocks and savings, are kept separate.

"You get the picture? I mean, no one's supporting me."

Stephen earns $130,000 a year. The biggest annual salary Elizabeth made was $56,000. In spite of that, she feels that she's managed her money remarkably well because she's so frugal.

But keeping up with Stephen and planning for retirement is creating conflicts for them. When Stephen decided that they should buy a rental property, he wanted her to pay for half of the down payment. She couldn't afford that much, but was able to come up with 30 percent of the total. "He wants me to pay him the other 20 percent when we retire, because he wants all his money back," she says.

When he retires, Stephen wants all of their expenses split down the middle. "He said to me, 'well you have more money than I do' but I said, 'You *make* more and you *spend* more. I make less and I really hold onto it.'"

One way she does that is by buying most of her clothes second-hand, at thrift stores.

Their financial future together, she says, is a bit cloudy, especially when it comes to the retirement years. "I don't know how it's all going to pan out. I'm hoping he mellows out when we get there and he's not so strict. We'll see what happens."

Stephen's financial acumen has its plus side, like when he got them to buy a duplex together in Sausalito, California at an auspicious time: just before the big dot.com boom. He put together the partner agreement and had it reviewed by a lawyer. The purchase benefited both of them.

"If it weren't for Stephen, that never would have happened," says Elizabeth.

She insisted that because she and Stephen are not married, they do estate planning, so that if anything happens to either one of them, everything would go to the other person. She's afraid that his family members would say that *they* were entitled to the money because the she and Stephen weren't married.

"Of course, he was completely insulted that I would think that. But I've seen what happens when somebody dies and people act stupid and greedy, and I don't trust them. You can see I have a little issue with trust."

She points out that if anything happened to Stephen, she wouldn't get a penny of his social security, which is twice as much as hers.

Future retirement problems aside, Elizabeth is financially fine in the here and now, although there are things about Stephen that aggravate her. For instance, he does not pay for her health insurance. If the situation were reversed and she made more money than he did, she would pay for his. She was on his health insurance plan until her portion went up to $450 a month, which she couldn't afford (she was laid off several years ago). She had to turn to Obamacare.

"But I'm not suffering. I make it work. Right now I'm living off part of my savings, but I saved and I invested well in the stock market, so I'm doing ok."

Her money smarts began when she was young. As a professional dancer who belonged to a union, she was paid well. She socked it away and then invested it, unlike many of her fellow dancers. She knows this because she's reconnected with some of them through Facebook.

"Unless they've married well, none of them are doing well. When they were on the road, they did drugs, they bought new clothes. They spent all the money. They spent it like they were going to make it forever. And I knew this wasn't forever. And none of them went back to college. I went back to college twice. And I'm not saying I'm better than them. They're happy people. They're great people. But I'm glad I didn't take their route. One of the girls got divorced and all she can get is an admin job because she has no college degree. And she's got to support herself on that."

"I had to surrender to the universe, to God."

When she was laid off from her job in the fashion industry during the recession, Sheryl went through a really rough financial patch. "The economy tanked. I was working at an apparel company. They decided to move all of the production offshore. Everybody who worked in that area got laid off. I got a decent severance package and had some money saved. I was able to collect unemployment, so I was ok for awhile."

She did some commission sales work, trying to make enough money to pay her mortgage and hang onto her house, but it was a struggle. When she reached the point where she had only enough money to support herself for one more month, she got a phone call from a recruiter about a position for which she was well qualified.

"I didn't want to get my hopes up, but I had a feeling that this might be it. I had to sort of surrender. I didn't know where I was going or what I was doing, but I had to surrender to the universe, to God."

Unexpectedly, Sheryl begins to cry as she recalls this time in her life. "I didn't think I'd get so emotional about it. I ended up getting this job. I was able to save my house and get back on my feet, so I'm really, really grateful for that."

Her situation improved further when a settlement from a car accident allowed her to refinance her house and pay off the second mortgage and her credit cards.

"It was like, boom! Everything shifted. I still feel a little unsettled because I went through that experience. I've always had this insecurity in the back of my head: I'm going to lose my job. It's a bad message to send to myself, I guess."

Sheryl doesn't feel as if she has planned sufficiently for her retirement. "One thing about the clothing business, there are not a lot of benefits, so even though I've been working in it a long time, most companies don't have 401Ks or investments. I haven't been overly prudent with my money over the years. I really don't have a retirement set up, so that's something that does concern me. I do have my house. I'll hold onto that. Time will tell if that remains a good investment."

Leaving Las Vegas

Debbie has also experienced the financial disadvantage of being a single woman, of having to rely solely on oneself when the chips are down. For years, the free spirit moved to new cities whenever she got the urge and was always able to find gainful employment pretty quickly. Within a few weeks of settling in Las Vegas, though, she realized that she'd made a big mistake. She couldn't find a supervisory position in her usual employment, hotel housekeeping, because she didn't speak Spanish.

"Financial security is important for me," Debbie says. "If I'm under pressure, that's when I'm the most gung ho or will work the hardest or will do whatever I have to do. But I could not get into a hotel to save my life."

Instead, she got a job in a factory, working on an assembly line, making slot machines. After that, she worked at a convenience store.

"Whenever I'd go for a job interview, I'd think, you know, this isn't really the kind of thing I want to do but if they're going to hire me, I'm going to take it, because I have to pay the rent or I have to make sure I've got this or that. I kind of got stuck. I was in Vegas for four years and it seemed like ten years."

She also experienced some social isolation while she was there. She couldn't afford a cell phone and didn't have a computer that she could use to email friends. Because she worked long hours, it was hard for her to get to a library to use a computer there. She lost contact with a lot of friends and family members.

"I felt that I wasn't even in this country anymore. It was just my little world of Vegas. It was: go to work, go to the gym, go home. I had enough money to pay my bills – barely anything extra – and I thought, 'I'm never ever going to get out of here.' I didn't want to go back to Michigan, but if I went somewhere else, I didn't have a line on a job. My brother told me to come back to Michigan. He said I could stay with him for awhile, and I could get a job."

In order to raise enough money to rent a truck to take her belongings back to Michigan, she worked every single day and many double shifts for the next few months.

"I would say, 'I'll work some more! Just give me another coffee.' My main goal was to get out of Vegas and the only way to do that was to work. Unless I robbed a bank. In another couple of months, I packed up my shit and left. I don't regret leaving Vegas. It was absolutely the best thing for me to do, because I was slowly killing myself there. But I didn't want to come back to Michigan."

It felt, to Debbie, like going back in time…and going back to winter. And Michigan had no palm trees, no oceans and no mountains – things she loves. However, she was able to reconnect with old friends and reestablish her social network, and today she is still there, living happily and staying busy.

"I feel very fortunate."

Ellen had a long career and managed her money well, but two factors had an effect on her financial stability: she took time off from her job to care for her ailing parents, and she became disabled after a bad fall. She's ok, but has to be careful about her spending.

"My parents wanted to leave my sisters and I something, so I have a little income from that and also IRA's from when I worked, in addition to decent disability from working as much as I did. I am better off to stay on disability the rest of my life given my age and other things. Sometimes I feel bad about it, but it is one of those things that you put into the system your whole life for in case something like my situation happens. I don't take advantage of anything."

Ellen's volunteer activities at a local food bank put her in touch with people who are down on their luck, often through no fault of their own. "I just hug them because they are so embarrassed sometimes. I tell them it is not their fault."

The hardworking Ellen had always planned to be employed until she was about 75 and have several different careers, whether or not she was married. She moved to Arizona to help her ailing parents when she was 50, at the peak of her earning power, but has no regrets.

"I am very happy I could help them and spend time with them after having a decent career and life, especially given all they did for me. Obviously things have changed, but I feel *very* fortunate. My parents were strong through tough times and passed that on to me."

"I would like to find some guy who is at least stable."

Suzanne's generous, trusting nature has led to her being financially exploited by a number of her boyfriends. Ryan, for instance, lived for years in a home she owned and refused to help with the mortgage payments, claiming that he was saving the money for *their* future together. Suzanne thought that future was going to include marriage, but Ryan never did pop the question and Suzanne eventually ended the relationship.

Other boyfriends borrowed money that they never repaid.

Suzanne today is in a shaky financial position, due to a number of circumstances. The retired firefighter has had several real estate setbacks, and regrets her decision to purchase a new home in the same year she began studying law at an expensive private school years ago. Some of her misfortune is due to things over which she had no control.

Suzanne feels that she has to factor money into her search for a mate.

"If I married a guy who had money, then I wouldn't have to worry so much," she says. "I don't want to hook up with a guy who doesn't have anything, with both of us trying to live on my pension. That would just be really hard on any kind of relationship. So I would like to find some guy who is at least stable."

Dating and Relationships

Once, on a first date, I went to a movie with a man named Greg. We found our seats and then he asked, "Would you like something from the concession stand?"

"Sure," I said. "A small popcorn, no butter." I'm a cheap date.

He was back in a few minutes with an extra large tub of popcorn so heavily dosed with that delightful combination of partially hydrogenated soybean oil, beta carotene, buttery flavoring, TBHQ and polydimethylsiloxane that movie theatres call "butter" that it looked as if the kernels were *drowning* in the viscous yellow liquid.

Greg was genuinely surprised when I declined to eat any. I hate soggy popcorn. I also hate sharing popcorn. Having to reach over into someone else's container is inconvenient. I'm a grown-up. I want my own popcorn.

Although I rarely do, I can go for a few hours without eating food, so I was fine with not munching on popcorn as I watched the movie. Greg was not. He was actually *hurt* that I refused to eat the snack that he had gone to the trouble and expense of getting for us. From his wounded reaction, it was clear that he'd intended for us to *bond* over the sharing of the popcorn. He wanted the two of us to become one, with food as means of achieving that transmutation. I wasn't just rejecting his popcorn; I was rejecting *him*. It didn't even occur to him that he'd completely ignored my preferences, or that I would spurn his offering because I didn't want to eat popcorn covered with unhealthy chemicals.

As trivial as it sounds – and I admit that it sounds trivial – the episode was emblematic of something referred to by several of the women featured in this book: an unwillingness to be *absorbed* into a relationship. As Leanne put it: "What happens to *me*, that I brought to the party?"

It reminds me of a disturbing episode of *Star Trek: The Next Generation*, in which Captain Jean Luc Picard is almost absorbed by the Borg, a race of aliens who suck in the intellects of other beings, robbing them of their individuality. Their motto is: "Resistance is futile."

Is the institution of marriage like the Borg?

There are, of course, lots of healthy, balanced relationships out there. But when a relationship is unbalanced, it's usually the woman who is forced to forego parts of herself in order to make the union work. Some always single women have decided that that is too great a price to pay for having a significant other.

That's not the only reason why women don't marry. In my completely unscientific research for this book – which consisted of talking with unmarried women from across the U.S. – I identified several categories of old maids: those unwilling to surrender their independence; those who came close to getting married but didn't (often to their subsequent relief); those with lousy taste in men (who at least have the sense not to seal the deal by making it permanent); and those who have never been in serious relationships.

"I would just be the banker's wife"

Travel professional Stephanie is in the first category. She refuses to embrace the relationship model in which one person's life gets fully absorbed into someone else's.

"To me that's not healthy, because it's not respecting the self. The self is a single entity that confronts this world in very unique expressions and ways, and to honor the self you need to have that immediate contact and direct contact with your world, not filtered through another human being, no matter how much you love them. And it doesn't mean that you don't love them. I believe you can have great love and still maintain some semblance of your personal relationship to your world, and I think that's necessary."

Stephanie was headed toward being wedded when she was young and living in Miami. The potential groom was a banker from Panama – a great catch, according to her friends.

"I was too young," she says. "I was in my early 20s and I just said 'No,' because I wasn't ready to get married. I wanted my life. I knew that if I got married at that age, I would just be the banker's wife. And that's not what I wanted to be. I knew that my life was still unfolding and developing and I was happy with that. I didn't want to just become a banker's wife."

Later, when another serious relationship ended, Stephanie was emotionally stricken at first, but rebounded quickly.

"I was sad for a little while, but then I said, 'Wow, this is kind of a blessing because I can go to graduate school – which I was already in — and then I can go anywhere I want. I always sensed that it gave me a freedom to realize things on my own and have my own life and I feel very lucky for that. I like it."

Stephanie's notion of an ideal relationship is one where both participants are independent. "They have their lives but they also have their areas where they come together, of course, as a relationship."

When she was in her early 20s, free spirit Debbie had a serious boyfriend whom she expected to marry. After breaking up with him, though, she was surprised to find that her parents were relieved. "He was a jerk and I didn't see it. But they never pressured me, which I was glad for." Since then, Debbie has had a number of boyfriends, but hasn't been tempted to tie the knot with any of them.

"It's not as if I haven't had opportunities"

When she was in college, Colorado ski instructor Marcy was the homecoming queen who was dating the captain of the football team. Sounds perfect, doesn't it? After graduation, he decided to pop the question at a house he had purchased for them to live in – a house she'd never seen. Surprise! It didn't go well, and not just because she'd played no part in the decision to buy the bungalow he'd chosen. The trouble started when her boyfriend became a Los Angeles police officer.

"Once he became a cop, he became more distant and didn't even understand what was going on in my life," she says. "And he pulled up in front of a house he had just bought, and he proposed to me and I'm like, 'No thank you.' And turned tail and went the other way. So it's not as if I haven't had opportunities."

Southern Californian Sheryl was almost *absorbed* into an Old World marriage in which, as the female part of the equation, she'd be a second-class citizen. Still, things with George – an immigrant from Syria – were promising at the beginning.

"George always had this twinkle in his eye," she remembers. "He was cute, and had a great sense of humor. He made me laugh. I thought, 'This guy is ok.'"

Even a language barrier couldn't put a damper on their romance. "He didn't speak that much English. It was a combination of English, French and Arabic, but somehow I could always understand him. I don't know how, but I did."

George had his own business and prospered in the U.S. He was a generous man, taking Sheryl out to dine in fine restaurants and buying her expensive gifts. His free-spending ways extended to loans made to friends and to a gambling problem, which made Sheryl feel anxious.

"He loved to go to Vegas and he loved to play the ponies," she says. "And I thought this would be a conflict if we ever married and had children, because I know I wouldn't starve, but to me, it would be wasting money that you could have put toward education or something. He would drop thousands of dollars – 30, 40 thousand dollars - on gambling."

George wanted to marry Sheryl and have children with her, but his ultra-traditional ideas about the role of women caused bitter conflicts between them. Even though he was only her boyfriend – not her husband – he had *a lot* to say about what he considered to be acceptable behavior on her part.

"He felt like girls should live with their parents, like you shouldn't live in an apartment and go out with your friends."

And so, after dating George for four and a half years, Sheryl broke it off.

"I just wasn't ready to get married and he was really pestering me to get married. He really loved me. He probably still loves me to this day."

"I come home from work and you're just sitting there."

Sheryl followed that up with another near-miss, with a man named Randy. She was very much in love with and would have married him, but…

"He quit working. That was the problem. We were living together and he just quit working."

Randy worked for a company that did special effects in the movie industry. The business went under, leaving him unemployed – a condition he didn't do much to remedy. He paid his half of the rent from savings, but Sheryl paid for everything else, like groceries and restaurant meals. She began to resent having to support him. Even her mother noticed the change in Sheryl's personality. She told her daughter; 'I know you're a hard worker, but Randy – I feel like he's taking advantage of you. And you don't seem happy anymore.'"

Things came to a head when Randy got an opportunity to work on an Arnold Schwarzenegger film.

"He gets on the phone and he was so wishy washy about it. After he hung up he said to me; 'They told me it was between me and somebody else.' And I said, 'Call back and tell them you want the job. You didn't sound interested.' He said, 'I don't know, it's only going to be temporary – for six weeks.' I said, 'You're going to be on a major movie with Arnold Schwarzenegger! You'll make contacts. You're not working at all. What's wrong with six weeks? Go *do* something!'"

At this point, Sheryl's fashion career was flourishing. She was tired of coming home from work to a messy house (which *she* had to clean) and a boyfriend who was watching TV.

"I said, 'Randy, I want to do some things, like get a house. I want to have a plan. It's not even about the money. You're not doing anything. Do *something*. Work at McDonald's. Do volunteer work. I feel like you're a smart man and you're becoming bitter against the world because you're not doing anything. You're digging yourself a hole. I feel like I'm becoming this nagging bitch. I don't really care about the money. I feel like I'm moving forward and you're just standing still. You won't take action to save yourself. That's what bothers me. You could make no money and do volunteer work all day and that would be productive for society. That wouldn't really bother me. But when I come home, you're just sitting there. You don't even get up to say hello. If that was me, and the situation was reversed, I would at least get up and *look* a little productive.'"

That outburst surprised them both and marked a turning point in their relationship. Sheryl suggested that she move out, and Randy said, "Maybe you should."

"I just started to cry, and I said, 'Ok. That's it.'"

Later on, when they were in bed together, she asked Randy if he would care if she left. If it would matter to him.

"He said; 'Well of course I care.' But I felt like he was so unemotional at that point."

After that, Sheryl decided to take a break and not date *anyone* for a couple of years. "I'd never had a break in between men," she laughs. "I just went from one to the other. I was never single. It was like I was married for 20 years, just not to the same person."

"There'll be a guy who's willing to unzip his pants for you, if that's really what you want."

She's back at it now and has met a few possibilities while salsa dancing. One man is nice, but… "His kissing is really flat, unfortunately. But he's a great guy. I like him as a person."

She did feel chemistry with a younger guy who asked her out, but it turned out that all he wanted was a booty call. She wasn't interested in that. "I think that at any age, if a woman wants that, she can find it. There'll be a guy who's willing to unzip his pants for you, if that's really what you want. That, to me, has never been the difficult part."

Finding something deeper, something that has lasting value, is a little more challenging.

"I think it's harder for men as well. For humans, it's harder to be intimate with yourself and with others."

She's gone out with lots of different men of different ages and finds that there's freedom to being single if one is open to new experiences. She goes to "weird little clubs" to listen to live music with Eric, who's two decades younger than her. They're not romantically involved, but they have the same taste in music.

"Most of the people in those clubs are in their 20s, but I think the music is pretty cool. It doesn't bother me, to be in that environment. But maybe if I was married and had kids, I'd think: 'I can't hang out with my kids.'"

Why Sheryl hasn't had sex in years

Dating can be confusing in other ways. "Just like the whole gender thing now seems to be very fluid, it seems that dating people of all ages is very fluid, at least in Los Angeles," Sheryl says.

She hasn't had sex with anyone in years. Part of the reason for that is that she wants to make healthier choices than she did in the past. "I know people think, oh, she's gay, or she's a prude, or my libido is gone. It *has* shifted, with the hormonal changes that come with age. But I'm really trying to see it differently now. It's a deep energy change. I don't want to be overly casual about it, because I have been in the past. I know what that's like. I know what sex is. Been there, done that. I figured that out when I was in my 20s. I want to be cautious with that and I want it to have some meaning.

"I want to make choices that are healthier for me and if that means that I'm single for the rest of my life and I don't have another relationship, so be it. It's better to be healthy and to feel better about yourself, in my opinion, than to grab a man just to have a body next to you."

"I don't want to be the object of someone else's sexual needs."

One thing that's kept Lucy single is that she can't stand the thought of men dating women for sex. "That just turns my stomach," says the Denver stockbroker. "That's part of why I don't do the dating sites. It is so overwhelmed with guys just wanting to find sex. I'd rather not date and be single than be pursued just for that reason. And we're so lucky that we don't have that drive. Most women, at least in my experience, are not as driven by sex as men are.

"I had a guy tell me that guys get married to have sex. And that's true even today. I don't want to be the object of someone else's sexual needs."

Although Lucy has had serious relationships, she's never lived with a man – or with *anyone*. "That's even more rare, and it kind of scares guys when we're learning about each other: 'You've never lived with anyone? Not even a roommate?'"

"I consider divorce the ultimate failure"

Andrea feels relieved when she looks at some near misses that she's had.

"In later years when I re-encountered the men, my reaction was usually, 'What was I thinking? That was a close call!' And that's happened three or four times."

In her 45 years of dating, during which she's gone out with – by her estimate – three or four men a year, Andrea said she can count on one hand the number of men she would ever have seriously considered staying with.

"None of them, when I look back on them, would have been right for me long term. Two or three of them I'm still in contact with and we're friends, but we wouldn't have been right for each other long term."

Another reason she's avoided marriage: "I have this real fear of failure. I consider divorce the ultimate failure, and I never wanted to go through that."

"In my soul, I didn't feel that he was the one"

Poet/writer Michelle has been engaged several times, to some "wonderful guys," but has yet to meet a man who understands her unique point of view.

"I wasn't that girl who dreamed about being married or one of those girls who would force a guy into marrying me. I was the total opposite. The guys wanted to marry me and I just didn't feel like that was for me."

When she got pregnant, members of her church tried to help by encouraging her to get married.

"People knew that I grew up in the church and it was unheard of to have a child out of wedlock during those times. I got a lot of marriage proposals because some of my friends wanted to keep me honest and pure," she laughs. "I had male friends that really respected me as a young woman and didn't want me to bring my child into the world without being married. But it was a choice that I made."

Her boyfriend at the time was not in the running. "He was an educated guy, he was in the service and all that. But in my soul, I didn't feel that he was the one. From a very young age I had different views about marriage and I felt like I don't ever want to get married unless I knew: this is my absolute partner that I want to be with for the rest of my life. That has put me in a position where I'm just not finding one or a partner is not finding me."

While many women of a certain age who've never married acknowledge – or even embrace – the idea that they will likely never marry, Michelle is spiritually preparing herself for the possibility, and has even given some thought to the specifics of the wedding ceremony. For example, she believes that each partner should come up with their own vows and not use traditional ones. "That would be something that I would definitely use in my marriage, to say something that's from me, to my partner."

Michelle rejects artificially-imposed romantic constructs, like Valentine's Day and all the hoopla that goes with them.

"Most of the guys that I do date, they test me because they don't believe they found a woman who won't celebrate Valentine's Day. It's not because I've been hurt or anything like that. It's because I've made a conscious decision that that is something that I don't need.

"I don't celebrate Valentine's Day or things of that nature because I feel like all of those things are set up for people to fail in their relationships. If you think about it, women get upset because men forget Valentine's Day or anniversaries or all of those things. My point is that they should create days that they commemorate together and celebrate together, not something that's predetermined by society. You create your own special days. That, to me, makes a spiritual connection – something that you decided together and in your union."

Michelle is not, however, immune to romantic gestures, such as one that was made by a man she'd been dating for awhile. They were shopping in a mall one day when he made an excuse to get away for a short time. He returned with something he'd seen in a jewelry store window: a crystal charm bracelet with charms in the shape of butterflies. (Michelle loves both charm bracelets and butterflies.)

"He said the moment that he saw it he knew he had to get it for me. And it wasn't for any particular day. It was just because he wanted me to have it. He knew that I would love it and appreciate that. And that was at a point in my life where I knew that I made the right decision because I would rather a person love me and think of me in those ways and remember the things that I like and say, hey, I want to get this for her because she's a very special person to me."

The relationship ended, however, when her boyfriend had to relocate for work – and Michelle wasn't willing to follow.

Michelle is one of those women who defy the stereotype of spinsters as being lonely and unfulfilled. "I don't think that I feel lonely. I'm so involved with stuff I guess I kind of drown loneliness out, if that makes sense. I don't really get to the point where I'm like, 'Oh my God, I wish I had someone.' And not to speak ill of anyone that may feel loneliness, I would just say that I haven't sat down in a moment in time and just said, 'Oh, I'm lonely.'"

"I had no great desire to marry."

Retiree and expensive car lover Tish dated her boyfriend Bob all through high school and fully expected that when he returned from serving in the Air Force during the Vietnam War they'd get hitched and start a family. However, like a lot of other veterans, Bob came home a changed man.

"He comes back and things are not the same. So we broke up, sad to say, after about seven years of being together. After him I was somewhat saddened, but maybe I was smart. I thought, 'Let's go on here.' And I went on for many years to date people, for many relationships of two and three years. But as I got older and more educated and made more money, guess what? The desire to be married was not there.

"I was independent," says the saucy 70-year-old. "As much as I liked having many of these long relationships, I had no great desire to marry. I don't know why. That's just the way it is."

Tish will never live with a man without being married to him. She is still open to the idea of marriage, although she has caveats. She is currently in a cozy relationship with a "gentleman friend" she met online. He has a business and a home in Philadelphia and comes to visit her on weekends.

"We go out to dinner, or if it's snowing, we have pizza and we stay here and he has beer. He brings a bottle of Beefeater for me," she laughs.

Would she like to see him every day? That's a no.

"I like my independence. I've worked very hard. So I always say, 'I take in weekend guests.' Is this terrible, or what?" she laughs.

Tish says the weekend-only nature of the relationship works well for her. "It serves our purposes. He was married once and has no desire to remarry, and he and I just get along very well."

If her friend changed his mind about getting married, she might reconsider marriage, but as a Catholic, she is reluctant to wed a man who's divorced. "I'm sorry, even in today's world, I'm just…very Irish Catholic."

If that were not a hindrance, would she tie the knot?

"Yes, possibly I would. At this point I can't say that for sure."

However, even as a married woman spending time with her husband in Philadelphia, Tish would keep her own apartment in her own town, "for my privacy and my contacts with the area where I live. That'd be a must. And both of us have the money to do that. But yes, I would give it a lot of consideration."

"I always knew it wasn't the right person at the right time"

Ellen has had offers. "I would have gotten married if I'd met the right person at the right time" she says. "I had several proposals of marriage but I always knew it wasn't the right person at the right time."

The obligation she felt to care for her parents was also a consideration in any decision she made about her future. "One of my goals was to make sure that if I got married and if anything ever happened with the family, that I would able to support them."

"I have never been in love like that again."

As mentioned previously Elizabeth has been in a committed relationship with Stephen for a long time – 20-plus years. Stephen doesn't want to get married. Elizabeth doesn't want to marry Stephen, either, because she has never recovered from losing the man she considers the true love of her life (who is *not* Stephen).

Now in her early 60s, the Washington state resident was deeply involved with a co-worker in her 20s, when she was a professional dancer.

"I was on the road, and he was on the road. When I was gone for a little bit of the tour and I came back on it, in that brief period of time he was sleeping with one of the other dancers, who I had to end up working with – and working with him. I've never gotten over that," she says.

"I have never been in love like that again. I thought it would happen again, but it didn't. It was horrible. A lot of the reason I think I didn't get married was a lack of trust. And because the person I wanted to marry didn't want to marry me. In the end, he did this awful thing. And I ended up being with somebody who didn't want to be married."

There are benefits to such an arrangement, but she's also experienced some of the drawbacks of marriage – or the negatives that make some women avoid marriage, as discussed in the chapter on finances.

When she meets new people and tells them that she and Stephen are not married despite being together for more than two decades, they are sometimes confused.

"This is what they almost always say: 'Well, that's just like being married.' I think what they're trying to say is; 'Good for you, that's a good long relationship.' It's also an awkward situation and they're trying to make it less awkward by saying that."

She and Stephen began their relationship as a business deal, intending to buy a duplex together and live separately, each in one half of the duplex. She couldn't afford the mortgage payments on her own, so it was a very practical arrangement. However, romance quickly entered the picture and they ended up living together.

After all these years, does Elizabeth have any regrets about never taking that walk down the aisle?

"No. The wedding part I don't regret. If we were ever to get married, yes, I would have a party. But that comes from me not wanting to spend that kind of money. I just think that's a waste of money. If it were me, I'd just go to City Hall and get the certificate and take that money and put it on a house as a down payment. I'm too practical. I don't have those kind of fantasies in my head. To me, what's more important is that I miss having that passionate love affair that will never happen again. You know, the kind that really only happens when you're young."

She doesn't feel like she's having that with Stephen?

"No, it's more, I mean, we love each other, but...we go through our day, trying to have fun, do fun things, but...I don't feel like it's the passionate affair."

If she pressured Stephen, she says, he'd probably agree to tie the knot for financial reasons, like to save on taxes. "I think he even said that to me once and I told him, 'I'm not getting married for that reason. I'm not.' I just won't. I'm a product of the 50s, you know?"

Passion and marriage should go together and besides, Elizabeth feels that by now there's too much water under the bridge.

Are there times when she wishes she was unattached? Footloose and fancy free?

Elizabeth laughs. "Oh, God, all the time! You know, I'm 61 now, and there are people from the past I like to reconnect with. I love Facebook for that, for finding old friends. It's been fantastic. I would like to be able to just get up and go see people from my past."

Additionally, Elizabeth longs for a simpler life. Stephen enjoys having a lot of belongings – a lifestyle choice that Elizabeth finds aggravating.

"The other part about being single is that my life would be less complicated. It just feels complicated right now in the respect that, there's all this *stuff* – and a lot of it is Stephen's stuff."

As discussed in the chapter on finances, Stephen insisted they buy a second home for them to own as a rental property..

"Having two houses – I would never do that," she says. "Stephen is very ambitious. I would make things way simpler. And then he wants me to keep up with that and understand things and be a part of that. It's way over my head."

She admits that she does benefit a lot by being with him, but would prefer to live a less complicated life.

"There's all this shit in the garage, and most of it's his. There's so much stuff in there I'm sure he's forgotten what's in there. And that's how I feel like life is. There's just so much stuff, and I want to know where everything is, what I have."

If she were single, she'd feel as if she had more control over her life. However, after being part of a pair for so long, she can't even imagine going solo.

"There are many times I've thought about wanting to leave and be on my own, but I don't even know the first thing about how to do that. We're so entwined now. It would take so much to disengage.

"The thing about Stephen, and why it's lasted so long, is that he hangs in there. I am not an easy person, nor is he. But you just… you have to realize there are good parts about this person. Are they perfect? No. Is this the great passion of your life you would wish it would be? No. But he makes a good life. He's really, really smart. He's very talented. He's very – which is kind of a pain in the ass – he's very meticulous about work on the house, so he insists on doing it all himself, and he does beautiful work. I'm very fortunate about a lot about him."

If she did strike out on her own, does she think she'd be lonely?

"I don't know. I'd have to be alone for awhile and see. It might be fantastic," she laughs. "The thing is, if I ever left, the dog is always considered *my* dog, so in that respect, I'd never feel like I'm alone because I'd have a dog with me."

"Why in the world would I want to pick one?"

Eleanore likes having a boyfriend, and has had a lot of them. When she talks about the joys of being single, it's not because she doesn't relish being in a relationship. She does. She also thinks that when a relationship has run its course, "it's time to go."

The marketing professional rejects the entire premise of marriage – something she's struggled to explain to the men who've tried to get her to join them in connubial bliss.

"The idea of marriage, the way it is done in the world, is insane," she says. "Who sat down and said, 'Now here's what you're going to do. There are a gazillion people in the world. You're going to find somebody and you're going to spend the rest of your life with that one person.' I would expect everybody to burst out laughing and say, 'That's ridiculous.' But for millennia, and all around the world and in every culture, that's what people do. Or are expected to do. I can't even imagine why I would want to do that. There are so many people out there who are interesting and amazing and fun. Why in the world would I want to pick *one* and spend the rest of my life with him?"

She realizes that her point of view puts her in the minority. "I don't know why that seems ridiculous to me when it doesn't seem ridiculous to most people."

She hasn't always had an easy time explaining this to her boyfriends. "It's awkward, because most of them I really loved. I would find myself in love with these guys, but I would try to picture us 15 years down the road, and I just could not get a clear vision of what that would be like. I'm not saying that necessarily had anything to do with them. It's clearly – or mostly – me. It could have had *something* to do with them."

The gist of it is that Eleanore has never met anybody that she wanted to be with for the rest of her life.

"You do become a little bit invisible as you get older."

The adventure of moving to Australia at the age of 60 was just what the thrill-seeker needed, although thinking about what her social life would be like there did cause her to contemplate how people's perceptions of women change as women grow older. *She* doesn't feel as if her best years are behind her, but she knows that some people do.

"I know that as a function of being both single and old, that's a whole other thing. I know that in the work world, I'm not as attractive. You do become a little bit invisible as you get older, particularly if you're a woman and you're single. I was starting to feel a little of that."

While her married friends also feel some anxiety about aging, Eleanore thinks her single status exacerbates hers.

"There're a lot of people my age who spend way too much time talking about what they used to do. How they used to be. I didn't ever want that to be me. I don't want to talk about, 'Oh my God, when I was 28, we used to hang out and party all the time.' A lot of older people do that."

Thus, the move to Australia could not have come at a better time in her life. "I feel like I'm doing Eleanore 2.0. It's all unknown, but it's exciting. It's an adventure, and it's really appropriate for this age, because I think a lot of people become less adventurous as they get older."

Still, given that she was a self-described "dating machine" for her entire adult life, she was surprised to find that her social life kind of "dried up" when she turned 55. She didn't have ready access to the array of candidates she was used to having. Online dating is an option for remedying that, even though she hates the idea. Eleanore is hoping Australia will offer a whole new dating pool from which to choose.

When she does go out somewhere by herself now, she believes it's much more important to get "glam" than it was when she was younger and could attract men wearing jeans and a t-shirt.

"I think I have to try a little bit harder now. I think because you're older you have to demonstrate that you've still got it. Nobody wants an old lady, unfortunately."

"He wouldn't even mention the 'm' word."

Marcy was in a relationship with a man off and on for 18 years. Despite the fact that they had little in common in terms of things they enjoyed doing, Marcy was, early on, eager to marry him.

"But he wouldn't even mention the 'm' word," says the Colorado ski instructor. "He never wanted to get married and I did at that point, 18 years ago."

When she realized that their relationship had stagnated, she broke it off with him.

"Now, I'm at the point where I want to grow old with somebody, but I don't necessarily want to be married," Marcy says.

She found another man that she spends a lot of time with, although there are no romantic sparks there – at least not on her part. He loves joining her in the outdoor activities she's passionate about – like skiing and playing golf – so in that sense, they're well-matched.

One night, as they were watching fireworks together, he asked where their relationship was going.

"I looked at him and said, 'We've already had this conversation. We are friends and if you want more than that then I can't have you as my friend because I'm not ready for a romantic relationship right now at all. I'm trying to dissolve one and just be me.'

"I'm happy with me and whenever I'm happy with me then men start coming around and I don't need them in my life. I love teaching skiing and being outdoors and doing stuff at the drop of a hat. And then when males pursue you, you don't necessarily need them but it's fun to be doing things with them. And of course the more standoffish you tend to be, and not falling all over them, the more they tend to come around."

"They want the younger women."

Lavender Moon has never had a relationship serious enough to lead to marriage – something she chalks up to low self-esteem. "I didn't think that I was capable or maybe even deserving of the type of man that I wanted. And then when I had my first two children, I was always thinking, 'Well you'll never get a husband or a man because you've already got a ready-made family.'"

She's a realist when it comes to choosing a partner, and has a list of characteristics that would rule out candidates. Of special interest to her: a healthy lifestyle – because she practices one herself.

"I don't want to be with anybody who eats pork or red meat because I don't, and I'm not cooking with two sets of dishes. I don't want to smell pork cooked in my house. And you have to be a healthy person, or at least be on the healthy bandwagon.

"I don't want to hook up with somebody who is not taking care of themselves, and I don't want to hook up with somebody who is smoking. I have never smoked. I don't like cigarette smoke. You can't smoke in my house or my car."

She finds it harder to meet men as she gets older, and believes that dating has really changed – and not for the better.

"Most men, they don't know how to treat a lady. And nowadays, I guess, especially when you reach a certain age, a lot of men are really not interested in a woman in her late 30s, early 40s. They want the younger women. So I don't really date."

She *would* like to get married and has given considerable thought to what her dream wedding would be like.

"I want to get married by the water," she muses. "I'm not the kind for realistic goals. I've always been a dreamer and always had big goals. I want a traditional African wedding with the jumping of the broom. At the reception I want to wear a yellow or maybe lavender wedding gown and some fairy wings that match the dress. The reception would be held in a flower garden. I'm a nature lover and I adore fairies. In one of my many lifetimes maybe I was one." She laughs. "No, I'm not crazy. I've just got a lot of imagination."

Fairy wings and flower gardens aside, being single is *not* making her miserable and lonely. "I'm just a happy person. I mean, I have my issues, but still, I still manage to come out with a smile and just be happy. That is my ultimate goal, to be at peace and be happy."

"It was always more trouble than it was worth."

Kay is in the 'I'm-glad-I-didn't-get-married-at-least-not-to-the-men-I've-dated camp.

"Guys I've had relationships with, I've always looked back and thought, 'Yeah, that wouldn't have worked in the long run. It's good that we broke up.' So I've found that each time I broke up with someone, I'd think; 'That was more pain, more trouble and aggravation than it was worth. Let's just put that aside and focus on my work, my life and taking care of me.'

"And then eventually, someone looks interesting again, or you get lonely and think, 'Oh, it would be nice,' but each time it's always more trouble than it's worth. So it just becomes; 'Get everything you need from your dog. Love and affection and snuggling.'" She laughs. "He listens. He doesn't complain. He's happy to see you. What more do you need?"

Kay is convinced that she hasn't chosen the right men.

"Men that I felt sexually attracted to weren't necessarily emotionally or intellectually good for me. I would find that out later. I was very picky because there weren't many men who I felt attracted to and when the rare man came along, I thought; 'this doesn't happen very often so this must be something to pay attention to.'"

Invariably, though, that man would turn out to be *not* a good fit for her. After awhile, she concluded that she was not good at choosing men for her, so she should just not do it. However, she's learned over time that telling herself that she's not good at picking the right guys is a negative thought process. A self-fulfilling prophesy, so to speak.

She is still friends with a man that she dated but who ultimately broke up with her. They had a great deal in common – both were animal rights activists, for instance – but that, it turned out, did not necessarily make them romantically suited to each other.

"We were more like brother and sister. We loved each other because of our deep commitment to the vegan movement but it was not romantic love in the full sense. But it was a learning process."

That man has since been married and divorced twice, so it's possible that he has trouble finding the right romantic partner as well.

Are there lifestyle issues that are dealbreakers for her? For instance, would the committed vegan date a carnivore?

"I would date someone who's vegan-friendly, who still eats meat. I've gone out with guys who do. Usually when they're around me and they hear about it and go to a vegan restaurant, they start to get inspired and want to try it. They don't go a hundred percent as fast as I'd like, but I'm open to someone who's eager to learn about it."

She wouldn't be with someone who smokes, or drinks to excess. She is a non-drinker and would prefer someone who doesn't drink at all.

"It would have to be someone who takes as good care of themselves as I take of me. That's a lifestyle match."

For right now, though, Kay is just practicing dating again. After a long time on the sidelines, she is re-learning what it's like to go out on dates, and figuring out how she wants to be treated by a man – and how she should treat him.

Learning how to bring out her feminine side

It's a process that includes finding the feminine within.

"When you're an independent woman you're very masculine, because you have to have that masculine energy to run your own business," Kay says. "And that's been a very difficult thing for me now: to learn to find my own feminine, and let the man be the masculine. And of course, not to change myself so much that I'm no longer me, but to realize I do have a feminine side and learn how to bring it out."

She found that difficult at first, because it was not part of her daily routine. The attitude she needed to survive and succeed in business was, as she puts it; "Being strong and tough and to heck with you if you don't like what I say or do. Becoming more malleable, more accepting and having a give and take kind of feeling with a guy was very difficult."

What she refuses to do is suppress her fun, outgoing, aggressive personality.

"But I'm realizing that I need to also make sure to allow the man to feel like a man, and that he sees my attractive feminine side. When you push that down for so many years, it takes a while to dig it back up and develop it. Dancing and yoga has helped a lot; it's made me feel better about my body, made me aware of my body. It just helps to get your mojo going again."

In her early 60s, Kay is undaunted about the potential difficulty of finding a partner at her age, mainly because she's fit and healthy and doesn't feel her age at all.

"I'm physically and anatomically so youthful that I feel I've got plenty of time to make new choices and go in different directions and start anew. I'm starting new careers now. I'm beginning to date, and I don't at all feel like I'm doing this at a late age in life. Because I just don't think of myself at that age. I truly am not. And if anyone else thinks differently, I don't care. I know how I feel and I'm going to outlive them."

She can, she says, run circles around those doubters, and do more pushups and more hours of yoga then they can.

"I had a date with someone yesterday who's 45 years old and it did not feel awkward at all. The fifteen year difference did not feel awkward. I'm in far better shape than him!"

She's tried online dating but was put off by the amount of time and effort it took, and by how judgmental the whole process felt.

"It felt weird. In a way, it's good because you're getting to know a person more than just based on their looks, but on the other hand, you don't have that in-person vibe to know from the get go if there is a vibe. So I decided it probably would be better for me to meet people either through the things I like – yoga, or dancing, or voiceover work – or through activism. Then you have that in person connection. Or you don't."

"I'm rusty at the whole process of communicating with a guy."

She's not meeting many men that way, but that's ok because she feels as if she's out of practice and needs time to figure things out. When she does go on a date, she's looking at it as a sort of exercise.

"It's me, taking a look at 'What did I do well, and what did I do not so well?' in that date? It's making me more careful about how I speak with him. And also I'm noticing what I do and don't like about men.

What I will accept. I know I'm not going to like 100 percent of him, or I'm never going to find a man to be with. What is a make or break habit or characteristic where I draw the line? So it's kind of feeling my way through that."

She admits that she's rusty at the whole process of communicating with a man and with flirting. "When is it comfortable for him to put his arm around me? When is it comfortable to kiss? What does that kiss feel like? Is there chemistry, and if there isn't, can there be chemistry the second time? Or is it there the first time or not? All those questions have come up. And probably some of these guys don't like that I'm really slow."

She is ok with that, though.

"I'm learning to have fun at this point in my life. Finally."

"You still have your space so you don't smother each other."

When she first tried internet dating, Kay felt as if she made a lot of mistakes with the men she went out with. She now prefers to date men who *aren't* a perfect match for her, so that she can make mistakes and get better at dating. That way, when men who are more in line with her values and her lifestyle come along, she'll be better able to put her best foot forward.

"I don't feel like I'm wasting their time," she says of her recent dates. "They probably need practice, too. And we're having a nice time. We're going hiking. We're going out to dinner. Nobody loses."

Having never lived with a man, she worries about the possibility of some day sharing a home with someone who may have a very different style and a different level of neatness.

"All of a sudden, you're in each others' space when you've always had your own space. You put things where you put them. And they're around all the time. So it is important to have your own things you go and do, or you go away with girlfriends, or you go off on your own for a few days. You have your own activities."

It's vital, she says, for a woman to have a room of her own. "You still have your space so you don't smother each other."

She does find it hard to imagine living with a man. "I just have to put it out of my mind because there's no sense spending energy or worry about it. If I come to that bridge, I'll just have to cross it then."

"Well, I like to wear pants"

Jo-Sue has never had a serious relationship. As noted earlier, she attributes that in part to her selection criteria, and in part to the fact that she lives and works in a small town where the pickings are slim.

"Probably the biggest thing, because of my faith and the things that I do, he would have to be a Christian, a solid Christian. And there just aren't many Christians who are truly committed in this area who are not already taken. Most men spend their time in the bars, and that's not who I am. And so I think maybe it's because I'm picky that there aren't many prospects."

Jo-Sue is also looking for a man who is as tall as she is – six feet. "So that's another little bit of an obstacle. There're not a lot of over six foot men that you meet here. I'm into sports, so it'd be nice if we had something in common along those lines. Those are the kinds of things I was looking for."

She tried online dating and in her late 20s met a man with whom she seemed to have a lot in common.

"I thought, 'Ok, I want to see if this is going to go anywhere. Let's meet.' But I didn't want to bring him here, so I went down to where he lived, in another state. I took a friend with me, because I wasn't going alone. We met, and I went to his church and found out that his church didn't believe in women wearing shorts. They had to wear dresses all the time and they had to have long hair and no makeup. And I thought: *this is good to know*. I'm a sports freak. So when I got back home, he asked me how that went, what we thought of his church. I said, 'Well, I like to wear pants.' I never heard from him again."

That was the only time she actually went so far as to meet somebody from an online dating site. "After that, it was a hit or miss kind of thing, and it just wasn't working out. So I haven't done that in a long time. I thought, 'You know what? If it happens, it happens, and if not, I'm good.'"

Jo-Sue has a close and loving family, a deep faith, a job she loves and, as a youth minister, a mission that she finds deeply satisfying. In other words, she has a pretty nice life. What, at this point, would tempt her to tie the knot?

"I'd have to be really in love to get married," she says. "I'd have to be head over heels in love with someone. The hesitation is that I've had people interested in me in the past and I've questioned myself, whether I've pushed them away because I wasn't really interested in them, or if I wasn't really interested in marriage. If I liked my freedom.

Sometimes I'm double-minded. I think; 'Yes, I really want to get married' and other times it's, 'I'm glad I'm not married.'

"I also think, too, that once you reach a certain age, you're so independent. Marriage is work, I guess, but how much change would I have to go through? Maybe I'm to the point where I'm too independent now to even make it work."

A series of train wrecks

Suzanne, the eternal optimist, has had many serious boyfriends and was *certain* that she'd be a wife and mother – two things she felt should go together. The retired firefighter desperately wanted children but wanted them in the context of marriage. Unfortunately, she found herself investing years in one relationship after another without achieving the results she desired. The ticking on her biological clock grew louder and then, finally, stopped. She is the favorite aunt of her many nieces and nephews and spoils them rotten, but she regrets not being able to lavish her attention on children of her own.

So what went wrong? Suzanne is a bright, attractive woman with an effervescent personality and a confident manner, but her romantic relationships can rightly be described as a series of train wrecks. Unlike some of the other women profiled in this book, Suzanne was not ambivalent about being married. She wanted it. Why didn't she get it?

The longest relationship she had was with Phil, who shared her love of sports and other activities but was emotionally manipulative. That characteristic, it turns out, was apparent from the start, but she ignored it. Suzanne's need to see the best in people causes her to overlook the worst, even when the red flags are wildly flapping.

"I always thought I'd marry Phil, but cheating was a big issue with him, so it just ended up fizzling out after I walked in on it."

Did she know Phil was a cheater when she first got together with him? "No, I didn't," she says, then corrects herself: "Well, yeah, I *did* kind of know it. Phil had asked me out on a date. He came over to my house to pick me up and he said, 'I have something to tell you. I slept with Sarah, my ex-girlfriend, last night. I have to make a choice now, between you two.' And I said, 'It seems to me you already made your choice. Bye-bye.' And I kicked him out."

However, six months later, Phil ended it with Sarah. He asked Suzanne out and she said yes. They started dating. When Sarah found out that Suzanne and Phil were dating, she came on to Phil again.

"Phil said, 'Well you made her interested in me.'"

Wait. Phil blamed *Suzanne*??

"I think Phil really loved Sarah. He thought she was beautiful. I think he really wanted Sarah but Sarah didn't want him, but because *I* found him attractive, she decided to take him back."

And he had no will of his own?

"No. He was an idiot!"

Suzanne did eventually break up with Phil – sort of – and began seeing a wonderful man named Karl, but Phil's machinations put an end to what could have been the true, deep relationship she was looking for.

"What happened to Karl was Phil," she admits. "At the time, I thought I was still in love with Phil. Phil kept calling me and interfering with my relationship with Karl. So it kind of fell apart – because of Phil."

"I think you've got to make them work for it."

A five-year-long relationship with Adam, a doctor, was promising at first. Suzanne is all about activity – no couch potato men for her – and in Adam she found a companion who wanted to do the things she liked doing, like going camping and traveling to Toronto for a romantic weekend that included seeing "Phantom of the Opera."

They actually did get engaged, but the "really sad proposal" that brought it about should have been a warning about what was to follow. Adam asked her to marry him while they were en route to the airport. He was about to leave for Africa to work for an NGO, so his absence from her would be an extended one.

"I was driving him to the airport and he kind of said, 'Will ya?' And I said, 'Ok,' and I took the ring. I should have never taken it, is the way I look at it, because I didn't make him work for it. You know? I think you've got to make them work for it."

He was gone for a month and a half and never contacted her once. "He said emailing from there was too difficult. So I'm waiting six weeks for a guy I just got engaged to, and…nothing," she says.

When he did return, things were not the same between them. A point of contention was the fact that he'd brought back gifts for others in his life, but not for his fiancé.

"He was showing me, 'Look at this stone chessboard I got for my brother.' He showed me all these things he bought for other people, for himself. And I waited. I was kind of getting perturbed because there was nothing for me. Nothing. And I finally said, 'Is that all of it? Did you get anything for me?' And he got really upset: 'You can have anything you want!' But he didn't have anything for *me*. So it made me feel like he didn't think about me the whole time he was gone."

A breakup was inevitable, but surprisingly, Suzanne wasn't the one who initiated it. Adam was the one who ended the relationship, and it had nothing to do with her being upset about his failure to bring her a gift from Malawi.

"Part of the reason we broke up was that he made what I call, 'man rules.' Most of my boyfriends did. They made these stupid man rules. One of Adam's man rules was that we didn't take separate vacations, and I agreed to that. I said, 'I'm fine with that. I'm not going to go to Paris or Cancun without you.'"

When Adam went to Florida to do an internship, however, Suzanne decided to visit a girlfriend of hers who lived in a different part of Florida. Furious, he reminded her of the no-separate-vacations rule.

"I said, 'Well, I'm going. You didn't have to do the internship in Florida. You could have stayed here.' He said, 'That was in internship.' I said, 'I don't care. You didn't have to go.'"

The episode cast a chill on the relationship from which it never recovered. Adam asked Suzanne to return the engagement ring, but she'd loaned him so much money by then that she told him he needed to pay her what he owed her first. He never did, and she still has the ring.

"I never realized that he lived with me"

Adam wasn't the only man in Suzanne's life to lay down "man rules." Ryan – who moved in with Suzanne surreptitiously (I'll explain in a minute) had a rule about not paying her any rent, so that he could put money aside for their future. It was a future that never came.

When Ryan came to work at the firehouse in which Suzanne worked, he asked her out a number of times before she said yes. They began dating exclusively pretty quickly, and Ryan soon did something which Suzanne thought was "cute" – mainly because she was young and naïve.

"He'd say, 'Suzanne, can I spend the night?' And I'd say 'Yeah, I hope you do.' Well he'd ask me every night."

They frequently ate dinner at his parents' house. One night, about three months into the relationship, his mother said, 'Suzanne, Ryan has three boxes of his stuff here. Can I send it over?' And I thought; oh, he *does* live with me! I never realized that he lived with me."

He'd been moving his things in all along, filling up drawers and closets without her being aware of it. "He just kind of did it on the sly," she says. In spite of the subterfuge, Suzanne accepted the boxes from his mother, because she liked Ryan so much. However, she did ask that he pay rent. Although he was working full-time, he refused.

"He was very selfish. He was working two jobs, making firefighter wages plus he did cement work, so he was making a lot of money. I said, 'You need to pay me rent if you're going to live here.' And he said, 'Well I'm doing this for the both of us. Holding onto it for now.' He was holding onto it all right."

Ryan *did* spend money on building a garage on her property – something she didn't want. He then filled it with his possessions. The garage, it turned out, was all for him. In addition to free rent, he also had someone to cook for him and do his laundry, courtesy of the possibly too accommodating Suzanne.

Finally, though, she issued an ultimatum.

"I said, 'I don't want to live with somebody without knowing that I'm going to get married, so Ryan you're going to have to move out. Or at least get engaged to me. I can wait to get married – I'm young. But I need to know that you *want* to get married.' And he said, 'I'm never going to be told what to do.'"

This conversation took place in May. Suzanne relented and gave Ryan until Christmas to put a ring on her finger or move out of her house. Christmas came and went and there was no ring. In fact, there was no gift from Ryan at all – something which became clear as the holiday festivities at his parents' house drew to a close.

As her present to him, Suzanne had had Ryan's grandfather's ring repaired so that he could wear it, because she knew how much it meant to him. "When I told Ryan's mother about the gift, her face went white. She said, 'Suzanne, *I* have his grandfather's ring.' I said, 'Well then what ring did I have repaired?' No one in his family knew."

It turned out to be a ring given to Ryan by his ex-girlfriend. He didn't think Suzanne would be happy about him keeping it, so he'd made up an elaborate story about it being his grandfather's ring.

Suzanne was furious. "Why would I be upset about something from the past?" she told him. "Lying is another story, though. And I spent money on your ex-girlfriend's ring, you asshole!"

Suzanne gave him *another* six months to move out. He was still around when she threw a party in the summer at which he flirted with one of her friends, Chris. Chris went to Suzanne and asked if it would be all right if she dated Ryan. She was worried about stepping on her friend's toes.

"I said, 'I'm never going to get back together with him but there are problems there. I don't want you to get hurt. Think about it. I don't see him being the guy for you.' I was worried about her. I thought he might be dating her to get back at me. I warned her: 'Chris, he might be using you. Don't do this. I want you to be happy. Remember: Ryan and I had problems, and you're probably going to have the same problems with him.'"

Chris did go out with Ryan, for about three months - then he dumped her. She and Suzanne have rarely spoken since. Suzanne thinks their estrangement is because Chris feels embarrassed about the whole episode.

All was well for the first three months...

I've mentioned that Suzanne really, *really* wanted to have children of her own. With time running out to do that, she pinned her hopes on Barry, a man she dated for about six years. They met at a party and she found him to be witty and intelligent – a great conversationalist. She did not consider him especially good-looking, but smarts go a long way with Suzanne. Despite the fact that he was nine years younger than her, they quickly fell into a fairly serious relationship that included social drinking. All was well for the first three months, and then...

"I couldn't figure out what changed but I knew the day it changed. I could tell. Barry must have decided he didn't really want this relationship. He wasn't sure about it. That was also the day he started drinking hard liquor around me, and that changed his personality. And once he started doing that, nothing was ever right."

Was it possible that Barry had been curbing his drinking because it was a new relationship?

"Yes. I do believe he did that. Then he couldn't suppress it anymore. He's such a raging alcoholic now that one Fourth of July, I had a bunch of friends over and he was visibly drunk. I didn't realize it until he took some people out on his pontoon boat and one friend refused to go because he was so drunk."

"She became better over time, in his memory"

His drinking habits weren't the only thing that changed. He became distant and withdrawn. Phone calls were shorter and less frequent. Nonetheless, Suzanne continued seeing him in the hopes that things would improve. About a year later, Barry told her he didn't think he could ever marry her, because he was still in love with his ex-wife. "They'd been divorced for ten years at that time, and she'd cheated on him," Suzanne said. "She was one of those things where, she wasn't great to begin with but she became better over time, in his memory."

Suzanne and Barry broke up – for the first time. On her birthday, though, he called to wish her a happy birthday and to tell her that he missed her. They resumed dating. Things took a turn when Suzanne had some unexpected financial setbacks and lost her house due to foreclosure. She moved in with Barry.

"He says he never invited me, but he did. I would have never moved in otherwise. He likes to change history. He's done that a lot, actually."

They were comfortable together. "I liked living with him. I spoiled him. Made him breakfast in bed. Made him his favorite meals. I did all his laundry and cleaned his house. I'd drive him to the airport for business trips and pick him up from the airport when he came home. I did the shopping. I did *a lot*."

"You're going to let me out of here now or I'm going to beat the living shit out of you."

Barry's alcoholism worsened, as did its affect on their relationship. He became prone to angry, middle-of-the night rants about things like cluttered kitchen counters or unfolded laundry.

"He started waking me up at 4:00 in the morning. My answer when he'd do that would be, 'Fuck you,' just because it was happening so often. So one day, the heat goes out in the furnace. He comes up to the bedroom and says, 'Come on.' So I followed him, and he kind of grabs me by the back of the head and guides me. He's not really hurting me, but he has his hand on the back of my neck, and he's sort of *guiding* me down the stairs. I get into the furnace room and I say; 'What?' He still has his hands on me and he says; 'Fix it!' Now I'm starting to wake up, and I say; 'Fix what, Barry?'"

He claimed that she'd done something to the furnace and demanded that she fix it.

Still half asleep, and in disbelief, she asked if he was kidding.

"He says, 'You sabotaged it. You fix it NOW!' I mean, he's screaming at me."

Suzanne told him she'd done nothing to the furnace and advised him to call a repair man. She said she was going back to bed.

"He put his hands on both sides of the doorway and said; 'You're not leaving until you fix it.' And I said; 'Barry, you're going to let me out of here now or I'm going to beat the living shit out of you.'"

She knocked his arm out of the way.

"You are not going to block me in a room, make me a prisoner. I don't feel like I did anything wrong. I'm very claustrophobic and he was holding me in a small room. And I went out. He was screaming at me. I went back to bed, pulled the covers over my head. He didn't come after me after that."

Why didn't Suzanne move out after that incident? She's not sure. "Maybe I was just hoping it would work out. Maybe I felt like Barry was my last chance for kids."

However, Barry was very ambivalent about having children.

"He'd go back and forth. He'd say something like, 'I would be a good dad.' And then later he'd say, 'I'm never going to have kids.'"

She wasn't even sure that she wanted them with Barry, but she was getting older and her options were dwindling. Her biological clock was ticking loudly and she wasn't meeting anybody else.

"He actually, I think, wanted to pull the trigger"

Another one of those drunken, middle-of-the-night wakeups happened a few months later – one that was much worse.

"It's 4:00 in the morning again. I'm sleeping and he comes in, screaming at me. My answer was, 'Fuck you.' But this time he decided to pull the gun out of the drawer and aim it at me."

Strangely, she didn't feel afraid at that moment because she didn't think Barry would actually pull the trigger. The source of his anger this time: he was upset about clutter on the kitchen counter, which turned out to be his laundry. Suzanne had folded it and left it on the counter, hoping he would put his own clothing away. For once.

"What scared me later was he said he felt like he was going to do it. He actually, I think, wanted to pull the trigger, which I never expected. I said; 'Barry, you really have a problem if you felt that way.'"

He expressed no remorse the next day. Suzanne considered calling the police and reporting the incident, but worried that if Barry got a criminal conviction, it would ruin his life because his company requires him to have a security clearance. Thus, she didn't pursue a legal consequence for his actions. She also didn't break up with Barry. She took the gun and hid it and continued to live with him. The following few months were relatively uneventful, almost peaceful. Barry even allowed her elderly father to move in with them while his own home was being remodeled – and he helped take care of him.

She did, eventually, find another place to live. After she moved out of Barry's house, he continued to call her.

"He was always kind of a loner, but I think he felt really alone after I moved out. Then he was stuck there with just dogs. Nobody was cleaning his house. Nobody was doing things for him, bringing him breakfast in bed. It just kind of fizzled out. We still talk, but there's never going to be a relationship there again. It's more of a friendship."

Looking back on the various men in her past, is there a takeaway that might explain why she is not married?

"I don't think I wanted to marry any of the guys that I broke up with, except for the good ones – the kind of really nice guys that would do things with you. The kind I've always been looking for. And I've had 'em. I don't know why I let them go. Different reasons."

An online love affair that turned out to be...

She's tried finding men online, but has discovered that they tend to ignore the important details in her profile. For instance, she's been contacted by lots of homebodies, despite the fact that she emphasizes – in her online description – her love of travel.

She also attracted a man who turned out to be scammer. Her friends warned her that there were too many inconsistencies in his various stories, but Suzanne texted him for quite awhile because it gave her something she needed at the time – romance, or at least, the *promise* of romance. He said he was in the military, in Special Forces, and he sent her lots of pictures of a handsome man in uniform. However, he used words like "mate" (when referring to a friend) and also asked her for money, explaining that because he was in a special operations unit, his paycheck was held so that he couldn't be tracked. When Suzanne asked for his APO box (for military mail), he said he didn't have one, also for security reasons. She pressed him for a phone call and he pressed her for money to buy the phone with which to call her, explaining that he wasn't allowed to call her from secure military phones.

"I knew that was bullshit. And yet, I enjoyed texting him. I was having a blast. It was fun, like a game," she says. "Later on, though, I think I scared myself. I thought; 'You shouldn't mess with him. He knows enough about you to track you and find out where you live.' I didn't want to make him angry, to have him come and kill me or something. But I wasn't going to give him any money, either."

After she delivered an ultimatum for him to come and meet her in person or they were through, he stopped texting her.

Despite the cheaters, scammers, users and the abusive alcoholic she's been with, Suzanne is still a romantic at heart. She remains hopeful that she will find the love of her life and get married.

"I guess they call it, serial monogamy."

Most of the men that Sheryl has been involved with have wanted to be her husband. It was her choice, she says, not to marry them.

After a childhood spent with a temperamental, alcoholic father, Sheryl did not enter into the dating phase at an early age. She found herself, at 17, sexually inexperienced, and decided in a strangely rational way to learn about the birds and the bees by experimenting with a foreign exchange student her family was hosting – a boy she didn't even like.

"We were not close, but at one point he sort of hit on me, made at a pass at me. This was my mindset at the time – I know it's very clinical – but I was thinking: I'm 17 and I haven't done anything with a boy. I need to figure out what's going on here, you know? With this side of my life. I'm very stupid, and I need to know a little bit because I want to go on with my life."

She started "messing around" with him – short of actually having sex – and found it enjoyable. There was no emotional attachment, though, because she didn't really like him as a person.

"I know that sounds cold and clinical. But I was just kind of fooling around with him. I was never going to have sex with him. If I'd had a guy I liked, I would have maybe pushed the boundaries a little more. So it wasn't that I didn't like it. I just didn't care for *him*. He was kind of an asshole. He was just a horny teenage boy and he was available."

Sheryl did push the boundaries with a boy she fell in love with during a school trip to Spain. "This guy kissed me and it was like, 'Whoa!' That was a whole different kind of thing."

She was so infatuated with him that she returned to Spain after that initial visit and stayed with his family for six weeks, at their invitation.

"He's the person I lost my virginity to. I was really crazy about him but I kept changing my mind because the actual deed was not very romantic. It was kind of flat, but I enjoyed being with him."

Back in the U.S.A., she dated a man that she worked with at a restaurant. He wanted to marry her, but she was only 20 years old. Additionally, she found some of his habits off-putting.

"He was a nice enough guy. He was pretty stable in the sense that he worked as a manager, but he smoked a lot of weed. I didn't want to get into that lifestyle. It wasn't really me. And he went to a lot of parties. I would go to parties with him, but I'd be the weird kid that wouldn't drink."

She then went through a twenty year period where she was never single. "I guess they call it, 'serial monogamy.' I was getting out of one relationship and I'd meet another guy and we'd go out and that'd be the next guy I'd date for four or five years. I just kept overlapping. I was never single. I just had different men that I either lived with or was in very serious relationships with."

One of those serious relationships was with Necmi, a Turkish citizen who was living in the U.S. Although he thought Sheryl was younger than him when they met, she was actually 13 years older. Dating a younger man was a new experience for her.

"I really, really fell in love with him. This was the one guy I thought I did want to marry. I was really crazy for him – to the point where I was unrecognizable."

Having an orgasm without touching

The relationship was intense. "Sex with him and being with him – I've never had anything like it before," Sheryl says. "I could feel his energy without touching him. We could *feel* each other. I know it sounds whoo-whoo. It was this intense thing – like this union that you hear about, a union of bodies that transcends into God. I've never had anything like it before, this connection.

"One time we were making love and we quit touching each other and we were just lying on the couch, taking a break. Without touching, I could feel his energy. I actually had an orgasm that way. I've never had anything like it before and I would have never thought it existed. It was just crazy. It was like he was really inside of me – almost to the point where it got spooky."

Sheryl thought they were going to get married. Necmi planned to start a business in the U.S. but had to move back to Turkey for awhile because he was having trouble earning enough money in the U.S. to put his plans in motion. Awhile turned into a long time. Sheryl continued to believe that he was the one for her.

"I think I held onto it for too long – probably eight or nine years. But he sort of never went away. And I never really dated in between. I went out a few times, but I think in essence, I was too loyal and I held on to that relationship for too long. I sat at home a lot, pining for this man who was never going to come back for good. I knew it was pretty much over, but he kept showing up. Every time I'd break it off, he'd show up and dangle the carrot again."

Her relationship with Necmi began to deteriorate. She felt as though he was using her for his business purposes, especially to introduce him to people she knew. As for her own career, Sheryl was laid off during the recession. Instead of being supportive, Necmi told her that she was too old to find another job – or another man.

"I was on the phone with him one day and I said, 'You know, I'm going to go shopping younger. You think I'm old? My next man is going to be 25.'"

Her prediction was *almost* accurate. Her next boyfriend, Mario, turned out to be 22 (28 years younger than her).

"It was really healthy for me, because for a young man, Mario had a lot of wisdom. He was really one of the smartest people I've ever met. He kind of stabilized me."

She was running out of money by then and had actually started to file for bankruptcy. Mario counseled her about some financial decisions she could make to improve her situation – like selling her car.

"People would look at the relationship like, he's the child, you're the adult, but he really woke me up. He said, 'Look, you've got to take care of yourself. You're on the edge. You're smart. You're an intelligent woman. You've done all this stuff for yourself. Now you need to take better care of yourself."

Their relationship came to a natural end, she says, with no hard feelings. She and Mario remained friends but not lovers.

"Mario had to go on his way, to go and do what he had to do. I'm always grateful for that relationship. I gave him certain things and he gave me certain things. It was unbalanced, in a way, but we both taught each other lessons. We came into each others' lives for a reason."

Sheryl was engaged once, but she didn't feel a strong enough connection to her fiancé and began to feel suffocated. Why did she get engaged to him?

"I guess I did it more or less because I was supposed to, and he really wanted to marry me," she says. "He was crazy about me. Ultimately, we were just not right for each other, and I shouldn't have said yes. It wasn't the right fit."

That could have been because her fiancé was counting on her earning potential – which he felt would be greater than his – to send the three kids he decided they would have to private schools.

"All this was going to be on *my* shoulders," said Sheryl. "He was ten years older than me. I felt like, 'Why is it going to be my responsibility?'"

A man she dated after that turned out to have a serious drinking problem, which eroded her feelings for him. Ironically, it was his sobriety that caused them to part ways, because it included his becoming an evangelical Christian – and him pressuring her to do the same.

"I'm glad he sobered up, but that was his path, not my path."

"I feel like I was working out issues with my father."

Sheryl has had a lot of boyfriends. Does she have any regrets about the way her relationships worked out (or didn't)?

"I feel like each person taught me something. With each relationship, I feel like I was working out issues with my father."

Is Los Angeles a good place to be single? To meet new men? Sheryl doesn't think so.

"I feel like it's hard to meet people in this city because we're really isolated in our car bubbles. You don't walk around and talk. I used to travel to Manhattan on business. One thing I noticed is that people talk in elevators. Or you bump into somebody in the lobby and you talk to them. Or you talk to people on the streets. It's much more vocal in New York. I would talk to people there and people would engage me in conversation. That's cool! That doesn't really happen in Los Angeles."

"I'm comfortable with the skin that I'm in."

Unlike Sheryl, Joan hasn't had a large number of boyfriends, and some of the ones she's had undermined her confidence.

"I have unfortunately found that with a lot of men, when you're my size, they think you're easy, that they can use you," Joan says. "They even act like they're offended that you have a standard. So I don't do much dating. I have a right to expect someone who loves me and treats me with the respect and love that I deserve. At this point in my life, given the way things are about to unfold for me, I don't really feel bad about it.

"I'm comfortable with the skin that I'm in. I have this wonderful vision and purpose that drives me and keeps me moving forward. If marriage happens, so be it, and if doesn't, so be it."

Because of her weight, Joan says that it took her years to reach the point where she knew that she was worthy of love. Before that happened, though, she was in some unhealthy relationships.

"Throughout my teen years, I was very unhappy and had very low self-esteem. As a result, I was preyed upon by two older men. One was just a dog. He took my virginity and dumped me when I was 18. The other one treated me better but he didn't have any business with me either because he was 20 years older than I was. He was grieving the loss of his wife. I was looking for love, for validation."

She didn't find it. Not yet, anyway. Throughout her 20s, Joan was depressed and burdened with a sense of low self-worth, which led to more weight gain. As a result, she hardly dated during that time period, and when she did, she did not make very good choices.

Now, she has a different perspective on herself and is meeting better men than those she attracted when she was younger – and weighed less.

"I think it's because I have more self-confidence now than I did when I was smaller and in my 20s and 30s. This has come from within, from an awakening and a recognition of what my value is. I am a priceless, platinum plated diamond and I'm not changing my mind about that for anything in this world."

So what qualities would Joan be looking for in a husband? For starters, he would have to see beyond her weight, to her true value.

"I grew up being criticized my entire life. I must have someone who sees beyond the physical. I used to not date men unless they preferred plus size women. There's a whole genre of men that prefer plus size women. Oh, my God, it's amazing! He does not have to be somebody that prefers a plus size women per se, but he has to see *me*."

After being verbally abused about her weight by family and friends throughout her life, Joan refuses to have that negativity in her own house.

"So, whoever comes into my life has got to love me at whatever weight I'm at. I need someone who will never criticize me or put me down. Someone that will love me with a passion and that is stable spiritually, emotionally, physically and financially."

"I'd like 20 years of good sex."

She also wants a man who takes care of himself and has a healthy lifestyle. "I'm older now and I'd like 20 years of good sex in a marriage. After 20 years, I'll be in my 60's, it won't be as important as before. I can look back and say; 'We had 20 good years.' Whoever comes into my life needs to understand, for the next 20 years, you've got to keep that working. I've waited and I could have been with a lot more men but it's not my style. I wanted the one God had for me, not just any man. I want the passionate sex and love. I want someone to just look at me and say, 'You are just drop dead gorgeous.'"

To Joan, respect is as important as love. She grew up in a household with an alcoholic, womanizing father who constantly humiliated his wife. That and other examples she saw as a child made vivid impressions on her.

"I've watched too many men beat their wives, cheat on their wives, because they don't have a respect and a value for what they have, despite the fact that the love is there. Yes, I want love and I mean no harm when I say this, but: love be damned. You respect and value me and we'll be all right. Because what you respect and value, you are going to cherish. You are going to treat it differently. When you respect and value your car, you get those oil changes, rotate those tires, and wash it on a regular basis."

What if Joan never finds that man who'll respect and value and cherish her? Who will tell her that she's drop dead gorgeous?

"I don't ever want to settle for less than what I know I deserve. That's where I am right now. As long as I know I have made a mark and lived my life to the fullest, I think I'll be ok with it."

"You're going to talk to me or I'm going to show up at your work."

Sally, who was molested as a child and stalked as a young woman, went on to date plenty of men, but did not always give a lot of thought to why she was choosing the men she dated.

"I went out with a lot of guys that, after I went out with them once, I never even wanted to talk to them again. I thought, 'Why did I even go out with him?' Drinking never helped, because when I'm drinking they're not as stupid, apparently, as when I'm sober." She laughs.

Sally is a very intelligent, strong-willed woman who doesn't suffer fools gladly, so men that reveal themselves to be intellectually inferior to her are cut from the herd pretty quickly. However, she hasn't always been the one doing the cutting. "I'm not brilliant, but I'm damn smart. I have a logical mind. I can retain book knowledge. I don't always have common sense, mind you, but I can see how things fit together. A lot of guys, they don't like that. Even intelligent guys."

Sally heard an aphorism as an adult that she wishes she'd known when she was young. It was: 'Don't date anyone you wouldn't want to be a parent with.' If she'd embraced that wisdom, she says, she wouldn't have dated half of the men she did.

"My first boyfriend – there's no way in hell. I wouldn't even have gone out with him if I'd been thinking: would I raise a child with this person? Because *he* was a child. And in reality, I would not have started going out with Frank, my current boyfriend, if I had used that concept, because I would never have raised a child with him, so it's a damn good thing we didn't have a kid."

She had serious boyfriends prior to Frank, including one that ended in a particularly traumatic breakup – when her boyfriend's sister informed her that he was engaged.

"When she told me that, it actually felt like someone punched me in the stomach. I'd never experienced that before."

"We'd only been going out a short time, but it was things like, one time we went to a St. Patrick's Day dance and afterwards we slept together. And the next day I had a cold or something and he said, 'I thought love cured everything.' So you know, my mind's thinking *love* but it was a short time after that that I found out from his sister he was engaged. I'm not a person to just let somebody do that to me. I had to talk to him."

Sally called him and said the two of them were going to have a conversation, one way or another. If he refused to see her, she would show up at his workplace. He agreed to have her come to his home, where his mother and sister were on hand for the meeting, "to make sure I didn't kill him or something."

Sally confronted him; "How dare you?" She reminded him that after his 'love cured all' comment, she'd asked him if he loved her and he'd answered yes. His explanation for why he was dating Sally when he was apparently engaged to another woman: his very traditional Albanian parents had chosen a woman from their church for him to marry.

"At one point in our conversation he actually said, 'Well how do you think *I* feel? I don't even know her.' And I'm thinking, '*Fuck you! I don't care how you feel!*'"

Perhaps to point out why Sally wouldn't be an appropriate mate for him, the man she'd been dating said; 'You know, sometimes you disagree with me.'

"I probably shouldn't have disagreed with some people as much as I did along the way, but who knows? Maybe I was testing him at that point."

"How are you going to take care of me?"

If Sally's goal in life was to be married, another boyfriend, Mario, would have sufficed. He was very, very nice – she uses that word a lot when she's describing him. But although he had graduated from college, he was unemployed and still living with his parents. Sally, in contrast, was living on her own, going to school (and paying for her own education), and working. She thought she loved him, but his lack of ambition was a problem for her.

"I said to him; 'Why don't you get a job? You should be doing *something*. You shouldn't not do anything for a whole year just because something doesn't match up to the job you thought you went to school for.' It possibly wasn't the nicest thing to have said to him. And I said, 'How are you going to take care of me? I mean, if you lose your job are you just not going to get another job? Are we going to move in with your parents?'"

Sally felt that Mario and his sister were very spoiled by their parents.

"His Mom actually said to me – because she probably thought I was a harlot or something, living on my own at 19 – 'Oh, with all those kids, your mom was probably happy as you each moved out.' And I'm thinking, 'You dumb bitch, no! She raised us to be *ready* to move out. Both our parents did. They prepared us to be our own people, and not have to rely on anybody.'"

It's hard to imagine someone with Mario's docile personality paired up with Sally's blunt but witty forcefulness. She admits that if they'd tied the knot, she definitely could have ruled the roost.

"But I don't want to always be in charge. I'd like other people to be in charge, damnit! It's tiring. Even at that age, I knew I did not want to be the one to always make the decisions. Apparently, ultimately, I do, but at least I'm only making them for me, versus for everybody else.

If all Sally wanted was to get married and have kids, she concedes that Mario would have fit the bill – for awhile. "We'd probably be divorced. I wouldn't be who I am because I wouldn't have gone to school, or finished school. And who knows what the hell he'd be?"

Ending the relationship with Mario wasn't easy. In order to make a clean break with him, she felt that she had to be cruel to be kind. That conversation went something like this:

Him: "I want to talk."

Her: "No, I don't have to talk to you."

Him: "I want to understand why"

Her: "No. I don't have to explain to anybody. I'm an adult. I don't have to explain to my parents. I sure don't have to explain to you. We're done."

Why did she do it that way? If she'd been nice to him, tried to let him down easy, Sally would have, in effect, been stringing him along. That wasn't the end of the story, though. Mario wrote her a letter, telling her that he was having trouble getting over her. In it, he said he tried to think of bad things to say about her, but admitted that he couldn't.

"I really wish I'd kept that letter he wrote me, after I broke up with him. Basically, it was saying I was perfect."

Sally's next serious relationship was with Gabe, who was ten years older than her and had commitment issues. And other issues. They broke up once because she threw him a surprise 40th birthday party. Yes, really. He said he didn't want one and she disregarded his wishes.

"He crushed me. I didn't expect it. I knew he might be mad about it, but I sure as hell didn't expect it."

Ironically, Sally had had the party videotaped – and Gabe wanted a copy of the tape. In retrospect, he loved the party.

"But he's just an ass. He wants things his way. And I tell him that all the time, as does his family. I'm still in touch with him. His family loves the hell out of me. He often tells people his family would choose me over him any day of the week. His parents are great people."

At first she stayed in touch with Gabe just to "stick the knife in," to remind him that he was an idiot for breaking up with her. It worked, she says. "Every day he was miserable over the fact that he let me go."

Gabe did eventually try to get back together with Sally, but it was too late. She had just begun going out with Frank, who would become the long-term love of her life (but not her husband).

"He thought I was just a screaming bitch."

Sally and Frank met at a party thrown by a mutual friend. Their first interactions certainly didn't hint at the decades-long relationship that would spring from that night. It wasn't, to say the least, an immediate attraction.

"Mind you, I was drunk," she says. "It's funny because my family, we're sarcastic. We joke with each other harshly, apparently. I thought he and I were on the same wavelength. He thought I was just a screaming bitch."

However, when it was time for her to leave the party, Frank said, 'You have a headlight out. I'd better ride with you.' And he jumped in my car." He came home with her, they started dating and the rest is history. They've parted ways a few times but have always gotten back together.

What has been the basis of such an enduring relationship? For one thing, Frank introduced Sally to lots of new experiences, like canoeing, and traveling to places she'd never been. One of their breakups, in fact, occurred during a trip to the northern part of their state, where they were sharing a cottage with two other couples. The nature of their dispute highlights the differences in their personalities and in how they approach problems. Someone in the group had burned a hole in a bathroom countertop of their rental house with a cigarette. Sally was sure she knew who the culprit was, but because Frank is so opposed to confrontation, he confessed that *he* could have been the one who did it.

That made Sally angry. "Grow a pair! And then don't make me the bitch! Say that it was not you! Be a man. It was *not* you, you idiot!"

Frank followed that up by failing to get her anything for her birthday – not even a card.

"In my family, birthdays are quite important. You don't have to shower me with things, but you have to at least acknowledge that it's my birthday. So, we're done. Get out."

"He had no problem helping me change my bandages."

Six months later, they saw each other at a party and started talking. Then started dating again. Frank more than made up for his birthday gaffe by taking care of Sally after she had surgery for fibroids in her uterus.

When her health later took a much more serious turn, Frank was there for her again. Diagnosed with breast cancer at the age of 43, Sally had a double mastectomy.

"I had read all sorts of things about how many relationships dissolve because of that, because the men are such assholes about what's important to them," she says. "He had no problem helping me change my bandages. Seeing what it was like at that point – and it was definitely not pretty. The scarring and everything. Yeah, he was there 100 percent."

He still is, according to Sally.

"Please don't curse me with that."

For Pat, a whirlwind romance turned into a transatlantic engagement that lasted a little more than a year.

"We just had different energy," she says as to why the relationship didn't last. "We weren't getting along. The way it ended was, I had been in England visiting him. We ended up fighting for 24 hours. And he made a comment like, 'I just don't know if I can do this.' And I said, 'Well why don't you call me when you know what you want to do?' and I hung up the phone on him. Then I didn't talk to him for six weeks."

She began to rebuild the life she'd begun shutting down in anticipation of moving permanently to England: doing things, seeing people. Their wedding plans hung in limbo. When her fiancé finally called her, he said, 'Why aren't you more broken up about this?'" Her answer: "I've had six weeks to get over you."

She has no regrets about what happened, because she knows they weren't meant to be together. "We had varying opinions on politics, on life, on everything. I have always been a spiritual Catholic and he was raised Catholic but didn't believe in God, necessarily. I don't believe you can make that difference work. You can if you're mature, but I wasn't mature back in those days."

Pat, who is in her 50s, is vivacious, funny, talented and intelligent. She has a strong network of friends, some of whom have told her that there's no man good enough for her.

"Which is nice, in one sense, and then it's like, that's bullshit. I don't see what smoke and mirrors you're seeing, but... It's not real. It's a nice thing to say, but please don't curse me with that."

Pat believes she is not married because she was never ready for it before this point in her life.

"Trust me: there're a lot of people that I wanted to marry and I thank God every day that I didn't marry any of them. Except maybe one – who I'm still curious about. I thought I was ready, but I was never ready. I'm ready now. I have a much more realistic view of what it takes to be in partnership with somebody, and I'm also much more healed and whole. You need two wholes to come together to have a decent relationship. No one else can fill me or complete me. That's bullshit."

What if she met Mr. Sort-of-Right, but would have to change herself in significant ways in order to make the union work?

"I'm adaptable," she says. "I went from being single in New York and having my own apartment to living with my sister and her husband and a baby. Every relationship takes compromise and understanding. I'm not particularly worried about that."

Pat has tried lots of ways to meet men, like online dating (never again, she says) and going to a matchmaker. At present, she's content to let things unfold.

"I'm going to shut up and let God do it. I have no doubt that a man will come and he'll be the right person."

As an African-American woman who grew up mainly around white people, Pat has predominantly dated white men. Her fantasy, though, used to be a boyfriend who was British and of East Indian descent – someone who'd get her whole British upbringing (as discussed earlier, she spent years at a boarding school in the English countryside), as well as understand being brown skinned. Now, at 52, her criteria is: Catholic and spiritual; well educated and intelligent (she put a qualifier on both as she feels that neither are necessarily synonymous) and good looking.

He must have integrity as well. "I don't ever want to know that someone is a really lovely man and then you hear that he's a total asshole at work." Honesty is another quality that's important to her. "I'm really honest. I'm really blunt. I have to have somebody who's on par. Who's not afraid to apologize. Not afraid to call me out on my shit or themselves out on their shit. Because I do that."

"I haven't shot anything down, but no one's really come knocking, either."

Leanne, who identifies as single because she declines to drag that "divorced" ball-and-chain-of-an-identity around with her for the rest of her life, got married when she was 23 and was married for eight years.

"At the time, it seemed like a good choice," she says. "He seemed like the right person. It was certainly not a high school sweetheart thing. This was someone I had met toward the end of college, outside of my college experience, and it seemed like a great thing. Ultimately it turned out *not* to be."

She feels that she stayed in the marriage longer than she should have. Once she got clear of it, though, she realized that she likes having time for herself.

"I haven't been really rabid about pursuing relationships since then. Not that I've been scarred, necessarily, but because I'm pretty comfortable and happy with the way my life goes without having to consider another person."

Leanne tried online dating twice since her divorce and found it to be a total bust.

"Other people may have tremendous success at it, but for me, that's just not how I roll. I guess I'm old-fashioned. I feel like your eyes should meet across a crowded room and you should go, 'Oh, that's interesting' and pursue it." She laughs and adds: "But apparently, that may not be the way either, since I'm still hopelessly single right now."

"I don't have time to dial it back for you, nor should I."

She does sometimes wonder why she hasn't had a relationship since her marriage. "I mean, I haven't shot anything down, but no one's really come knocking, either." Her theory (which has been suggested to her by other people as well): she's confident, strong, intelligent and self-sufficient – qualities which are intimidating to some men.

"To me that's sad, but I guess part of me is like, 'If that is a deal-breaker for you, then, yeah, you *do* need to keep walking! I don't have time to dial it back for you, nor should I.' I guess there's a part of me that does keep hoping that I'll someday be in the right place at the right time and magic will click, but am I wandering the internet looking for Mr. Right? No. I don't pursue it in that capacity."

What kind of man could tempt Leanne into a serious relationship – maybe even marriage – at this point? The man she describes sounds like a male version of her: he needs to be independent and have his own identity and hobbies. He must be intelligent and self-sufficient.

"I'd like somebody who could support me, and I, in turn, would support them back," she says. "And someone who would challenge me. Who would push me beyond where I am into new things, new experiences, perceptions, hobbies. Something new in my life that would enhance what I'm already good at and feel comfortable with.

"I think once you meet someone who is also comfortable in his or her own identity and still wants to share that with someone else but with the understanding that we are still two people, that's a tricky combination. That's what I'm waiting for. Someone who gets that."

"They just considered me a convenient fuck."

Atheria has never had a serious relationship.

"I've never dated," she says. "I've always been alone. I had one official boyfriend, from April 2002 to February 2003. There was a guy in Oregon that was almost a boyfriend but not quite. I've mostly just pined for men from afar. Thanks to the internet, I've gone out on a couple of dates here and there, but usually it was like just one date and I didn't feel it. And then there were some guys that I really did like, but they just considered me a convenient fuck. It's hard to explain it but I have not had a normal life, where you date people that you actually like and you are a couple. I've never had that."

She thinks that's because she fell for the wrong men: *players* and commitment-phobic types who didn't even like her.

"I always wanted somebody. It's depressing now at age 48 but I remember being in my early 20s and at that point I was still a virgin and had never had any boyfriends or dated or anything and I was going through a very hard time. I was extremely depressed and somewhat suicidal, probably. And I remember being hysterical on the phone with my mom, talking about why don't men ever love me and why doesn't anybody want to be with me. And back then, she said what was natural for a mom to say: 'It's just not the right time. It'll happen when it's meant to happen. You're still young.' You, know, typical stuff. Trying to make me feel better. Now, 25 years later, I'm in the same boat. And I haven't met anybody who really wants to be with me. There are men who find me attractive and they'd like to have sex with me a couple of times and then go on to the next woman, but that's it."

"We went to have sex, and in the middle of it I got physically repulsed."

She did date a man about ten years ago that she felt no attraction for, because people kept telling her that she had to "get past the physical."

"I remember, we started to have sex, and in the middle of it I got physically repulsed. And in my mind, I'm panicking, going, 'Oh my God, can we just please get this over with? Can I just get through this?' Because he physically repulsed me. Not only because he was so overweight, but because he was unhealthy. Because of his smoking, he wheezed. It was just awful. And after that, I thought, I am never going to do that again. If I'm not physically attracted to the guy, I can't date him. I'm sorry."

Atheria admits that as she gets older, she does feel lonely, but is still not willing to "settle."

"Now at this age, many men my age are so unattractive. Men just do not hold up with age. I really saw that at my 30th high school reunion."

"I'm more and more to the point where, if it's meant to happen it's going to happen"

Online dating hasn't worked well for Atheria. "I feel like it's too forced. In real life, if you meet somebody, it's more natural. In online dating, there's the immediate pressure, where you exchange emails a little bit, you go meet for coffee. You're sitting across the table from this stranger that you're just meeting for coffee and you're thinking, 'Ok, am I attracted to him? Am I going to want to have sex with him?' It's too pressured."

She doesn't like the bar scene either, but is a big fan of Meetup groups – although she says she doesn't join them to try and meet men. "I join them to hopefully make some friends and have fun. But if I meet a man through one of them, then great! But it's not my main intention."

"I'm more and more to the point where, if it's meant to happen it's going to happen and God's going to arrange it. I don't make tons of effort anymore. I don't."

Atheria does feel as if it's harder to meet men as she (and we) get older, and that the old adage of all the good ones being gone is true. She remembers having a conversation with her boss a few years ago, when she was upset about being single and he was trying to make her feel better by noting that because of divorces, there are men becoming eligible all the time.

"I was complaining about being alone and he says to me – and he said it with genuine sincerity in his voice: 'Men are always being recycled. Divorce isn't always the guy's fault. Sometimes it's the women's fault.' So he's telling me, by late 40s, men are getting divorced from their first marriage, so there should be a guy for you who might not be a jerk. He was trying to help. He meant well."

She's encountered lots of men in their late 40s who are broke and bitter because they're divorced and their ex wives took half of everything.

"They tend to be much more leery that you're going to take the other half of their stuff. They tend to be more guarded. And a lot of them are flat out not willing to pay for anything. There was this one asshole in Santa Fe who said, 'I'm not paying for anything. Don't think you're getting money out of me.' To be honest, especially if you've just met somebody on the internet, I don't want a guy to pay for everything because I don't want to be indebted, so I usually do offer to chip in. But this guy, he was so cheap, it was disgusting. So there is a lot of that.

"The interesting thing is, when people divorce around age 50 – 40s or 50s – the women often have the attitude of, 'I'm done. I can be totally fine without a man for the rest of my life.' But the men, once they're middle aged, they panic. They will latch onto the first woman who walks by and marry her."

"It's possible that on a spiritual level I'm meant to be alone"

After a man she had feelings for – a man who told her he "didn't do relationships" went and married someone else, Atheria had an epiphany. It took her a long time to get over him, but she finally realized that if she'd ended up with him, she wouldn't have had the freedom she needs to be able to move around.

"I am a bit of a gypsy. And I do have a spiritual calling that it's been predicted is going to come to fruition. I have a feeling when I'm older that I'm going to be traveling around a lot and probably teaching people spiritual stuff, so if I was rooted with a man and locked into a city, it wouldn't give me that freedom. It's possible that on a spiritual level I'm meant to be alone because I need the freedom to move around and possibly be a teacher. That's kind of been my realization lately.

"I will admit: At this point, I do like my freedom. I like being able to do what I want, when I want, how I want, never answering to anybody. I don't need to give an explanation of where I'm going and who I'm doing it with. If I do meet somebody now it's going to be really hard to learn to take someone else into consideration. It's going to be difficult."

Atheria is a bit sad that she's never found a man who loved her, but she's also heard enough horror stories about bad marriages and dysfunctional relationships to make her think that being single is pretty great. She saw an interview several years ago in which Stevie Nicks echoed her own feelings.

"She said she never wants to have to ask permission to do something, go somewhere, or to answer to anyone about what she's been doing, who she has been with, and when she's coming back."

Friendships

I've got wonderful friends. They are male and female, married and single, young and old, straight and gay. They serve different purposes in my life. There are friends I call when I'm having a crisis and need a shoulder to cry on, friends who call me when they get tickets to the symphony, friends that I catch up with at parties, friends who put up with my crankiness, friends who know how bad I am with directions and don't make fun of me when I use a gps to go somewhere I've been to many times before, friends who come to see my plays in order to support me, friends who share my political views, friends I disagree with, friends who let me be an honorary aunt to their kids and friends who give me good advice when I need it and sometimes when I don't.

There was a time in my life when most of my friends were getting married and I wasn't that I felt like an outcast. No one *made* me feel that way, but our interests diverged and I was often left out of things. It was only natural. Couples tend to do things with other couples. People with children gravitate, quite naturally, toward other people with children. They have a lot to talk about. I had nothing to contribute to conversations about breastfeeding, potty training and preschools. When several sets of married friends went off on a cruise together and I wasn't invited to join them, I was a bit hurt. Did they not want a fifth wheel around? Were they assuming that I wouldn't want to pay double the fare to compensate for the "missing" passenger in my cabin? Or, did it just not occur to them to ask me, because going on a cruise was a couples thing and I was not part of a couple?

This was just one of the ways in which I was confronted by the fact that by being single, I was taking the road less traveled by. Even though I didn't particularly want to get married, being in the minority was psychologically difficult at times.

It's less so now. Maybe that's because some friends have gotten divorced, or because marriages have matured and can make room for single friends in a way they couldn't when the couple was finding their way together and busy with raising a family. Now, I am included in everything. My married friends are welcoming and accepting of me, and I love them for it.

But does staying single change friendships? For some women, it does.

"That's the only thing I think I miss"

When Jo-Sue's three best friends from college got married and moved away, she found it difficult to stay in touch with them. "Facebook makes it a little easier," she says. "You can at least see what's going on in their lives, but it's not the same. We don't really talk a whole lot anymore.

"I don't have a ton of friends because most of my friends are married and have kids, so sometimes it's hard to connect with them and do things with them."

Her closest friend at this time is a woman who's divorced. Her son recently graduated from high school, which allows her to spend more time with Jo-Sue. "For me, it's been nice that I finally have someone that I can hang out with. But mostly I don't hang out a whole lot with people who are single. It's always married couples."

When Marcy moved to Colorado nearly three decades ago, she had a large group of close friends. "Then they started settling down and having kids, and then you're no longer included, even though you still see each other at the gym. They have a different set of friends – married friends. That's the only thing I think I miss – the connections with girlfriends I had prior to them getting married. Now that they're married and have kids, you don't have that tight knit connection."

Marcy has three close friends and then lots of acquaintances that she can "just pick up the phone and do things with."

It made her wish she had close girlfriends to talk to

Kay also found that once friends got coupled up and started having children, their lifestyles became very different and she had less in common with them. Sometimes she was the one who'd changed. Once, on a trip to her home state she reconnected with an old friend. "She was divorced and had grown kids, but most of all – and this may just be the difference between Pennsylvania and California – she hadn't changed a bit. She just wanted to go out drinking. And I thought, 'I don't do that anymore.' Her friend wanted to do the things they did when they were in their 20s. Kay had moved past that.

The friends Kay has these days are people with whom she feels a strong bond. "I make friends fast and deep. I connect fast. Like one of my yoga teachers, we've become friends in just five months."

When her friends are having problems or going through an emotional time, Kay wants to help, but all that empathy for others can keep her from dealing with her own issues.

"I want to be there for them," she says. "I'm really good at that, although I'm discovering that I'm avoiding taking care of my stuff, because I want to help fix that other person. I don't know if that's a single woman thing, or if that's my thing. I'm finally recognizing that I need to focus on me, to get my life in order and stop avoiding it by being the helper and the service person for everybody. That depletes me and gives away all my energy and then I wonder why I'm behind on things. I'm not giving myself top priority and taking care of me and my life."

Throughout most of her life, Kay has had more male friends than female ones – guys who were like brothers to her. It made her wish she had close girlfriends to talk to. These days, she's got more of them. They tend to be divorced or single women focused on their careers, animal lovers or animal activists, women who hike or women who do yoga. In other words, women that she shares a common interest with. She does not have a close friend who has children.

"Seems like when people become a couple, they're a unit. It's always 'we, we, we.' It's probably really important to maintain your individuality. It's still your life, within this couplehood."

"I know they're supposed to think of themselves as a unit"

Eleanore, the Spinsterlicious marketing professional, always suspected that married women didn't particularly like having attractive single women around. That impression was confirmed when a friend of hers got married at the age of 48 and found that her social life blossomed. Suddenly she was being invited to *everything*.

She told Eleanore; "I didn't know I was missing stuff. Not being invited to stuff. As soon as I got married, people that I know or know of, suddenly started including me in ways that they never did when I was single."

Eleanore did notice that when some of her male friends got married, they drifted out of her life because "the wife just couldn't be bothered with including me anymore, and the guy would just go along because it's just easier."

She is surprised at the way couples tend to think of themselves as a unit. "I forget that sometimes. There have been countless times when I have invited a girlfriend to do something and they showed up with their husband and I'm thinking, 'We didn't talk about that.' And then I realize when you say, 'Do you want to do dinner Thursday night?' I sometimes forget that that means, 'Do *y'all* want to do dinner

Thursday night? – not you by yourself.' I am still surprised sometimes when I don't remember to figure out this is a 'we' thing."

On several occasions, Eleanore was actually paying for dinner and she ended up buying the husband dinner as well. For instance, a girlfriend of hers did her a favor, so Eleanore offered to treat her to dinner.

"Now as it turns out, when she did the favor for me, she brought along her husband. She didn't need to, but she did. And so they both did the favor for me. But when it came to dinner and he shows up, I'm thinking…? I certainly was not intending to treat two people to dinner. I didn't want to say anything because it sounded petty, and they did do me a favor and I never said, 'Well when you do this for me, don't bring your husband.' It never occurred to me. But it just got weird.

"That's a common thinking thing that married people do. And I know they're supposed to think of themselves as unit, but sometimes maybe you could be unit lite, you know?"

"We have to make appointments to see each other"

Sheryl is in the process of trying to create a strong and supportive social network for herself. While she was waiting for a man she was in love with to come back into her life (he didn't), she went through a period of being withdrawn.

"I feel like in that time frame, I lost a lot of friends, a lot of interests. I lost a lot of things. I just kind of let myself float away."

With her next boyfriend, she began to feel as if she was getting back to herself and healing, but… "I felt like I needed to be quiet. Like I didn't have to seek out social connections or crowds or noise. I kind of wanted to putter in my yard. Go to work and come home."

Now, though, she's ready to be more social, but that's not always easy to do in Southern California.

"I just feel like L.A. is so spread out and people really get caught up in their lives here," she says. "Everyone I know is exceedingly busy. They work long hours. If they do have kids or a husband, we have to make appointments to see each other. I feel like that's kind of sad. I would like to build a community. I don't know how to do that, but that would be kind of nice. I really like the friends that I do have, I just don't see them that often."

"What the hell is wrong with men that they can't see the attractiveness?"

Leanne has a few very close friends and a lot of small social networks. "I'm not uber-social. I'm very much an introvert, so I'm not seeking social interaction a lot, but I have my theatre friends, and then I have my work friends, and then I have my lifelong friends. So when I want one, it's there. When I want to be alone, people know to just let me be. I don't surround myself with people, but I have people I can rely on."

Most of her male friends are married. Most of her female friends are single, widowed or divorced. "Some were divorced ages ago and have not remarried," she says. "There are a lot of single women in my life. We all kind of get together and sort of high five each other and go, 'Yeah, right, everybody good? We're happy? Everybody ok?'"

Her single friends, she says, are single with a capital 'S.'

"They are divorced, they are widowed, they are whatever, but they are no longer in a long-term relationship. And what I find is that all the single women that I am friends with and that I hang out with, from the entire age bracket of adult women – I'm talking former students who are in their 20s all the way through to 67-year-old women – they are all so amazing, intelligent and attractive. They've got so much to offer and so many interests and so many fun things that they do. As a betrayal of that, part of me is thinking, 'why are these women single?'" She laughs. "What the hell is wrong with men that they can't see the attractiveness? Here's a whole roomful of – you name it – and they are *all* a catch. Every single one of them."

She wonders what is causing this phenomenon, this plethora of amazing single women who've been overlooked by men.

"I think it's easy to say, 'Well, it's the women. They don't want a relationship.' Not necessarily. They don't want *any* relationship. I think these are discerning women who, like me, want something that's going to enhance who they are, not take away from it or eclipse it. Or, at this stage of my life, come in and want to be mothered or taken care of or nurtured. A clingy, vine-y thing.

"But I find that most single women are really awesome, incredibly cool people. They're not losers or wallflowers."

Are all of Leanne's single female friends as ok with being single as she is? She thinks so.

"I mean, we all go through our 'pity me' phases, where somebody will call and go, 'Wahhh.' But I think, by and large, yeah, we're good with it. We're all homeowners or condo owners. We all have our own space on this planet, literally, our own real estate on this planet. And I think a lot of us are proud of that accomplishment. We are grateful to have the independence to make our own way. Very few mature single women are longing for some sort of knight in shining armor to come out of nowhere. If George Clooney calls, we're all going, but by and large, we're ok with it. I don't think anybody's going through depressive episodes. If they are, they're hiding it very well."

"As you get older it gets harder to make friends"

Because she was busy raising four children by herself, Lavender Moon didn't have time to develop and nurture friendships. Babysitting was a problem. She didn't like to leave her children with non-family members, and her mother "wasn't the babysitting type."

Her kids weren't the only reason, though, that she wasn't able to cultivate the kind of friendships she would have liked to have.

"I don't know why I was never able to make friends. I didn't really get out. I didn't go to college, didn't socialize. And as you get older it gets harder to make friends because most times people are friends with someone on the job, or where you went to college, or you have to be in a church. Some sort of activity. And you have to – I guess – grow up with people."

These days, with her kids grown, she is able to engage in activities where she's meeting more people.

"I still try to make friends. I do have some places that I go to. I wouldn't necessarily say that I have anybody that I can call up or go to their house. I go to activities and I know people there but that's it.

"I didn't have any friends growing up. And once I had kids, I didn't have the time."

"I'm either a doormat or I'm a bitch"

Elizabeth blames herself for not having as many friends as she'd like to have. "As my cousin says, 'Your dukes are always up all the time. You're always on the defensive.'"

She admits that there's some truth in that observation. "I'm always waiting for that punch to fly. I so badly want to have friends, but then they'll say something snarky to me and I 'm ready to drop them. I have to be more giving and forgiving. I wish I had a lot of close loving friends, but I really only have a couple of them. I have a dog that I adore and whose company I cherish.

"I'm either a doormat or I'm a bitch. One extreme or the other. I have to bite my tongue, and then I'm just being taken advantage of, or if I stand up for myself, all of a sudden I'm this horrible person. I haven't figured that one out."

She does have a group of friends who are all lesbians. "I adore their humor, strength, courage, acceptance and lack of judgment. I wish all women would possess their qualities."

"People don't invite you out"

Pat moved to New York when she was 34 in part because her friends in Detroit were getting younger and younger. "If you weren't married or coupled, you were a leper. No one's inviting you to dinner parties because you're the single woman. And if you're a single woman who's relatively attractive and intelligent and can hold a conversation with a man and one who doesn't care about gender roles – which still exist – people don't invite you out."

Did other women perceive her as a threat? "I think I was, yeah," she says. "I wouldn't have thought that, at the time. I was way too insecure then to think that. But in hindsight, yes."

She's not the only one to have been on the receiving end of jealousy.

Most of Eleanore's friends – both single and married – enjoy entertaining and are very good at including Eleanore, but *their* girlfriends are not necessarily enthusiastic about having an attractive single woman in the mix.

"And it just cracks me up, because so many of their husbands – I just want to say to them, 'I wouldn't have your husband if you gave him to me on a plate.' There is this ridiculous expectation that somehow the single woman in the room is going to poach their husband. And it's just pretty funny to me."

Either the marriage isn't solid or the wife has no confidence in herself. "Or she also, in my opinion, doesn't have an accurate perception of me or her husband, because most of them I look at and I'm like, I'm not the least bit interested in him."

Lucy has definitely noticed that she's been excluded from some events because she was single.

"There were social cliques that I was involved with in the past where it was all couples, and a single pretty girl was threatening, so I would be left out of things. Or girlfriends who had boyfriends didn't want me around their boyfriends because I'm pretty and petite.

"That's my interpretation of why I wouldn't be included in couples things. It hurt my feelings, but I brushed it off very quickly."

Stephanie has not felt the sting of exclusion because of her single status. "I've had great married friends who've always invited me over. There was never a feeling of being a third wheel."

Atheria gets invited to lots of social events but over time, she has enjoyed going to them without a partner less and less. "It did get tiring. I had this one friend, especially, in Los Angeles, she had a lot of parties, was very social. It did get old, year after year, decade after decade to go to parties by myself. But I'd still go, and nobody made me feel weird or anything. Not everybody who went was partnered."

"They feel a little threatened"

Michelle has been excluded from social events by some of her married friends.

"People don't always see it as a good idea for single people to hang with married people. I get that in some cases, but not in all cases. I *have* felt left out of activities because I was a single woman."

She believes that her male friends may unwittingly be inspiring jealousy in their wives.

"A lot of times, married men see single women as remarkable women. I have male friends who I knew before they were married to their wives. Sometimes I've had the problem where my male friends will talk of me so highly that it can come across as something else and that causes a problem. So I kind of try to stay away but I can't stop people from talking. In that aspect the women feel a little threatened, because their spouse is admiring somebody only for who they are as an individual, but not because they want any type of romantic relationship with me."

Tish dismisses the notion that anyone would leave her out of *anything*.

"You'd have to know me to appreciate that yes, I am very much a part of things. Every once in a while, the couple I travel with – they would get together for dinner or something where I may not have been included. It doesn't mean that I didn't have a date and wasn't doing something. So I really didn't resent it or anything."

"They don't want to invite the single person"

As a firefighter, Suzanne worked in a predominantly male environment. When it came time to socialize with co-workers, she found herself on the receiving end of jealousy and other negative reactions from her colleagues' wives.

"I think people think something's wrong with you if you're not married at my age. Like, oh, she's bizarre. She's strange. People treat you differently. They don't invite you places. If I was in a couple, I'd get invited to those places. They don't want to invite the single person: 'We're not going to invite Suzanne, she might hit on the men.' I find that happens a lot."

Firemen's wives never invite single women to their social events, but Suzanne says that as soon as a "firegirl" gets married, she's regularly included in things.

"It's like you're less of a threat if you're married, I guess."

She also speculates that she doesn't get invited to dinner parties because she might make the gathering come out to an odd number.

Leanne hasn't been left out, but sometimes being *included* can feel strange. She goes back to her wedding reception example. "Sometimes when it's a bunch of couples getting together, everybody's paired off and then there's the extra chair. I don't feel excluded, exactly, just awkward. Just because…a table for five." She laughs, and then reflects; "I've never *not* been included because I'm single. I'm surrounded by people who like me for me and whether I bring a partner or not is irrelevant, but it sometimes does feel awkward."

Being Single and Aging

What happens to all of our single-woman-independence when we get older, especially if we have no children? Will we be able to maintain the lifestyles we enjoy when our physical and mental abilities are diminished by age?

When my mother was diagnosed with Alzheimer's, my father took care of her. Because of him, she was able to continue living in their apartment for years longer than she otherwise would have. Eventually, though, her condition worsened and it became necessary to place her in a nursing home. She refused to eat for the attendants there so my father, brother and sister and I timed our visits so that we could feed her her meals. She could no longer remember our names, but it was clear by the big smile on her face when she saw one of us that she remembered who we were. She knew that she was loved and cared for.

We talked to her and sang to her, to keep her engaged. We combed her hair and rubbed moisture lotion onto her dry skin. Watched Lawrence Welk re-runs with her (she responded to music to the very end). At night, when she curled up in bed as if she were a child, we covered her with a blanket and kissed her good-night.

When she finally passed away, we leaned on each other for strength. None of us were alone in our grief.

My father recently passed away at the age of 94. Through his health crises, my siblings and I made his medical decisions for him and helped to take care of him.

My father was an athlete for his entire life; a runner and tennis player who ate a healthy diet and who worked out at a local fitness center into his 90s, serving as an inspiration for many of the center's younger members. He maintained his fitness and muscle tone and mental clarity a lot longer than most people, but even he was not immune to the inevitability of the aging process.

His journey is also my journey, because it helped to dispel my I'll-never-get-old-and-suffer illusion – a protective bubble with which all of us, to some extent, surround ourselves. It enables us to function, to get on with today without being paralyzed by fears about tomorrow, but sooner or later, it will – it must – yield to reality. What will that be reality be like when one is alone? It's not only always single women (or men) who must contemplate this possibility. People who are divorced or widowed must also think about it – particularly if they have no children.

"That whole picture is fuzzy"

Like my father did, Kay is using healthy habits as a strategy to delay the effects of aging. She doesn't expect to need anyone to help her with things for a very long time, but...

"I do wonder about that. I think, 'What does that look like? Going into your final days. Especially when you're really healthy and everyone else you know has passed away. You'd better have money to pay someone to take care of you." She laughs at the thought. "That whole picture is fuzzy. I'm not the kind of person who'll spend energy and time dwelling and wondering and worrying. I just put it aside and say, 'Let's take care of today. Let's take care of what I need to do now and figure it out as I go along.'"

She may not be alone as she figures it out, though, because over time, she's changed her mind and is now, potentially, open to marriage.

"My opinions have shifted. For my entire life, the "m" word was not in my vocabulary. I'd think, 'Well maybe someday I'll live with somebody, but I wouldn't get married until we were together for a long time, or probably never get married.' And that shifted – I'm not sure exactly when. I think during the last few years."

What's caused the change in attitude? Positive examples of healthy, nurturing relationships that she's seen among her friends and acquaintances.

"They're very supportive of each other, they do businesses together and they're raising very conscious children. I look at that and go, 'Gosh, that's really nice!' They take trips together, do things for each other. They're affectionate. You can see in their eyes how much they care about each other."

One woman she knows was in a terrible accident and sustained serious injuries. The way her husband of 20-plus years took tender loving care of her made a strong impression on Kay.

"I thought, 'Wow. What would I do, if somebody hit me crossing the street? Who would help me?' So I do think of those things. I don't focus on them. I just put it aside and think, 'It's not going to happen.' But you do wonder. You're happy that that person did have someone who was able to step in and pick up the slack. To take care of her."

Of course, if she were with someone who was not as healthy as she is, she might have to become their caretaker too soon.

"So it's kind of a two-edged sword. You don't know at what point someone's going to need help. But most of all, I think it's a matter of companionship and having enough things in common that you like to do together."

"I believe all of us should be all the more picky as we get older"

A lot of people, she says, make the mistake of falling in love because they're attracted to each other, but they don't have common interests, so they don't end up spending that much time together.

"So that's partially in the back of my mind, at this age, and as I look toward dating. I do think about who would be a good match for me and what would be fair for me and fair for him. It's not just, do we get along, do we like the same things, are we attracted to each other? It's also, how healthy is this person? Can they keep up with me? Are they going to stay healthy as long as I am (or plan to)? And some people have got a long way to go to catch up to me."

What happens if she never gets married? Will she regret it?

"No. It's simply now a matter of, it *could* happen. It would have to be a very specific guy. It should always be a very specific guy. I believe all of us should be all the more picky as we get older, because we are that much more formed as a human being, and there's maybe less flexibility or less we want to put up with or are willing to put up with. That's why people get divorced. They find things they are not willing to put up with."

Finding her direction – at 60

At 60, Kay feels as if she still has a LOT to do yet. "Most people would think this is the time you slow down in your life. No! I feel like I'm just getting going. I'm really finding my direction, finally. It's like everything I've done has brought me to this point, and I've learned things, but I feel like there are a lot of beginnings now."

Previously age was just a number that Kay ignored but turning 60 was a bigger motivator for her than other birthdays had been. "For some reason, I'm like, ok, I'm going to prove to the world how fit a 60-year-old vegan can be. I'm going to start dating. I'm going to start having fun, so I'll go out dancing. I'm going to put a priority on that."

Her new attitude pleased her friends – especially those whose problems she'd spent considerable time and energy trying to fix. They were happy to see her doing things for herself for a change. "Yeah," she told them. "I'm actually having a life."

"I'm ok with the aging process"

Sheryl has given a great deal of thought to what it's like to be a middle-aged woman.

"Now that I'm older, I feel like, in a way, like my value has gone down a little bit, as a woman," she says. "You're not reproductive anymore. This is in a societal sense, not necessarily how I feel about myself. You go out, you don't really get hit on as much. You don't get noticed. It's like the new flower is always prettier and more interesting."

However, Sheryl finds a richness to being older and having accumulated life experiences. "I wouldn't want to go back and be my 25-year-old self or my 35-year-old self. I'm ok with the aging process. I love to read. I don't like the fact that I can't see as well as I used to. That annoys me. Other than that, I feel like I'm a better person. I have more to offer. I actually would be a better parent now."

"I don't want to miss out on that"

Lucy does not plan to be alone in her golden years. She wants to be with – even live with – a man during that time.

"I don't know if I'd get married at that point, but I do want a life companion in retirement. And I'm thinking, ok, I'd better get moving on that when I hit like, 58, 59. Because right now I do absolutely nothing to inspire relationships or to look for relationships. I mean, I do absolutely nothing whatsoever. But yes, that is a concern for retirement. I think it would be a loss to be single at that time. I think I'll feel the pain of that, if you will."

She believes that in many ways, a relationship among people of a certain age is easier to start and to cultivate.

"Let's say I meet the man of my dreams at 58. And he's 60, for an example. We're both mature at that point. We're over the dramas of life. We're over the pettiness that couples go through today, at a younger age, and the immaturities of relationships. Most of the pain that couples go through is just due to immaturity, and not knowing how to behave and how to live a happy life. I just think when we age, our relationships can get richer and better, and I don't want to miss out on that. *That* I will make happen."

Does she worry that she might be out of practice when it comes to being in a relationship? Not at all.

"I think being single for so long has made me better at relationships when I do go into them. Much better."

"They won't throw me in a cheap old folks' home and let me rot"

When she needs help as she ages, Andrea is counting on family members to take care of her. Thanks to her long corporate career, she has financial security in place for her golden years. Despite that, she says her biggest concern about aging is that she doesn't want to run out of money.

"I kind of joke with my nephew and my niece – we live within about an hour of each other. I tease them, 'You know you have to take care of me when I'm old, right?' And I think they will. They're not going to abandon me. I kid them: 'You know you're in my will.' And they are. They are my heirs. I promise them that the money won't run out. They know I'm the one in the family with a little bit of money – because I haven't spent it on kids. So it's half joking, half serious, but they care about me and I trust them. They won't throw me in a cheap old folks' home and let me rot. That's kind of a crude way of saying it, but I trust them."

"That is the ultimate independence for a woman"

Stephanie also cites financial security as a factor that makes her more comfortable with contemplating her well-being in the years ahead.

"I think it would be terrible to be a single woman and have financial problems, and I feel very lucky that I don't," she says. She credits her parents with giving her the foundation for that security. "They knew that if I got started with seed money at an early age and had property, then that would help me in my future. I think my father recognized that. That is the ultimate independence for a woman. You've got to be able to have a place to live. Renting is not always a solution. Owning property, I think, helps women be independent."

Relying too much on children

Tish has absolutely no concerns about getting older, being single and not having any offspring. In fact, she thinks people rely too much on their children to take care of them when they get older. That, she says, doesn't always pay off.

"I have friends who are far more caring and will take care of business more than a child."

Because she's from a close and loving family, Jo-Sue is confident that she has a strong support system in place – one that will be there for her when she gets older.

"I have thought about it, actually, a little bit, only because there are some kids that I'm extremely close with. They call me their second mom," she says. "Their *real* mom said to me one time, 'You know, my girls told me that they always want you in their life and that, since you don't have any kids, when you get older, they're going to take care of you.' And I just started to laugh, because I'd never thought of it before. I was like, 'Oh, who *will* take care of me when I get older?'"

The example her mother set for her brings her a great deal of reassurance. "My mom has such a giving heart toward elderly people. She had an aunt and uncle that had no kids and she took care of them when they got older and made sure things were done for them. So I'll just trust that someone will be there to take care of me. I'm not going to worry about it. If something happens, it happens."

Joan has a niece and nephew who will be there for her when she needs some assistance. Because she's been working towards a healthier lifestyle, she hopes that won't be anytime soon.

"This is why I'm so adamant about my health now," she says. "I honestly believe that if I remain single, God will keep me healthy till the end. I had an aunt who was 91 when she finally passed. She was still living at home and had the most gorgeous set of pearly white teeth. She drove her own car and she cooked every day. That was her life until she dropped down dead of a heart attack. I want to live the exact same way."

"Who's going to make sure that I've got slippers and I'm not wearing my clothes backwards?"

Leanne *is* worried about who is going to take care of her when she can't live by herself anymore, perhaps because the subject is on her mind; her father passed away recently and her mother is in an assisted living facility. The decline in her parents' health made the passing of time – including her own – difficult to ignore.

"I can't imagine losing my independence anyway, but this is less scary for people with children or a spouse in the picture. I am a little haunted about what happens to me when I am not safe to live by myself and I go live in some place. Who's going to check on me? Who's going to make sure that I've got slippers and I'm not wearing my clothes backwards and all of that? That bothers me a little bit.

I don't know how it's all going to end, but really, between now and like, 80, I don't have anything that concerns me."

Like many of the other women profiled in this book, Leanne doesn't have children who could take care of her in her old age – but is that something that people can really count on? Children may have moved to another state, be too busy with their own families to help or even be estranged from their parents.

"That's almost more heartbreaking, because you would have relied on something that didn't happen, rather than not having it at all," she says.

Leanne is focused on the near future rather than on what may happen way down the line. She looks forward to retiring in a few years and then being able to *really* do what she wants with her time.

"If that includes a someone else, that's great. If not, think of all the things that I can do that I didn't have time for before."

"Having kids is no guarantee whatsoever that your kids are going to be there the way you need them to"

Eleanore dismisses the idea that having children automatically provides you with someone who will take care of you in your old age.

"The nursing homes are full of people whose kids don't visit them enough. So let's start with that. Having a child is absolutely no guarantee whatsoever that your old age is going to be amazing, for a lot of reasons. Sometimes your kids are assholes. Sometimes your kids live far away or they have their own kids and lives that they have to manage. Having kids is no guarantee whatsoever that your kids are going to be there the way you need them to. And sometimes kids die. You may have them and then outlive them."

Then, too, she points out that kids don't always do what their parents want them to do.

"That's just the reality. We all know of a situation where kids could have done better for their parents and they didn't.

"So just like I don't know who's going to take care of me when I'm old, nobody does. You just don't know. Any of the situations that I've described could happen."

One thing she's sure of: having someone to look after you in your old age is definitely *not* a good reason to have kids.

"I'm just going to trust God"

Despite a disabling illness that caused a career loss and necessitated a move away from a city she loved, Pat does not have concerns about being single and getting older. The things she's been through have changed her perspective on life.

"I stopped thinking and planning about my future to a certain extent because I have given it all over to God," she says. "That's not to say that I didn't do a power of attorney, and it's not like I'm not going to do a will.

"You know what? My life is so not where I thought it was going to be. It's so amazing and so much better that I thought. I'm just going to stop dictating. I'm just going to trust God."

An Army of Spinsters

When I first started tweeting as @TheNewOldMaid, a fellow Twitter user joked about being intimidated by this "army of spinsters" that he felt was out there, growing in numbers and rising in prominence. It's interesting that he used a term that made unmarried women seem combative, or at least, *dangerous*.

I suppose our sheer numbers may indicate that the status quo is changing, but is that necessarily a bad thing? Don't many of society's mores change over time? Still, the fact that there are more single women in the U.S. than there used to be doesn't mean that people have stopped getting married.

In addition to there being more women who are single these days, there are more women who *identify* as single and want to discuss what that means. A recent Google search of "spinster blog" returned 4,260,000 results, including Diary of a Modern Day Spinster, DC Spinster, Hollywood Spinster, Diary of a Spinster Aunt, The Spinsterhood Diaries and Spinster Jane. (Keep in mind that blogs come and go. By the time this book goes to print, some of those mentioned above may no longer be active. However, chances are good that new ones will have gone online.)

There are countless books about being single being published every month, with lots of different angles. While there are still plenty of tomes aimed at helping someone who's single find Mr. or Ms. Right and shed their onerous solo status, they're being numerically overtaken by the ones that advise people on how to be happy *as singletons*.

So how big is this "army of spinsters"? According to U.S. Census Bureau data, in 2010 there were 52 million unmarried women in this country.[2] This figure represents a demographic trend that is on the upswing; the percentage of never-married women aged 25-34 rose from 11.3 percent in 1950 to 29.7 percent in 2000.[3] In the 2010 census, 61 percent of U.S. residents over the age of 18 said they'd never been married.

That doesn't surprise Eleanore, who was taken aback by the large number of women who responded when she began blogging about being single. "There are a million of us, or more, but you don't always have somebody to talk about this stuff to," she said. "I was just amazed, once I started talking about it on my blog, how many women said, 'Oh my God, this is the first time I've given voice to that.'"

A Pew article[4] published in 2011 noted that barely half of all adults in the U.S. were married at that time – a record low. (It also pointed out that the same trend was occurring in other post-industrialist countries.) The age group showing the least inclination to get married? Young adults. As a matter of fact, the difference in marriage rates between contemporary millennials and their counterparts in the past is dramatic. The Pew article reported that "just 20% of adults ages 18 to 29 are married, compared with 59% in 1960."

Sociologists, economists and psychologists have all weighed in as to why 20-somethings are avoiding matrimony, or at least delaying it. There are tangible reasons. The burden of having to pay off college loans, for instance, can make it financially impossible for young people to move forward into the next phase of their life. Additionally, women are having children later in life and so may not be in a hurry to get married, which some believe is the necessary foundation on which to raise children. Of course, young women who want children don't *have* to be married in order to have them.

"If a woman makes enough money on her own and wants a kid, she can have one now," Elizabeth says. "It's not like it used to be. So that kind of takes away the importance of being married, for that generation."

Elizabeth's young nieces and nephews are a lot more confident about relationships than she was at their age.

"Remember the movie *When Harry Met Sally*?" she asks. "When some guy broke up with Sally and Harry was like, 'Did you want to marry him?' And she said, 'Nooooooo! But he didn't want me!' I suffer from that a lot. You feel like, well if they wanted to marry you, you felt accepted. And I don't think these kids need that."

I also get the sense from my 20-something friends that they feel no sense of urgency in taking on the title of "Mrs." Society's expectations don't register strongly with them, or at least, don't affect them much. If they're in a committed relationship, they don't need a legal change in marital status to confer legitimacy on it.

Leanne, the high school teacher, has had a lot of students whose parents are divorced. She believes that also contributes to a lack of enthusiasm for marriage on the part of younger people.

"They're seeing what a divorce looks like, and so are hesitating – and rightly so – to say, 'Do I want to go through that?'"

Having been married and divorced herself, what advice would she give them? "I don't know that we are the same person our whole lives, so I don't know that it's fair to not only promise a partner that you will never change and you will always be true and faithful to who you are, and in return, expect them to do the same thing, when at age 20 or God knows now, age 30, you're not who you are 20, 30 years down the road.

"So I guess I would say, 'If you're going to choose marriage, that's great. I support that. If you manage to make that work, that's outstanding , as long as it's not at the expense of your safety, your sanity or your health. But recognize that what you're promising – before whatever faith or religion or creed you follow –may not be a fair promise. Nobody has a crystal ball that will let them see where they'll be in 40, 50 years. And to say that 'I will still love you, and I will still be with you in spite of everything,' I think that's a big ask.'"

There was a time, she says, when people found their niche and stayed there, whether it was a marriage that lasted unto death, a job one held until retirement or a house a family lived in their whole lives.

"In a more sedentary time, that made sense. But with the globalization that goes on here, that's a big old world out there, and there's a lot in it that can affect you. I'm not sure that marriage, long-term, is necessarily a realistic institution anymore."

Famous Old Maids

Louisa May Alcott
"Liberty is a better husband than love to many of us."

Louisa May Alcott was a successful writer because she had to be. Her father was a brilliant philosopher and transcendentalist, an ardent abolitionist and supporter of women's rights, but he was a lousy provider. He was passionate about many causes but what he *wasn't* passionate about was gainful employment. Thus, his family lived in poverty.

Born in 1932 in Philadelphia, Pennsylvania, Louisa had to work hard from a young age; as a domestic servant and teacher and then as a nurse during the Civil War. That last job provided her with the material she needed to write *Hospital Sketches*, an account of her experiences nursing wounded soldiers that launched her professional writing career in a big way.

Then came *Little Women*, a commercial and critical success that finally gave Louisa the financial security she'd craved for so long, as well as the independence to sustain a lifetime writing career. That much-loved novel, which is still read widely today, has been the basis for six films, several television series, a musical, an opera and even a web video.

Alcott is believed to be the inspiration for the main character of Jo, a strong-willed, boyish young woman who loves literature and longs to be a writer.

In this passage from *Little Women*, Jo predicts that she'll be an old maid (although the character, unlike her creator, does ultimately get married):

"'Well, I needn't be a sour saint nor a selfish sinner, and, I dare say, old maids are very comfortable when they get used to it, but…' And there Jo sighed, as if the prospect was not inviting."

In addition to her writing, Louisa worked toward the emancipation of women and the prohibition of alcohol. She died at the age of 55 of a stroke.

Susan B. Anthony

"The woman who will not be ruled must live without marriage."

American women have the right to vote today largely due to the efforts of early crusaders like Susan B. Anthony. She was a relentless activist who devoted her considerable energy and organizing skills to the cause of women's suffrage, the abolition of slavery, and the temperance movement.

Born in February 15, 1820, Anthony grew up in a socially conscious Quaker family and became a teacher. When she wasn't allowed to speak at a temperance meeting because she was a woman, she joined the women's rights movement. She endured arrests, abuse and scorn for her efforts to secure women the right to vote, own their own property and keep the money they earned. By the time she turned 80, though, the pendulum of public opinion had swung in her favor, and she was celebrated at the White House by President William McKinley.

Although she didn't live long enough to see women actually get to vote, in 1920 Anthony and her colleague Susan Cady Stanton got Congress to pass the "Anthony Amendment" – the Nineteenth Amendment to the U.S. Constitution. It prohibits citizens from being denied the right to vote on the basis of gender.

Susan's detractors accused her of trying to destroy the institution of marriage. It's true that she does not appear to have been a *fan* of marriage, at least not of the version that existed during her day.

"If women will not accept marriage with subjection, nor men proffer it without, there is, there can be, no alternative." she said. "The women who will not be ruled must live without marriage. And during this transition period...single women make comfortable and attractive homes for themselves."[5]

She was often asked why she never married. One answer she gave: "I never felt I could give up my life of freedom to become a man's housekeeper. When I was young, if a girl married poor, she became a housekeeper and a drudge. If she married wealth she became a pet and a doll. Just think, had I married at twenty, I would have been a drudge or a doll for fifty-nine years. Think of it!"[6]

Anthony may have been demographically prescient; she predicted "an epoch of single women."[7] She died in 1877 at the age of 86.

Jane Austen
"A single woman, of good fortune, is always respectable"

Jane Austen gave the world stories so romantic that they still reso-
nate with readers and filmgoers today, yet she herself never married,
and a youthful relationship that could have produced a satisfying real
life love story was thwarted by circumstance.

The author of the novels *Pride and Prejudice, Sense and Sensibility,
Emma* and *Persuasion*, among others, was born in Steventon, England
in 1775 and grew up at a time when women were wholly dependent
on marriage for their financial survival. Despite this stark reality, the
heroines she created never settle for mere matrimony. They bravely
– often defiantly – pursue true love, and by the end of each book,
they find it.

Unlike her characters, Jane did not experience a deeply romantic
relationship during her uneventful and tragically short life. A budding
love affair with a man when she was 20 years old was cut short by
his family, because neither Jane nor her suitor had any money and a
marriage between them would have been impractical.

An engagement to an old family friend seven years later *would have*
resulted in a practical marriage – one which would have provided Jane
and her family with financial security – but she ended the engagement
after only one day because she did not have feelings for her fiancé.

With so much of her writing focused on the power and excitement
of romance, Jane may not have been happy as an always single woman.
She may, however, have made the best of things, particularly after
success as a novelist freed her and her family from money worries.

Perhaps her view of her own status can be seen in a passage from
Emma, in which the title character responds to a friend's worry about
her becoming an old maid by noting that she won't be a *poor* old
maid, "and it is poverty only which makes celibacy contemptible to a
generous public! A single woman, with a very narrow income, must
be a ridiculous, disagreeable old maid! – the proper sport of boys and
girls – but a single woman, of good fortune, is always respectable,
and may be as sensible and pleasant as anybody else."

Tyra Banks

"My mom never taught me to be waiting for some prince on a white horse to swipe me off my feet."

Although Tyra Banks has described herself as an "ugly duckling" as a child, that phase didn't last; she grew up to become one of the top-earning models in the world, walking runways in Milan, appearing on the cover of the *Sports Illustrated* swimsuit issue and working as one of Victoria's Secret's famous Angels.

That was just the beginning of what has been a multi-faceted career for Banks. Modeling led to acting roles in films and TV shows. She then created and hosted the reality TV show *America's Next Top Model* and co-created the show *True Beauty*. Her outgoing, highly opinionated personality was put to good use as host of her own talk show, *The Tyra Banks Show*, which won two Daytime Emmy Awards. She also wrote a young adult novel, *Modelland*, which made the *New York Times* Best Seller list in 2011.

Of her drive and determination to succeed in her various business endeavors, Banks has said: "My mom never taught me to be waiting for some prince on a white horse to swipe me off my feet."[8]

She has been romantically linked to a number of men, including musician Seal, film director John Singleton, actor Will Smith, basketball player Chris Webber and hockey player Mark Messier. As of this writing, she has never been married.

Clara Barton

"I may sometimes be willing to teach for nothing, but if paid at all, I shall never do a man's work for less than a man's pay."

Shy and timid as a child, Clara Barton grew up to be fearless and assertive. She defied convention in order to nurse wounded soldiers near the front lines of major battles, opened and taught at the first free public school in New Jersey, was the first woman to earn a federal government salary equal to a man's, worked for civil rights for all people and, in her spare time, founded the American Red Cross.

Clara's nursing ambitions were apparent early on. She was only ten when her brother David was severely injured in a fall from the roof of a barn. Clara appointed herself his nurse and learned how to give him the required medication and treatments, which included "bleeding" him with leeches. Contrary to his doctor's grim prognosis, David made a full recovery.

Born in 1821, Clara must have chafed under the restrictions that limited opportunities for women at the time. That school she originated? She made it so successful in one year that the town opted to build an expensive new building for it – and replace her with a male principal who was paid twice her salary. The clerkship she had in the U.S. Patent office, where she earned more than women usually did? The position was eliminated.

During the Civil War, it was not considered appropriate – or safe – for women to be close to the front lines, but Clara knew that was where nurses were most needed, so she persisted until she got permission from military higher-ups to get right in the thick of things. Surgeons and soldiers came to be grateful. When she was not nursing, the "Angel of the Battlefield" was conveying wagonloads of supplies to field hospitals, often arriving after bandages, first aid and even food had run out.

After the war, Barton headed up an effort that helped find or identify thousands of soldiers who were killed or missing in action – an initiative that gave closure and comfort to their families. She also directed her energies toward the women's suffrage and abolitionist movements. She was instrumental in founding the American Red Cross – once she'd convinced President Chester Arthur that it would be useful in responding to natural disasters in addition to its wartime functions (Arthur thought the U.S. would never again face the kind of conditions it endured during the Civil War).

Clara never married, although she did reportedly have a romantic relationship with a married military officer, Colonel John J. Elwell. She died at the age of 90.

Jacqueline Bisset

"I had the urge to nest and I've always been domestic. But not toward marriage."

Jacqueline Bisset started acting and modeling when she was very young in order to pay for the ballet lessons she loved. That smart choice led to an acting career that includes a Golden Globe award, an Emmy nomination and even the Légion d'honneur from France.

Born in 1944, the English actress had her first major roles in 1965, starring in *The Detective* opposite Frank Sinatra and in *Bullitt* with Steve McQueen. Her résumé also includes *The Sweet Ride*, Francois Truffaut's *Day for Night*, *Murder on the Orient Express*, *The Deep*, *Who is Killing the Great Chefs of Europe?*, *Rich and Famous*, and *Under the Volcano*.

Although she's had long-term relationships with actors Michael Sarrazin and Vincent Pérez, and dancer and actor Alexander Godunov, Bisset is an always single woman.

In a 2008 interview[9] with Marshall Fine of the website *Hollywood & Fine*, she mused that her parents' unhappy marriage had influenced her attitudes. Her mother, she said, had urged her to get educated – but not to get married.

"My parents were both very intelligent. But they didn't pull out the best out of each other. I didn't see a lot of affection there."

Jacqueline said that serious relationships sometimes make her feel "claustrophobic." "Like many people who don't easily commit, I think I had a fear of being known; I was not sure there was anybody inside there."

However, Jacqueline– at that time – said that she was still open to the idea of marriage.

Susan Boyle

A moment in the spotlight changed everything.

Susan Boyle stunned the ten million viewers of the TV show *Britain's Got Talent* when she stepped out on the stage in April of 2009 and sang "I Dreamed a Dream" from *Les Misérables*. The middle-aged, bushy-eyebrowed, unfashionably dressed woman delivered a stunning performance that brought the audience in Glasgow's Clyde Auditorium to its feet in a standing ovation.

That moment in the spotlight propelled Boyle – who'd previously sung mainly in church, karaoke bars and local singing competitions – into a successful music career that has included best-selling albums and her own television special, *I Dreamed a Dream: the Susan Boyle Story*.

Boyle is an always single woman (as of this writing) who still lives in her childhood home, which she bought with her music industry earnings.

Having rather famously admitted earlier that she'd never been kissed, Boyle revealed in a 2014 interview with *The Sun* – which was reported by *The Daily Mail* – that at 53, she was dating her first boyfriend, an American doctor around her age.[10]

Coco Chanel
"Women have always been the strong ones of the world."

Although Gabrielle Bonheur (aka Coco) Chanel died in 1971, the French fashion designer left behind a legacy of style that continues to reverberate through the fashion industry to this day. Despite being born illegitimate and enduring a poverty-stricken childhood – or perhaps because of it – Coco's ambition and determination drove her to found the Chanel brand which transformed the female silhouette from corseted to elegantly suited and gave the world the little black dress and the iconic fragrance Chanel No. 5.

She was described by those who knew her as passionate, focused and fiercely independent. She was also a drug user who injected herself with morphine on a daily basis[11] and an anti-Semite who may have collaborated with the Germans occupying France during World War II[11].

Born in 1883, Coco learned to sew at the convent where she was sent to live at the age of 11 after her mother died. As an adult she pursued a career as a cabaret singer while working as a seamstress. She failed as a singer, but working in a nightclub brought her into contact with the first of several men who would influence her. Étienne Balsan showered her with expensive dresses and jewelry and introduced her to the hard-partying, indulgent lifestyle of the wealthy.

An affair with a different man got her a posh apartment in Paris and financing for her first shop – a millinery store that sold the hats she was designing at the time. She then turned her attention toward casual yet stylish clothes and advertised her creations by having models walk through town while wearing them. It was the type of shrewd business move which – along with alliances with well-connected people – helped her build a business empire that employed thousands of people and revolutionized the fashion industry.

Throughout her lifetime, Coco had numerous affairs and relationships with some of the most influential and aristocratic men of her time.

"Women have always been the strong ones of the world," she said. "The men are always seeking from women a little pillow to put their heads down on. They are always longing for the mother who held them as infants."[12]

Sheryl Crow
"Are you strong enough to be my man?"

Sheryl Crow has written and/or recorded the kind of songs that make you want to hear them again and again: "All I Wanna Do," "Leaving Las Vegas," "If it Makes You Happy," "Strong Enough" and many more. The singer, songwriter, multi-instrumentalist and actor has sold more than 50 million albums worldwide and won nine Grammy Awards to date and has had roles in *30 Rock*, *Cougar Town*, *Hannah Montana*, *NCIS New Orleans* and *One Tree Hill*.

Although Crow's rise from Missouri music teacher to international recording artist seems magical, she paid her dues along the way, like singing jingles for TV commercials and touring with Michael Jackson as a backup vocalist. Established artists like Kenny Loggins, Celine Dion and Tina Turner began to record songs written by Crow. The success of "All I Wanna Do" launched her career into high gear.

Crow has faced challenges in her personal life. She's dealt with breast cancer and a brain tumor and has seen her relationships become fodder for tabloids and celebrity gossip shows. Her high-profile romances with actor Owen Wilson, musician Eric Clapton and later-disgraced bicyclist Lance Armstrong have garnered nearly as much attention as her hit songs.

Lyrics from Crow's hit song, "Strong Enough" speak to a relationship dilemma faced by many women: "You can't change the way I am/ Are you strong enough to be my man?"

In a 2014 interview[13] in *Good Housekeeping* magazine, Crow said dating highly successful men always resulted in her feeling somehow diminished.

Although Crow has been engaged several times (to Armstrong, for one), she's never ended up tying the knot with anyone. She lives on a farm outside of Nashville with her two adopted sons.

Kristin Davis
Actress, mother, animal activist

There's considerable irony in the fact that in a role she made famous, that of Charlotte York Goldenblatt in HBO's *Sex and the City*, Kristen Davis played a character who was hell bent on finding love and getting married (and remarried). In real life, marriage is not a priority for Davis.

The actress said in a 2013 interview[14] that she didn't make a deliberate choice to remain single, but hasn't had the type of relationship that would tempt her into marriage.

Born in 1965 to parents who divorced when she was a baby, Davis was later adopted by her stepfather. After college, she waited tables and taught yoga before finding success in the entertainment industry. In addition to her role on *Sex and the City*, Davis has appeared in TV's *Melrose Place*, in a variety of movies and in the stage version of *Fatal Attraction*.

A recovering alcoholic who got sober at the ripe old age of 22, Davis has an adopted daughter.

Davis has devoted tremendous time and energy working with The David Sheldrick Wildlife Trust to help raise awareness about the tremendous cruelty involved in the worldwide ivory trade, for which elephants are being poached to extinction.

Bessie and Sarah Delany
Sisters who made history

Sisters Bessie and Sarah Delany were remarkable in many ways, not the least of which was that they became famous when both were over 100 years old.

Born in Raleigh, North Carolina in the late 1880s, Bessie and Sarah never married and lived together nearly their entire lives. Bessie, the younger of the two, became only the second black woman to work as a dentist in New York State. Sarah was an educator, the first black person allowed to teach domestic science in New York City high schools.

Both sisters were active in the civil rights movement and participated in numerous marches and protests.

In 1991, journalist Amy Hill Hearth wrote a feature article about the sisters' lives for the *New York Times*. It inspired a full-length book, *Having Our Say: The Delany Sisters' First 100 Years*[15], which was a best-seller. Next came the stage play adaptation of the book by Emily Mann, which debuted on Broadway n 1995 and later toured the United States.

After having lived together in Harlem and then the Bronx, the Delanys moved to a house with a garden in Mt. Vernon, New York.

Bessie Delany died in 1995 at the age 104. Sadie Delany died in 1999 at the age of 109.

Emily Dickinson
An intense inner life

By all accounts, Emily Dickinson's existence was quiet and uneventful, as befitting the "reclusive" description she's usually tagged with. In fact, for the last 21 years of her life, Emily rarely left the grounds of her family's home.

But the woman who would become America's foremost female poet had an intense *inner* life which informed her work, enabling her to challenge and transform poetic conventions as she meditated upon happiness, grief, loss and mortality.

Born in 1830 in Amherst, Massachusetts, Emily's intellect was stimulated by an education that was unusually extensive for a girl at that time. The end of that schooling, though, thrust Emily into the role expected of young unmarried women in the early nineteenth century: keeper of the family home. She chafed against dull domestic duties ("God keep me from what they call households," she wrote in a letter in 1850) and demonstrated a rebellious streak by refusing to participate in the endless social calls women in her social circle made to one another. She preferred to spend her time studying botany and writing poetry.[16]

Still, young Emily sounded confident when she observed; "I am growing handsome very fast indeed! I expect I shall be the belle of Amherst when I reach my 17th year. I don't doubt that I shall have perfect crowds of admirers at that age. Then how I shall delight to make them await my bidding, and with what delight shall I witness their suspense while I make my final decision."[17]

However, as she grew older Dickinson reportedly felt "different" from others.[18] Nonetheless, she enjoyed her family (she was a beloved aunt to her brother's three children) and had a number of close friends. She also cultivated relationships with some well-chosen mentors who encouraged her in her writing.

Emily never married, although she did have a romance with a widower, Judge Otis Phillips Lord, whom biographers say she considered marrying. She is also believed to have received a marriage proposal from a man who went to the same college she did (Amherst College).

She died in 1886 at the age of 56. Sadly, only a handful of the 1,800 poems Dickinson wrote were published during her lifetime. When the first volume of her poetry was published four years after her death, it became a best-seller.

Edie Falco
It's ok to have an unconventional life

Edie Falco worked at her craft for years before becoming an "overnight" success. Playing Carmela Soprano in HBO's hit series, *The Sopranos* brought her to the public's attention in a big way – although she'd been earning praise for her work in TV and films for a long time prior to that unforgettable role of a tough-as-nails wife who stood up to her philandering mob boss husband.

Born in 1963 in Brooklyn, New York, Falco appeared in TV shows like *Law & Order*, *Oz* and *Homicide: Life on the Street* before being cast in Woody Allen's movie, *Bullets over Broadway*. She followed up *The Sopranos* with *Nurse Jackie*, a Showtime series in which she plays the title character, a drug-addicted health care provider. She also acts in stage plays, and received a Tony nomination for her work in the Broadway revival of *House of Blue Leaves*.

Falco has won four Emmys, two Golden Globes and five Screen Actors Guild Awards to date. She has dealt with breast cancer (after a 2003 diagnosis) and achieved sobriety after struggling with alcohol. She is the mother of two adopted children.

Falco has told interviewers[19] that she isn't unhappy with being single, although it did take her a long time to realize that it was all right to have an unconventional life – one that isn't at all what she expected.

Greta Garbo
"I was afraid he would tell me what to do and boss me."

In the 1930s, screen star Greta Garbo was one of the highest paid women in America. Decades later, her luster hadn't dimmed; in 1954, she was named "the most beautiful woman that ever lived."[20]

Garbo was one of the few actors to successfully make the leap from silent films to talkies. She is also the one who introduced what is now known as "method acting." Her ability to bewitch audiences came from a potent mix of mystery, magnetism and extraordinary beauty.

After training at the Academy of the Royal Dramatic Theatre in Sweden, Garbo gained success in European cinema, which brought her to the attention of MGM President Louis B. Mayer. He signed her to a contract and put her in films that turned her into an international film star.

Her first "talkie" was *Ana Christie*, released in 1930. She made thirteen more films for MGM, winning special acclaim for her performances in *Camille* (1937) and *Ninotchka* (1939).

Unlike many of her peers who courted publicity as a means of furthering their careers, Garbo craved privacy and gave few interviews. She had a reputation for being a loner and lived alone for most of her adult life – yet she had many friends and lovers. Actor John Gilbert tried to move his romance with Garbo to a more permanent footing by proposing marriage numerous times. Garbo reportedly accepted his proposals and then changed her mind. "I was in love with him," she said. "But I froze. I was afraid he would tell me what to do and boss me. *I* always wanted to be the boss."[21]

There were also rumored love affairs with both men and women: conductor Leopold Stokowski, writer Erich Maria Remarque, photographer Cecil Beaton, actresses Lilyan Tashman and Louise Brooks, and writer Mercedes de Acosta (some biographers believe that Garbo was bisexual or a lesbian).

Garbo was nominated for the Academy Award for Best Actress four times. She was awarded a special Oscar for her work in 1954.

Garbo made her last movie in 1941 when she was [36]. Directed by George Cukor, the romantic comedy *Two-Faced Woman* was a critical failure. During World War II, Garbo took what was intended to be a break from filmmaking. It turned out to be, in effect, a permanent retirement.

She died in 1990 at the age of 84 of pneumonia and renal failure.

Chelsea Handler
From class clown to star

Brash, blunt and hilariously vulgar, comic Chelsea Handler has conquered the entertainment industry with a successful standup touring act, roles on television shows, her own talk show and bestselling books.

Handler was born in 1975 in Livingston, New Jersey to a Mormon mother and a Jewish father. She moved to Los Angeles at 19 to become an actress, but a drunk driving arrest sent her in a different direction. Forced to take a DUI class, Handler entertained her fellow students with her wisecracks, which inspired her to pursue comedy.

After sharpening her act – and her wit – in comedy clubs, Handler's big breakthrough came in the form of a part on the cable sketch comedy show *Girls Behaving Badly* in 2002. She followed that up with guest appearances on a variety of sitcoms, a short-lived sketch comedy show, *The Chelsea Handler Show*, a long-running late night talk show, *Chelsea Lately*, a scripted series about her long-running late night talk show, *After Lately* and a series of best-selling books.

Handler has not lacked for male companionship; she's used her plentiful and diverse sexual encounters as fodder for her comedy (as in her book, *My Horizontal Life: A Collection of One-Night Stands*). She has reportedly dated Comcast CEO Ted Harbert and rapper 50 Cent, among others.

Handler has said that marriage and motherhood are not on her radar, and that she's happiest when she can focus her energies on her friends, family and career.[22]

Daryl Hannah
Assassin, android and activist

Born in Chicago in 1960, Daryl Hannah has described herself as a shy child who suffered from insomnia when she was young. She studied acting and ballet, and graduated from the University of Southern California School of Theatre.[23]

Hannah's more exotic roles include a mermaid (in *Splash*), a one-eyed assassin (*Kill Bill*) a violent android (*Blade Runner*) and a cave woman (*Clan of the Cave Bear*). Her acting resume also includes memorable characters in *Roxanne*, *Wall Street*, *Legal Eagles*, *High Spirits*, *Crimes and Misdemeanors*, *Grumpy Old Men*, *Grumpier Old Men*, and *Steel Magnolias*.

And, although she's had high-profile relationships with men like John F. Kennedy Jr., Jackson Browne, Val Kilmer and Neil Young[24], the role she has *not* taken on in real life is that of wife.

When she's not making movies, Hannah is an environmental activist who works to raise awareness about climate change and promote renewable energy. Her activism sometimes lands her in jail; she's has been arrested for protesting against the bulldozing of a large urban farm in south-central Los Angeles and the removal of mountaintops (a practice in the mining industry) in West Virginia.

Hannah practices the sustainability principles that she preaches, living in a solar-powered home and driving a biodiesel fuel-powered car.

Debbie Harry
Owning it

Surprisingly, the woman who would become a punk rock icon began her musical career singing backup for a *folk* rock group, The Wind in the Willows.[25]

Debbie Harry – whose "day jobs" included secretary, waitress, go-go dancer and Playboy bunny – moved on to other bands, eventually forming Blondie with her boyfriend, guitarist Chris Stein. Blondie quickly became popular in the club music scene but the group found international success in 1976 with the release of its debut self-titled album.

The burgeoning music video industry boosted Blondie's profile even higher – and Harry's pouty lips, chiseled cheekbones and platinum hair had a lot to do with that. She understood that her appearance was a part of the band's success, but unlike some female singers who preceded her, she took ownership of her sex appeal, setting her own style and refusing to let record companies dictate it to her. That attitude is credited with paving the way for many female artists who followed, like Lady Gaga and Miley Cyrus, although Harry says she doesn't consider herself a role model.[26]

In addition to fronting Blondie, Harry has released five solo albums and acted in TV shows and dozens of films, like 1988's *Hairspray*, *Copland* and *A Good Day to Die*.

Debbie has not married, nor has she had children. She's had relationships with both men and women.[27]

There've been setbacks and missed opportunities. Despite years of hits, in 1982 Blondie was suddenly found to be financially strapped, reportedly because of lax money management. Harry spent years during the 80s nursing Stein through an autoimmune disease. She passed on the role of the robot Pris in *Blade Runner* because her record company didn't want her to take time out to do a movie (the role then went to Darryl Hannah). She split with Stein, although they remain good friends.

She's done drugs. Lots of them. A heroin addiction landed her in rehab. Although she is happy that she's had such a tremendous variety of experiences – including drugs –these days she's pursuing a healthier lifestyle. Clean living is enabling her, in her 70s, to continue performing with Blondie. As this book went to print, the band was in the midst of the "Pollinator Tour 2017."

Dr. Mae C. Jemison
Astronaut

Dr. Mae C. Jemison is the first African-American female astronaut and the first one to make it into space – which she did in 1992, aboard the *Endeavour*. She is also a physician.

Born in Decatur, Alabama, but raised primarily in Chicago, Mae was a voracious reader as a child and – no surprise – an honors student. While pursuing a BS in chemical engineering from Stanford, she found time to be involved with dance and theater productions and serve as head of the Black Student Union.

With her undergraduate degree under her belt, she changed direction and became an M.D., working as a doctor first in Southern California and then as a Peace Corps medical officer in Sierra Leone and Liberia.

When she returned to the U.S., it was time for another career change. Jemison was accepted into NASA's astronaut training program and went on to make history.

As science mission specialist aboard the *Endeavor*, Mae was responsible for conducting scientific experiments on weightlessness and motion sickness on the crew and herself. She spent 190 hours in space before returning to Earth on September 20, 1992.

Since her adventures in space, Jemison has taught at Dartmouth. She also founded the Jemison Group, a company that develops advanced technologies.

Diane Keaton
Single and satisfied

The fact that Diane Keaton didn't marry any of the high profile men she's dated (like Woody Allen, Warren Beatty and Al Pacino) seems to mystify many interviewers.

The Academy Award-winning actress shines in both comedic and dramatic roles; she's created unforgettable characters in iconic films like *The Godfather*, *Baby Boom*, *Annie Hall*, *Looking for Mr. Goodbar*, *Father of the Bride* and *Marvin's Room*. In addition to being an actress she's a mother, photographer, writer, real estate developer and singer. And yet, it's the fact that an attractive, accomplished woman has remained single that seems to fascinate the media the most.

People magazine thought it was such an important subject that they ran an article about her entitled: "Diane Keaton: Why I Never Got Married."[28] In it, Keaton refused to characterize being unmarried as a tragedy. With her trademark mix of goofy humor and thoughtfulness, she said that her earlier idealistic notions about love had evolved into an understanding that a committed relationship is based on teamwork.

IMDb declared in 2001 that "Diane Keaton's Given Up On Men."[29] The title is, predictably, misleading. In the article, Keaton does say marriage is not likely in her future, but does not rule out relationships. She also calls the old maid myth "garbage," pointing out that her life is no less satisfying because she is single.

Harper Lee
A private person

To Kill a Mockingbird is considered by many to be the best work of fiction ever produced by an American writer.

Its author, Nellie Harper Lee, was born in 1926 in Monroeville, Alabama. Lee reportedly based her best-selling novel on characters and events she knew and witnessed as a child. *To Kill a Mockingbird* won the 1961 Pulitzer Prize and earned her the Presidential Medal of Freedom. It was made into a 1962 movie by the same name which is also regarded as a classic.

Another of Lee's accomplishments: she helped her close friend Truman Capote (who inspired the character Dill in *To Kill a Mocking-bird*") do research for what would become his best-selling 1966 book, *In Cold Blood*.

The only other novel Lee released was *Go Set a Watchman*, which was published in 2015 and received mixed reviews.

Lee was an intensely private person. Reportedly overwhelmed by the attention she received after the publication of *To Kill a Mockingbird*, she refused – for most of her long life – to make public appearances or do interviews. She died in 2016 at the age of 89.

Janet Napolitano
A lot of firsts

Janet Napolitano has broken a lot of glass ceilings throughout her career. She was the first woman to serve as Attorney General of Arizona, the first female president of the University of California and the first woman to head up the Department of Homeland Security.

During the Obama administration, she was rumored to be a potential nominee for U.S. Supreme Court Justice.

Napolitano has responded to questions about whether or not she is gay by describing herself as a heterosexual, single workaholic.

Dr. Condoleeza Rice
Miles to go

The first African-American female U.S. Secretary of State and first female National Security Advisor originally intended to be a concert pianist before politics and policy-making beckoned. Nonetheless, she plays piano well enough to have performed with cellist Yo-Yo Ma and for Queen Elizabeth II.

As one of the most highly visible members of the George W. Bush administration, Rice was active in Middle East affairs and advised Bush during the breakup of the Soviet Union and the reunification of Germany. She logged more miles of travel than any previous Secretary of State.

Rice was engaged for a short time in the 1970s to pro football player Rick Upchurch, but broke off the relationship. Like many other famous always single women, she has found herself in the position of having to explain why she's never tied the knot.

She told Piers Morgan during a 2011 interview[30] that she always expected to grow up and be married, but that she'd never found somebody she wanted to spend the rest of her life with. When Morgan pressed her for more details through a series of idiotic questions about whether or not she still held out hope or dreamed of a fairy tale wedding, Rice laughed and gave him a gracious answer about being beyond the fairy tale marriage stage.

Since leaving public office Rice has taught at Stanford and served as a director of a think tank.

Winona Ryder
Bullied into stardom

Winona Ryder has attracted as much attention for her off-screen romances and a shoplifting arrest as she has for her film work, which leans heavily toward movies in the black comedy genre such as *Heathers*, *Edward Scissorhands* and *Beetlejuice*. She's also starred in: *Mermaids*, *Bram Sroker's Dracula*, *Reality Bites*, *Star Trek*, and *The Age of Innocence*, for which she won a Golden Globe Award.

Ryder spent a good part of her childhood in a commune in California with no electricity. When her family moved to a more conventional setting and sent her to junior high school, she was bullied by fellow students who mistook her for being a gay male (something she attributes to the pixie hair cut she had at the time).[31] Her parents decided to homeschool her. It was a move that proved fortuitous, because her new flexible schedule allowed her to accept her first movie role, as a band nerd in 1986' *Lucas*, when she was only 15 years old. It was the beginning of a long and varied career.

Ryder's relationships with Johnny Depp and Matt Damon came under intense scrutiny by the tabloids. So did her arrest for shoplifting more than $5,000 worth of merchandise from Saks Fifth Avenue in Beverly Hills. Ryder blamed the incident on clinical depression and various prescription medications she was on at the time. She performed community service and paid fines and restitution for convictions related to the theft.

Ryder has said she'd rather remain unmarried than get divorced.[32]

The Timmerman Sisters
A happy childhood

None of the seven Timmerman sisters of Geronimo Creek, Texas ever married, nor did any of them move away from the family homestead in which they'd grown up. Tekla, Estella, Hulda, Miletta, Wanda, Meta and Willie Mae lived together in the weathered farmhouse until the end of their days, operating a successful floral shop together at one end of the house and even dressing alike (whichever sister arose first selected the outfit for the day).

They were popular in their community for more than their quirkiness; the sisters were noted for their generosity and philanthropy and their involvement in church and civic affairs. They opened their home at Christmas time to let visitors enjoy their elaborate decorations, sang in the church choir, were enthusiastic boosters of the local high school football team and taught Sunday school.

They got lots of media attention and even appeared on game shows and *Good Morning America*.

Melitta Timmerman once said the sisters' single status was rooted in a happy childhood, with a father who gave them such a happy home that they felt no need to ever leave it. [33]

The last surviving sister, Wanda Timmerman, died in 2012 at the age of 102 – at the family homestead.

Elizabeth I Tudor
"Beggar-woman and single, far rather than queen and married."

Elizabeth I Tudor had even more pressure on her to get married than do most single women. As queen of England, she was expected to select a suitable husband and produce heirs in order to continue the Tudor line. She did neither.

Elizabeth, known as "The Virgin Queen," ruled England and Ireland for the second half of the 19th century. She established the English Protestant Church – which would become the Church of England – and named herself Supreme Governor of it. Nevertheless, she was fairly tolerant in religious matters at a time when religious tolerance was not much in evidence. In foreign affairs she had to contend with England's contemporary superpowers, France and Spain. She was credited with England's defeat of the Spanish Armada in 1588 – one of England's greatest military victories.

Toward the end of her reign, though, there were military failures and economic downturns that tarnished her reputation. Elizabeth could be ruthless; she had her rival, Mary Queen of Scots, executed in 1587 after keeping her prisoner for nearly 20 years.

Was "The Virgin Queen" really a virgin? Although her chastity was celebrated by some of her subjects, many others – including her enemies – called her the "whore" of Europe, because of the affairs she allegedly had with men like Robert Dudley, Earl of Leicester and Robert Devereux, Earl of Essex.[34] Because of these liaisons, Elizabeth attracted gossip in the same way modern celebrities attract tabloid news coverage.

Regardless of her sex life, why didn't she ever marry? This quote, which has been attributed to her, tells us something about her opinion of matrimony; "If I follow the inclination of my nature, it is this: beggar-woman and single, far rather than queen and married."

Eudora Welty
Pulitzer Prize winner

One of America's most prominent and most honored writers of fiction, Welty grew up in Jackson, Mississippi in a close-knit family that valued education. Like the Timmerman sisters, Welty lived in the home in which she'd grown up for most of her 92 years, although she did travel extensively.

The editor of the literary magazine that published her very first short story, *Death of a Traveling Salesman*, said it was one of the best stories he'd ever read.[35] Welty's subsequent work would include short story collections and novels that captured the flavor, characters and dialect of her native Mississippi as well as things she experienced and people she met while traveling through Europe. Her works include *The Wide Net and Other Stories*, *The Golden Apples*, *The Bride of the Innisfallen and Other Stories*, *The Robber Bridegroom*, *Delta Wedding* and *The Optimist's Daughter*. She won the Pulitzer Prize and was awarded the Presidential Medal of Freedom and the French Legion of Honor for her writing.

Welty was also a talented photographer whose photos were published in a number of books.

She never married, but Welty reportedly had two long-term relationships with two writers, John Robinson and Kenneth Millar (whose pseudonym was Ross MacDonald).

Oprah Winfrey
Non-conformist

Oprah Winfrey is the queen of unmarried women – after Elizabeth I, who was an actual queen. The media mogul was born into poverty in Mississippi and raised in inner city Milwaukee. As a child she endured sexual molestation. As a young teen she had an unwanted pregnancy which produced in a baby who died in infancy. Despite these challenges, Winfrey created a business empire that has made her one of the richest, most influential women in the world.

Oprah told one interviewer that she has never gotten married because marriage requires a degree of conformity, and she doesn't conform well to other people's ideas about who she should be.[36] She added that if she had gotten married, it probably wouldn't have lasted.

Some have speculated that Oprah has remained single because she is a lesbian – something she's consistently denied.

Her relationships with men have been well-documented – especially the one she's had with businessman Stedman Graham for more than three decades. They were engaged to be married in November 1992, but did not end up exchanging vows. Engagement rumors regularly swirl around the two. By the time this book is published, Winfrey could well be married.

Or not.

Fictional Old Maids

Mary Richards was the coolest single girl ever. She had a career in television, a studio apartment that she managed to make look chic and a fabulous wardrobe (watching what she wore each episode was one of my favorite things about the series). She was attractive but didn't seem to know it. Her friends and co-workers adored her – and why shouldn't they? She was warm, witty and caring. She was over 30 and unmarried, but was not – over the seven-year span of *The Mary Tyler Moore Show* – ever willing to "settle" for a man she didn't love.

Granted, Mary Richards was too young to be considered an old maid. Nonetheless, in a sweetly funny way, the show blazed a trail by showing us an unmarried, career-oriented woman who was likable, pretty and happy. She wasn't desperate for a man. She wasn't single because she couldn't get a man. Her single status didn't make her miserable and lonely. She loved her work and her co-workers, hung out with her friends Phyllis and Rhoda and dated interesting and handsome men.

The Mary Tyler Moore Show offered up a new prototype of the single woman, one that contrasted sharply with fictional spinsters of the past, when women without husbands were written or portrayed as either sexually frustrated, unfulfilled misfits desperate to find a man or man-haters who were probably closeted lesbians.

How unmarried women are portrayed in popular culture matters. It both reflects and affects how people view single women. It also influences how we single women view ourselves. Too often, in books, plays and movies, unmarried women are characterized as abnormal, pitiful and dissatisfied. In some ways, such portrayals have changed over time in order to keep up with evolving social mores. A sexually free, marriage averse character like Samantha in the TV series *Sex and the City*, for instance, would never have appeared in books or television series in previous decades (or if she did, she would have been a slut – an outcast – instead of a valued friend and successful businesswoman).

That doesn't mean that contemporary characterizations are all positive. In the opening scene of the movie *Heat* (1995), a tough cop played by Sandra Bullock is leading a group of male cops on a raid of a house in which weapons are being illegally trafficked. Her male colleagues clearly resent her and openly mock her. Although she is obviously very good at her job, her competence gets her rewarded by the ultimate insult; "No wonder she's single." That, of course, says more about the male cops than it does about Bullock's character. As a woman working in what is still predominantly a male-dominated career field, Bullock's tough cop is probably used to misogynistic insults.

But let's go back in time a bit, to the novel *Emma* (1815), by Jane Austen, which includes a character who demonstrates the folly of failing to get married. Miss Bates is a middle-aged spinster who is forced to depend upon the kindness of others after her father and brother die, because she doesn't have a husband to support her. She's got a nice personality and everybody likes her, but her life without a man proves difficult.

Romantic disappointment ruined her life

Charles Dickens' acclaimed 1861 novel, *Great Expectations* has in it the famous spinster Miss Havisham, a bitter and deranged woman who lives in her moldering mansion, wearing the fraying, tattered wedding dress from a long-ago ceremony that never took place (she found out that her suitor had been after her only for her money). That romantic disappointment ruined her life and caused her to live out her life as a despondent old maid.

Miss Almira Gulch in *The Wizard of Oz* movie (1939) tormented Dorothy, the young heroine of the piece. (The character of Almira Gulch did not appear in the book by Frank Oz.) Gulch is ugly and unfriendly, frightening when she's threatening poor little Toto and even more terrifying when she morphs into the Wicked Witch of the West, after Dorothy travels to Munchkinland by way of a tornado.

She may be a bit crusty, but Agatha Christie's famous spinster sleuth Miss Marple is a far cry from the odious Almira Gulch. Unburdened by a husband or children, Miss Marple is free to spend her time solving crimes. Although the source of her financial independence isn't clear, she doesn't work and doesn't have to depend on a husband to pay her bills. She is a fairly positive representation of an old maid for her time (1927-1954); one who is intelligent and knowledgeable and who performs a vital service for the apparently crime-ridden communities in which she finds herself.

The same can't be said for Charlotte Vale, the dowdy, repressed spinster played by Bette Davis in the 1942 film, *Now Voyager*. It is only when Charlotte falls in love that she comes into her own and is transformed into a fashion forward, confident woman with a purpose who's able to assert herself against her bully of a mother. The screenwriter still doesn't let her have a truly happy ending, though.

Charlotte never gets to be with the man she loves, but she is allowed to vicariously mother his daughter.

A frightened, homely librarian who wears thick glasses and ugly clothing

The 1946 movie *It's a Wonderful Life* is a popular Christmastime staple with a heartwarming central message, as well as a not-so-heartwarming image of a single woman. The plot has George Bailey getting a chance to see what the lives of his family members and friends would be like if he'd never existed. In the alternate reality that he's shown by his guardian angel, Clarence, George encounters his wife Mary (played by Donna Reed). Clarence warns him beforehand; "You're not going to like it, George. She's an old maid." And she is. Instead of being the lovely and witty woman that George knows, Alternate Reality Mary is a frightened, homely librarian who wears thick glasses and ugly clothing. When George insists that he's her husband, she screams and faints. In an effort to show George a really grim alternate reality, Mary had to be a wretched spinster – so sheltered and shy that she's terrified when a strange man speaks to her.

The 1953 stage play and 1955 musical *Picnic* has an old maid character who is an angry, disruptive drunk. Rosemary is a middle-aged schoolteacher living in a rented room; a woman who throws herself at men and stirs up trouble among the people she knows. She begs a man to marry her and eventually, he gives in and takes her away.

Dangerously different

In *The Prime of Miss Jean Brodie* (a 1961 novel, 1968 stage play and 1969 movie), the titular main character's defiance of convention goes way beyond her refusal to accept her boyfriend's marriage proposal. She insists on remaining fiercely independent and nonconformist in her opinions and teaching style. The unusual influence she exerts over her young students borders on the sinister. It gets one of them killed and ultimately results in her being fired from her job. A woman who doesn't wish to get married is depicted as dangerously different.

Until she falls in love in 1951's *The African Queen* (based on a 1935 novel), Katherine Hepburn's character Rose is an irritatingly proper spinster, prim and humorless. Once Rose gets involved in an opposites-attract romance with Charlie – Humphrey Bogart's rough-hewn captain – she is transformed. She lets down her guard and becomes adventurous and resourceful, even though she and Charlie are almost killed during their wartime adventures. Without a man = uptight and repressed. With a man = passionate and daring.

The novel *Judith Hearne* – later changed to *The Lonely Passion of Judith Hearne* – was published in 1955. (The film by the same name was released in 1987.) Judith is an old maid living a dreary life in Belfast, Ireland; a middle-aged alcoholic who tries to find love and companionship and to cope with the rage she feels at the church over what she regards as her wasted life.

Prim, proper and repressed

In the 1957 stage play *The Music Man* (the movie version came along in 1962), Marian the librarian is another prim and proper spinster who doesn't really start living until she finds love. Like Rose in *The African Queen*, Marian ends up with a man that she originally disapproves of. It adds a great deal of charm to the story.

Rachel, Rachel, a 1968 movie based on a 1966 novel, features a repressed spinster schoolteacher who doesn't really come into her own until she falls in love, with a man who pretty quickly breaks her heart. Rachel Cameron lives with her bossy, widowed mother in an apartment above a funeral home. (Could her life be worse?) She loses her virginity – at 35 – to a colleague who dumps her when he realizes that she's taking their relationship seriously. That devastating rejection and a pregnancy scare that turns out to be false cause Rachel to make big changes in her life. She decides to move across the country and start anew – a bold move that she wouldn't have been capable of making prior to her sexual awakening.

Real life old maid Diane Keaton has played old maids in both dramatic and comedic films. In 1991's *Marvin's Room*, her character, Bessie, is an unmarried woman who's been caring for her bedridden father for decades. Naturally the job fell to her instead of to her married sister because she wasn't busy raising a family. When Bessie has a health crisis of her own, she is forced to contact her sister for help with their father.

Baby Boom (1987) had Keaton playing a driven career woman whose life is thrown into turmoil when she "inherits" a toddler from a deceased cousin. Instant mom J.C. Wiatt must radically change her life in order to accommodate the needs of her new daughter. Challenges and catastrophes ensue, but J.C. manages to summon up her business acumen and use it to reinvent herself. She falls for a small town veterinarian (played by Sam Shephard), which seals the deal;

she's staying where she is, in the new life she's created. It's a very satisfying ending.

Yes, I admit it; I LOVE romantic comedies. Good ones, anyway. And a happy ending that is based on an unmarried person finally finding a mate is how romantic comedies are usually resolved. That is a basic, and even logical part of the genre. Romantic comedies and romances in general can be terrific entertainment – and there's nothing wrong with plots involving characters striving to find a husband or wife. There *is* something wrong with portraying women who aren't married as losers.

A happy ending...alone.

There *are* a few movies that defy romantic comedy conventions. In *My Best Friend's Wedding*, Julia Roberts' character Julianne ends up dancing not with the man she loves but with her gay best friend George, after the man she loves marries someone else. Julianne is too young to be considered an old maid, but there are hints that she's headed in that direction.

Another romantic comedy that ends up with the leading lady going solo in the end is *Private Benjamin*. In the movie's final scene, Judy Benjamin (who is a widow, not a spinster) leaves her tall, dark and handsome (but overbearing) fiancé standing at the altar and skips off alone, ready to enjoy her independence.

Over the years, TV shows have had their fair share of old maids. The cast of *The Dick Van Dyke Show* (1961 to 1966) included Rose Marie, who played wisecracking TV comedy writer Sally Rogers. Sally's desperation to find a husband was a running gag. So was the fact that she often scared men off with her strong personality. Marie played a similarly man-hungry spinster, Myrna Gibbons, in *The Doris Day Show* (1969-71).

The Beverly Hillbillies, which ran from 1962-71, introduced us to Miss Jane Hathaway. A plain Jane spinster with a short, severe haircut and a closet full of unflattering tweed suits, Jane was the moral compass of the show. Her efficiency and smarts as a secretary were rarely appreciated, although she often used them to bail out her boss, bank president Mr. Drysdale, when his schemes got him into trouble. Jane harbored a secret crush on Jethro Clampett.

Alice the housekeeper was a constant presence in the suburban split level home inhabited by *The Brady Bunch* (1969-74). Always ready to drop her mop and listen to a family member's problems, Alice was a steady presence in the fictional family. Her romance with Sam the butcher progressed slowly and was kind of hard to imagine: did she change out of that crisp blue uniform and let down her tidy, upswept hairdo when they went bowling? By the way: the wonderful character actress who played Alice, Ann B. Davis, was an always single woman.

New old maids

Murphy Brown was a different kind of spinster; a not entirely likable lead instead of a peripheral helpmate, a tough-as-nails career woman who'd gotten to the top of the heap in the broadcasting industry and made no apologies for it. A recovering alcoholic with a somewhat abrasive personality, Murphy was much more successful at her job than in her personal life. Although her character had a series of relationships with men throughout the ten year run of the show (1988-98), by the time the last episode wrapped Murphy was still unmarried. She did have a baby, which sparked a national debate about single mothers and family values.

The character of Samantha Jones in *Sex and the City* is a successful businesswoman who runs her own public relations firm, but her main focus in life is on sex. To call her sexually liberated would be an understatement. Ignoring society's disapproval of promiscuity, she pursues sex for its own sake, reveling in its variety and eager for frequency and multiple partners. Not only does she avoid the kinds of emotional attachments that often accompany physical relationships, she turns down a marriage proposal from a good-looking, famous and younger (than her) actor, because she just *does not want to be married*.

Is the character of Samantha, with her over-the-top sexuality, admirable? Or appalling? However you view her, she does represent a newer, bolder version of the ever-evolving old maid as she appears in popular culture.

Coming Full Circle

When I began working on this book, I wasn't sure what to expect. I hoped that it would help bring a much-needed update to the perception of single women. I aspired to change some widely held negative notions into positive ones. For purely selfish reasons, I wanted to gather tips on the art of living well as a single woman from those who've achieved that goal.

However, I worried that the women who were asked to participate in this venture would be unwilling to speak candidly, perhaps because I was projecting my own insecurities about being single onto them. A few who I approached did turn me down. Maybe they didn't want to delve too deeply into that particular part of their self-identify. Maybe they were tired of strangers giving them *that look*.

Most of those I asked, though, were eager to talk. They were open and sometimes painfully honest as they patiently answered my intrusive questions and spoke about the experiences that shaped them and the people whose lives intersected with theirs in powerful ways. Some of their stories are heartbreaking, others are hilarious. I came away from these interviews feeling a tremendous responsibility to do justice to the stories that they entrusted to me.

Their personalities, backgrounds and geographical locations may differ, but the always single women in this book have one thing in common: they own their lives and make no apologies for who they are, in spite of society's lingering discomfort with unmarried women. Although most are still open to the idea of getting hitched (what a phrase that is!), they are not waiting for someone to complete them. They are living life to the fullest, right now. The things they have overcome – whether financial difficulties, low self-esteem, a physical disability – they have overcome on their own.

I did not anticipate the extent to which my own views would be transformed by this book and by the extraordinary women who contributed to the conversation at its core. Talking with them gave me a new perspective on my own single status – something about which I'd always felt defensive. I'm not going to apologize anymore. Not going to explain. Going forward, when strangers give me *that look* and ask me the annoying HIITYNBM question, I'm going to borrow Marcy's standard response: "Who wants to settle down? I want to keep going!"

About the Women in this Book

Atheria is a psychic medium who blogs at *On Angels' Wings*

Productions (https://bridge4spirit.word-press.com/). You can also find her on Instagram at: https://www.instagram.com/atheria444/.

Atheria

Michelle E. Alford is a poet (known by the pen name "Poetic Energy"), author and stage director. Michelle founded the Spokenword Billboard Awards and is Executive State Director of the Miss Missouri Plus America Pageant. Her resume also includes being a plus size model, radio host, certified life coach and real estate agent. Michelle can be found on Facebook (Michelle Alford Pg II) and on Linkedin.

Pat Jones is a writer, producer, director and brand strate-gist who has been telling the stories of people and brands for over 25 years. With a Bachelor of Fine Arts in Theatre from Wayne State University in Detroit, she has applied her gift of storytelling to a multi-faceted career in media that includes theatre, television, fiction and marketing. Pat has worked with brands as diverse as General Motors to Reebok, produced TV shows that have appeared on IFC, Spike TV and Oxygen, and has written, produced and directed Off-Off-Broadway shows. She is also the creator of The Brand Root

Pat Jones
aka P. J. Edghill
(photo by Garlia Jones-Ly)

Method (thebrandrootmethod.com), a branding methodology. Under her pen name, P.J. Edghill, Pat will soon launch a fiction podcast – *Ovid's Flea*, based on her novel of the same name (ovidsflea.com). *Ovid's Flea* tells the story of seven people wrestling with pride while trying not to destroy themselves or each other, as they converge one weekend in New York during Gay Pride.

Dr. Karen Gail Lewis is a family therapist, marriage counselor and author of books like, *With or without a Man: Single Women Taking Control of Their Lives* and *Why Don't You Understand? A Gender Relationship Dictionary*. Visit her website (http://www.drkgl.com/) for information about her books and audiotapes and about the seminars and retreats she conducts for women.

Dr. Karen Gail Lewis

Debbie Roszkowski is such an ardent concert goer that her friends call her "Rocker Chick" and "Concert Debbie." She's also a foodie and enthusiastic traveler. You can follow her adventures on Facebook.

Debbie Roszkowski
Glacier National Park
Montana, 1996

Debbie Roszkowski
at a rock concert, circa 1981

Stephanie Schneiderman's tours of Mexico, Columbia, Guatemala and other countries allow travelers to experience the culinary and textile traditions, art history and festivals of those areas with the help of knowledgeable guides and local partners. Learn more about Tia Stephanie Tours at: http://tiastephani-etours.com/

Stephanie
Schneiderman

Eleanore Wells

Eleanore Wells writes about being single on her popular blog, *The Spinsterlicious Life (eleanorewells.com/blog)*. She has also chronicled her adventures in a book by the same name: *The Spinsterlicious Life: 20 Life Lessons for Living Happily Single & Childfree*. Her book can be found on Amazon at: https://www.amazon.com/Spinsterlicious-Life-Child-free-Eleanore-2012-03-14/dp/B01FIX7RMM/ref=sr_1_2?ie=UTF8&qid=1499702103&sr=8-2&keywords=spinsterlicious

Joan White is a fashion and inspirational blogger. She is developing a line of fashions for plus size women called Voluptuous Diva, Inc., which you can find on Facebook and at voluptuousdiva.com.

Works cited

1. Nanos, Janelle. "Single by Choice." *Boston Magazine*, January 2012. Web June 20, 2017 http://www.bostonmagazine.com/2012/01/single-by-choice-why-more-of-us-than-ever-before-are-happy-to-never-get-married/

2. U.S. Census Bureau, Housing and Household Economic Statistics Division, Fertility & Family Statistics Branch. "America's Families and Living Arrangements: 2010." Web June 20, 2017 https://www.census.gov/population/www/socdemo/hh-fam/cps2010.html

3. Kreider, Rose M. and Tavia Simmons. "Marital Status: 2000." U.S. Census Bureau, U.S. Department of Commerce Economics and Statistics Administration, October 2003. Web June 20, 2017 www.census.gov/prod/2003pubs/c2kbr-30.pdf

4. Cohn, D'vera, et al. "Barely Half of U.S. Adults Are Married – A Record Low." *Pew Research Center, Social and Demographic Trends*, December 14, 2011. Web June 20, 2017 www.pewsocialtrends.org/2011/12/14/barely-half-of-u-s-adults-are-married-a-record-low/

5. Anthony, Susan B. "Susan B. Anthony Quotes." *Brainy Quote*. Date unknown. BrainyMedia, Web June 20, 2017. www.brainyquote.com/quotes/authors/s/susan_b_anthony.htm

6. Harper, Ida Husted. *The Life and Work of Susan B. Anthony Vol. 2*. Indianapolis, IN, Bowen-Merrill/The Hollenbeck Press, 1898, pp. 858–860.

7. Stanton, Elizabeth Cady and Susan B. Anthony. *The Elizabeth Cady Stanton-Susan B. Anthony Reader*. Edited and critical commentary by Carol Ellen DuBois. Northeastern University Press, 1981 and 1992, p. 148.

8. Banks, Tyra. "Tyra Banks Quotes." Famous Quotes and Quotations at Brainy Quote. Web June 20, 2017 www.brainyquote.com/quotes/quotes/t/tyrabanks369506.html

9. Fine, Marshall. "Giving thanks for Jacqueline Bisset." *Hollywood & Fine with Marshall Fine*. November 21, 2008. *Web June 20, 2017* www.hollywoodandfine.com/giving-thanks-for-jacqueline-bisset/

10. Reporter, Mailonline. "'It's very early days…but he's a very nice guy!' Chart-topper Susan Boyle finds her first-ever boyfriend at 53." *Daily Mail.com*. November 2014. Web June 20, 2017 www.dailymail.co.uk/tvshowbiz/article-2853877

11. Vaughan, Hal. *Sleeping with the Enemy: Coco Chanel's Secret War.* Knopf, 2011, pp. 80-81.

12. Chanel, Coco. "Coco Chanel Quotes." Famous Quotes and Quotations at *Brainy Quote*. Date unknown. BrainyMedia, Web June 20, 2017 www.brainyquote.com/quotes/quotes/c/coco-chanel414003.html

13. Weller, Sheila. "At Home with Superstar Sheryl Crow." *Good Housekeeping*, July 11, 2014.

14. Rothman, Michael. "Why Kristin Davis Can't Imagine Getting Married." *ABC News* via *Good Morning America,* December 3, 2013.

15. Delany, Sarah L., Elizabeth A. Delany and Amy Hill Hearth. *Having Our Say: The Delany Sisters' First 100 Years*. Dell Publishing, 1994.

16. Emily Dickinson Museum. "Emily Dickinson: Her Childhood and Youth (1830-1855)" Web June 20, 2017 https://www.emilydickinsonmuseum.org/childhood_youth

17. Dickinson, Emily. "Emily Dickinson Quotes." Famous Quotes and Quotations at *Brainy Quote*. Date unknown. BrainyMedia, Web June 20, 2017 https://www.brainyquote.com/quotes/quotes/e/emilydicki717917.html

18. Emily Dickinson Museum. "Emily Dickinson: The Later Years (1865-1886)." http://www.emilydickinsonmuseum.org/later_years

19. Sessums, Kevin. "Edie Falco Comes Clean." *Daily Beast*, May 16, 2010. Web June 20, 2017 www.thedailybeast.com/articles/2010/05/16/edie-falco-comes-clean.html

20. "Greta Garbo Biography." Official Website of Greta Garbo. Harriet Brown & Company, Inc. Web June 20, 2017 www.gretagarbo.com/Offical_Website_of_Greta_Garbo/BIOGRAPHY.html.

21. Gross, Michael *(*May 21, 1990) "Garbo's Last Days," *New York Magazine,* pp. 39-46.

22. Messer, Lesley. "Chelsea Handler Reveals Why She's Not 'The Marrying Kind'." *ABC News,* March 12, 2014. Web June 20, 2017 http://abcnews.go.com/Entertainment/chelsea-handler-reveals-shes-marrying-kind/story?id=22880312

23. Dicker, Matt. "Darryl Hannah Biography." *IMDb.* Web June 20, 2017 http://www.imdb.com/name/nm0000435/bio

24. Biography.com. "Daryl Hannah." Web June 20, 2017 https://www.biography.com/people/daryl-hannah-240976

25. "The Wind in the Willows." Discogs. (discography)." www.discogs.com/artist/1333895.

26. *Wilde, Jon.* "How I survived heroin, a serial killer and losing all money - to play Glastonbury... at 68: Debbie Harry on her amazing career." *Daily Mail,* June 13, 2014. Web June 20, 2017 www.dailymail.co.uk/home/event/article-2656274/Debbie-Harry-How-I-survived-heroin-serial-killer-losing-money-play-Glastonbury.html.

27. *Hastings, Chris. "My 'sensual' nights with women, by Debbie Harry: Blondie star reveals she is bisexual despite relationship with band-mate." Daily Mail, April 5, 2014. Web June 20, 2017* http://www.dailymail.co.uk/tvshowbiz/article-2597774/My-sensual-nights-women-Debbie-Harry-Blondie-star-reveals-bisexual-despite-relationship-bandmate.html

28. *Peoplestaff.* "Diane Keaton: Why I Never Got Married." *People Magazine,* April 24, 2014. Web June 20, 2017 http://people.com/celebrity/diane-keaton-why-i-never-got-married/

29. WENN News. "Diane Keaton's Given Up On Men" *IMDB,* July 2, 2001. Web June 20, 2017 http://www.imdb.com/news/ni0066410/

30. Rice, Condoleeza. Interview by Piers Morgan. "Condoleeza Rice Talks Marriage." *CNN,* published on *YouTube* Jan. 19, 2011. CNN Official Interview. Web June 20, 2017 https://www.youtube.com/watch?v=vXRVrZcLsxl

31. Daily Mail Reporter. "Winona Ryder reveals the homophobic attack that made her quit high school... after pixie crop led to her being mistaken for a gay teen boy." *Daily Mail*, Nov. 7, 2013. Web June 20, 2017 http://www.dailymail.co.uk/tvshowbiz/article-2491889/Winona-Ryder-reveals-homophobic-attack-forced-quit-high-school--indirectly-win-Hollywood-role.html

32. Bueno, Antoinette. "Wynona Ryder Explains Why She's Never Been Married." *ET Online*, July 14, 2016. Web June 20, 2017 www.etonline.com/news/193224_winona_ryder_explains_why_she_never_been_married/

33. McBride, Stewart. "A Matching Set of Seven Sisters." *Christian Science Monitor*, Jan. 22, 1981. Web June 20, 2017 https://www.csmonitor.com/1981/0122/012256.html

34. Mason, Emma. "Elizabeth I's love life: was she really a 'Virgin Queen'?" *HistoryExtra*, April 14, 2015. Web June 20, 2017 http://www.historyextra.com/article/elizabeth-i/elizabeth-i-love-life-was-she-really-virgin-queen

35. Marrs, Suzanne. "Biography." *The Eudora Welty Foundation*. Web June 20, 2017 https://eudorawelty.org/biography/

36. Dutt, Barkha. "In conversation with Oprah Winfrey at the Jaipur LitFest." *NDTV*, Jan. 22, 2012. Web June 20, 2017 https://www.youtube.com/watch?v=sIMVT49JSeQ

About the Author

Maureen Paraventi is a journalist, novelist and award-winning playwright whose works include _Palm Tree Pipe Dreams_ (a novel available on Amazon.com) and _The Bucket List of Booze Club_ (a stage play). She is also an actor and singer who performers with McLaughlin's Alley, a Detroit pop/rock/Irish band (www.mclaughlinsalley.com). Visit Maureen's website at: www.maureenparaventi.com.

Photo by Jan Cartwright

Made in the USA
Columbia, SC
04 April 2018